D0894361
This ... an
to ... or
the ... were approved by Little Rock
voters on 12/11/07. Thanks, Little Rock!

They Said It Couldn't Be Done

by

Colonel Lynn A. Davis

They Said It Couldn't Be Done

Closing Down "The Biggest Illegal Casino Operation in America - Hot Springs, Arkansas - 1967" in 120 Days

by Colonel Lynn A. Davis

Days Creek Press
P.O. Box 7815
Little Rock, Arkansas 72217
1-888-854-8513

A percentage of each sale is donated to the
ARKANSAS STATE POLICE ASSOCIATION
SCHOLARSHIP FUND

ISBN 978-0-578-01955-0

TABLE OF CONTENTS

In Memory of nineteen Troopers who died in the line of duty

Trooper Sidney Pavatt

Trooper Ermon Cox

Trooper Harry Locke

Trooper Allen Bufford

Trooper Ron Brooks

Sergeant Kelly Pigue

Sergeant Glenn Bailey

Trooper William Rose, Jr.

Trooper Louis Bryant

Investigator Robbie Klien

Investigator Michael Bassing

Trooper Wilson Atkins, Jr.

Trooper Clark Simpson

Corporal John Scarberough

Captain Tom Craig

Trooper Herbert Smith

Trooper Jimmie White

Corporal Mark Carthron

Sergeant Richard LeBow

FOREWORD

I first began studying the history of Hot Springs, Arkansas in the summer of 2007. I was in the City to research and develop a project known as *The Gangster Museum of America*. "On the way to the forum," so to speak, a funny thing happened. The past revealed itself as one of the most fascinating mosaics of gambling, prostitution, bootlegging, and political corruption that everyone from some of the former governors of Arkansas to the dealers of the Southern Club and a dozen others, considered encouraging tourism. The fight to clean up a hundred year old institution of extreme pleasures remained a split decision between the gamblers and the non-gambling Christians. The "business," after all, seemed to be the only industry in town. The policemen and the firemen made more money working in the casinos as their avocation than they possibly could exercising their vocation. Especially when they exercised both. The rolling of the dice, the clunk of the slot machines and the spinning of the roulette wheels put food on the table for the favored families of judges, gangsters, politicians and some Christians alike. Any time the question of ridding the spa city of gambling made it into any conversation in America, most would agree *it couldn't be done* and that very thought was what brought Colonel Lynn Davis into my life and that of Arkansas and the life of *The Gangster Museum of America.*

This blow by blow account of Lynn Davis' history making closure of the mob's playground reads like a Mickey Spillane novel and will leave you with the feeling that you were riding in the Arkansas State Police Command Car when Davis and his Troopers drove old Dixie down.

Little did Colonel Davis know that in the heat of the night, in the summer of 1967, that his efforts would play a key role in the overwhelming success of the first *Gangster Museum of America* as well as closing down the biggest illegal casino operation in America.

Robert Raines
Executive Director,
The Gangster Museum of America
Hot Springs, Arkansas

DEDICATION

Dedicated to all those many who have given their lives to serve their country in many different ways and also to those who wait:

HENDERSON HENCE GILES, a great uncle who was shot three times, ambushed by a fugitive on the streets of Texarkana, Arkansas on July 16, 1926.

JOHNNY HALSELL, US Marine Corps, Killed in Action July, 1968, DaNang, Viet Nam; (Son of Major "Buck" Halsell, Arkansas State Police (Deceased) and Virginia Halsell (Deceased) (Friends)

WILLIAM "BILL" POTTS, Deputy Sheriff, Green River County, Wyoming (Deceased) Died With His Boots On, 2008

BENJAMIN GROGAN, Special Agent, FBI, Killed in gun battle, April 11, 1986, Miami, Florida. (Classmate, New Agents Class #3, FBI, EOD September 18, 1961).

W. E. DAVIS, Sheriff, Miller County, Arkansas. 16 years, (deceased) A lawman's lawman, a kind and gentle spirit proud to call him my uncle; shot in the heart and survived; had his thumb shot off apprehending 2 bank robbers at the Red River bridge in Fulton, Arkansas.

CLARENCE AND ESTELLE DAVIS, My parents who led by example.

SPECIAL THANKS TO:

Steve Arrison, Commissioner, Arkansas Parks and Tourism and Director, Hot Springs Visitors Bureau,

Martha Chadwick Lindvall,

Clay White, Special Agent, FBI (Retired), Garland County, AR

Robert Raines, Executive Director, *The Gangster Museum of America*, Hot Springs, AR

Garland County Historical Society, Hot Springs, AR

All others who know who they are, the ones who encouraged me throughout this process.

THEY SAID IT COULDN'T BE DONE

Colonel Lynn A. Davis

Hot Springs or "Bubbles" or "Hot Town"? No matter the name, the mobsters found it, and it was to their liking. From the number of out of state thugs who visited or took shelter in Hot Springs, some came to invest in the action, some to create the action, some to take away the profits, some just came to take the baths and enjoy the action and relative freedom from the legitimate lawmen and maybe other gangsters looking for some of them. Some of the "baddest" of the bad were, for example: Charles "Lucky" Luciano, Al Capone, Frank Nitti, Dutch Schultz, "Pretty Boy" Floyd, Jesse and Frank James, Richard "Tallman" Gallatas, "Bugsy" Siegle, Alvin "Creepy" Karpis, Bonnie and Clyde, Frank Costello, Owney "The Killer" Madden and many more.

Those came from the recent past. Some remain.

THE DEBATE OUTSIDE THE SAFEWAY STORE YOU KNOW THEY CAN KILL YOU!

You are sitting in a white unmarked command car, decorated with a whole "corn row" of antennae just to the East side of the Safeway Store located about three blocks from the Oaklawn Race Track and about six blocks from downtown Hot Springs, Arkansas. "They" can kill you, the only question is "when." You do know they have killed a number of your friends, all of them believing it wouldn't happen to them and the fact that you have a Smith & Wesson .357 Magnum pistol with six widow makers in the chamber on your hip makes no difference.

This was the beginning of the entire episode.

Lynn Davis Is Man Governor Wants for State Police Job

LITTLE ROCK (AP) — Lynn A. Davis, 33, an FBI agent at Los Angeles, is the man Gov. Winthrop Rockefeller wants as director of the State Police, the Associated Press learned Tuesday.

Davis' appointment, however, depends on whether he meets the requirement that the State Police director must have lived in Arkansas in the 10 years prior to his appointment.

Atty. Gen. Joe Purcell has been asked by the governor's office to rule on whether Davis meets this requirement. Davis told The Associated Press Tuesday that he has maintained a residence in Texarkana although he actually has not lived in Arkansas for about six years.

"The attorney general has the ball and the decision rests on his opinion," a Rockefeller aide said.

He said Davis was the person the governor described in a news conference Monday as the man he wanted for the position, but he said he wasn't sure Davis was the only person under consideration.

Davis would neither confirm nor deny that he had been appointed to the position, but he acknowledged that he was under consideration. He said he wanted the job and would consider it an honor to succeed Col. Herman Lindsey, who is retiring as director next month.

He said he was not at liberty to disclose any conversations he has had about the position, but that he had not heard from the governor's office recently. He said he was "looking forward to hearing from the governor."

Davis, a native of Texarkana, joined the FBI in September of 1961 at Texarkana and has been assigned to the Springfield, Ill., and Denver, Colo., divisions and was resident agent at Rock Springs, Wyo., in 1964-66. He has been at Los Angeles for a year.

He was at one time manager of the membership and public relations department of the Texarkana Chamber of Commerce and taught school two years at Genoa in Miller County.

"I own property in Texarkana and consider it my hometown," he said.

His parents are Mr. and Mrs. Clarence T. Davis of 1001 Ferguson St. His father is a building contractor and his uncle, the late W. E. Davis, was sheriff of Miller County for many years.

Rockefeller told a news conference that the man he wanted for the job attended the University of Arkansas and graduated from Henderson State Teachers College, now Henderson State College, at Arkadelphia.

The governor implied that the man either was presently or had been with the FBI, but declined to reveal his name pending an opinion from the attorney general's office on whether he passed the residence test.

Davis said he attended the University of Arkansas two years and gr aduated fromHenderson in 1955.

Davis, married and the father of two children, said he did not actively seek the job but "it is commonly known. . . that I wanted to get back to Arkansas."

"Law enforcement is my career and this (the director's job) seems to me to be a pretty good opportunity," he said.

Davis was an infantry captain in the Army.

"I don't know the man, but if he's the governor's selection, I'm sure he will be a capable person," said Clark H. "Rusty" Ralston, chairman of the State Police Commission.

"Naming the director is strictly the governor's prerogative. All the other hiring and firing out there is done by the commission, but that's the governor's prerogative."

LYNN DAVIS

You know down deep in your gut that if you don't stop taking chances, "They" will kill you for sure even if you have six or sixty bullets, but how do you conquer the habit of putting yourself in danger. Come on now, Lynn, quit being a crybaby and don't let one of those demon Lucky Strike cigarettes get the best of you... continue to set your mind to it. You answered that question about three weeks earlier. You quit smoking and promised yourself that you had smoked your last cigarette. Well, so far, so good, but if you were ever going to quit quitting, this would be the day, promises or no promises.

The smoke coming from the back seat doesn't help your resolve; your promise to yourself. All you have to do is "bum" one from the Captain in the back seat. It will settle your nerves, etc. etc. using all the excuses from the past. Let's see, you are now thirty-four years of age, and you started smoking when you were sixteen, so that makes you, after eighteen years of smoking, a good candidate for an early demise. Even as a high profile candidate for a "whacking" by the mob, you know you stand an even better chance of going the short breath route.

All I have to ask the ASP Captain in the backseat is to kindly stop smoking. That would be unfair, though, bearing in mind that there is nothing more righteous than a reformed "lady of the evening," and the same goes for smokers who have quit. They do their dead level best to convert everyone to nonsmoking status.

Seeing a young attorney lighting up years later, I asked if he knew that his babies would be born naked if he kept smoking. He said, yes, he knew that, but his grandfather lived to be ninety-two years of age. I, naturally, asked him if his grandfather smoked. He replied with a smile on his face, "No, but he minded his own business." Since then, you might think I have slowed down my preaching, but I haven't.

Concentration is called for now. Enough evading of the question. How are we, the Arkansas State Police going to close down the illegal casinos which have existed for years, closing only when the political heat is applied, then coming back to life after elections, but in the meantime corrupting Hot Springs' Mayor, judges, prosecutors, police, the Sheriffs Department and just about everybody else in authority in Garland County during that time—1967 and years before.

Now quit whining about smoking. It's do or die time. Literally and figuratively.

But still, there must be ten million people out there smoking away, but how many of these people are sitting in a State Police command car waiting for reports from eight or ten undercover officers to report on their efforts to gain entrance to Hot Springs' illegal casinos? These are the casinos which have been dubbed by the United States Department of Justice, U.S. Attorney General Bobby Kennedy and J. Edgar Hoover, as "The biggest illegal casino operation in America … Hot Springs, Arkansas." We are here to close them down, something that has not been done in over 100 years, give or take a few years when they sometimes closed for political reasons ... but not for long. At least 52 FBI special agents were in Hot Springs at one time in an attempt to close the operations. Evidently, they failed. Owney Madden kept operating.

It's early August, 1967, shortly after midnight. The steam can be seen rising from the forty-seven hot springs around the Valley of the Vapors. It seems, in the hazy early morning, that later in the day it will be even hotter than a Texas Blue blazer. It's hot and getting hotter, but having the choice of five lakes to swim in made it worth it, yet the only problem was that we were not likely to be swimming unless we let them get the drop on us.

Ridding Hot Springs, Arkansas, of illegal gambling can't be any harder than quitting those demon cigarettes or can it? It's time to concentrate! The decision I have to make tonight isn't to decide whether I was to continue torturing myself by quitting those demon smokes, but whether we are going after the prize—over 300 slot machines and related casino equipment, roulette wheels, crap tables and all those accoutrements to be found in at least eight or ten clubs? That outcome remains to be seen. Based on history and memory, it isn't a certainty by any means. As a matter of fact,

ration before the McClellan committee exposed the syndicate's racing wire.

at 315 Park Avenue.

hern Club at 250 Central Avenue.

Another full house of gambling customers in a downtown club.

floor rolls out
nder the band-
then on it's
ainment, for a
mum per per-
ay have dinner
of drinks for
of the great
business have
rs, from Sophie
rge Jessel to
s Diller and
nnett, with a
tween.

Vapors is responsible or not is an open question, but some of Hot Springs' old-time — and possibly old-fashioned — casinos have been left out in the cold. The Belvedere Country Club, which operates only during racing seasons, and the Tower Club, for example, now stand dark and shuttered, without so much as the clatter of the dice coming from them.

All these places also serve liquor in mixed drinks as do many of the restaurants and cafes of Hot Springs.

Hot Springs, June 16. — The customers are practically lining up behind the 37 "one-arm bandits" at the plush Vapors Theater-Supper Club here, and if there's any problem, it's simply that the gilt-edged casino isn't big enough.

There might be one other complaint: There aren't enough nickel slot machines to satisfy the demand, but this probably is more by design than error. The alternatives are dime, quarter or half-dollar machines, with payoffs

"EXPOSED?" Anyone on the street could have told them that Owney Madden owned and operated a sports racing wire which came from New Orleans owned by Mafia boss, Carlos Marcello. And illegal gambling ran rampant, including Owney's casino, The Southern Club,

Supposedly, 800 plus slots and related gambling paraphernalia in Arkansas. Just a partial list — An example of illegal activities being taxed by the federal government via gambling tax stamps.

Gaz. Aug. 14-60

Gambling

Gaming Machines Thrive

Arkansas cafes, night clubs and other establishments have paid federal taxes of $150,500 in order to operate 602 coin - operated gambling devices during the fiscal year 1960-61, according to records of the Internal Revenue Service at Little Rock.

The devices—pin ball machines equipped for gambling and slot machines—operate despite a state law which prohibits their use. The $250 federal tax on each machine applies regardless of whether the state law is enforced.

Altogether 321 establishments have paid the gambling tax. They operate anywhere from one to dozens of machines. The Southern Club at Hot Springs sets the pace with 31, and its affiliated firms, the Southern Bar and New Southern Grill, account for eight more. Their tax bill: $9,750.

The tax is reduced proportionately when machines are placed in operation later in the fiscal year, which ends June 30. Many the Hot Springs cafes and clubs place additional machines in operation in February just in time for the horse racing season at Oaklawn Park.

The Belvedere Club at Hot Springs began the 1959-60 fiscal year by paying $3,000 in taxes to operate 12 machines, but on February 13 installed 74 more and paid taxes of $7,703.21 on them for the balance of the fiscal year.

The Southern Club, Southern Bar and New Southern Grill started last year with 21 machines and completed it with 44. Their bill came to about $8,000.

By the end of the 1959-60 fiscal 846 coin-operated gambling devices were operating in Arkansas. They could be found in 450 places of business, which shelled out a total of $189,139.75 for tax stamps.

Hot Springs Leads

Hot Springs, with its casinos, perennially leads the Arkansas cities in the number of coin-operated gambling devices. Slot machines, also known as "one-arm bandits," are the most popular there.

This year tax stamps have been issued for 234 gambling machines at Hot Springs, 101 at Little Rock, 88 at Fort Smith, and 4[illegible] at North Little Rock. Next comes Springdale with 19, a large number considering its size, Texarkana 18 and Fayetteville 17. The remaining 81 are divided among many cities and towns.

Pine Bluff, the state's fourth largest city, has no gambling machines, according to IRS tax stamp records. Neither does

number of machines at each place:

Little Rock

James E. Allen, Community Club House, 114 West Capitol Avenue, 2; James L. Angel, Angel's Cafe, 614 West Ninth Street, 6; James L. Angel, Burger Bar, 514 West Ninth Street, 6; Lola Martin Baker, Lola's Steak House, New Benton Highway, 1; B. F. Bennett, Main Recreation Parlor, 117 Main Street, 2; Jack Braswell, Braswell's Diner, 824 West Ninth Street, 2; Rose Brinkley, 106 Louisiana Street, 3; Cecil Burks, Burk's Mobile Service, 2524 West Twelfth Street, 1; Thelma W. Campbell, Thema's Cafe, 2230 Arch Street, 1; A. B. Cassinei, Brunswick Billard, 118 Main Street 3; L. C. Cassinelli Harlem Bar, 600 West Ninth Street, 2; Donald D. Cummins, Center Bowling Lanes, 415 Center Street, 3; Columbus Club Association, Inc., 215 East Ninth Street, 3; Roy and Pat Cook, Cook's Cafe, 119 East Third Street, 2; R. C. Coulter, Blue Bowl Cafe, 814 Main Street, 1; Ex-Serviceman's Club, 120½ West Markham Street, 2; Max H. Ezell, Ship Ahoy, 1108 Battery Street, 2; H. C. Faucett, Citizens Cigar Store, 316 West Capitol Avenue, 3; 3; Phillip F. Geller, The Purple Cow, 714 Broadway, 1; Dorothy C. Graves, Stifft Station Recreation, 3015 West Markham Street, 1; T. J. Graves, Pastime Pool Hall, 1204 West Seventh Street, 2; J. O. Hale, Jim's Place, 1207 West Thirty-third Street, 1; C. L. Hendricks, Lowber's Billiards, 5302 Asher Avenue, 4; Coy L. Hively, Circle B, 2001 East Roosevelt Road, 2; Gurley Javada and Frances M. Sullivan, Sully's Cafe, 5308 Asher Avenue, 2; Carl William Knoedl, Joe's Grill, 6322 West Twelfth Street, 1; Ralph M. Kuykendall, 3100 West Roosevelt Road, 2; J. W. Land, Courthouse Cafe, 323 West Second Street, 1; H. A. McMurry, Mac's Drive Inn, 2520 West Twelfth Street, 2; Marie Maher, Bismark Cafe, 1210 West Seventh Street, 2; Thomas V. Marbut, The Band Box, 1623 Main Street, 1; Paul M. Maus, American Grill, 113 Main Street, 1; Mrs. Mike Miller, Miller's Coffee Shop, 212 Main Street, 1; Gene O'Kelley, Red Gate Inn, 1437 Stagecoach Road, 1; W. T. Parks, Amoco Service Station, Roosevelt Road and Arch Street, 1; Freddie Perciful, Freddie's Drive Inn, 515 West Eighth Street, 1; George Peters, Majestice Confection, 800 Main Street, 1; Pla-Mor Bowling Lanes, Inc., 901 West Seventh Street, 1; Cleon L. Rogers, Anchor Cafe, 2727 Arch [illegible] Country Club, Hot Springs Highway, 2; Gladys Williams, Summerfield's Restaurant, 1123 Main Street, 2; J. P. Willis, Jimmy's Billiard Parlor, 1105 Main Street, 3; E. E. Wycott, Pitcher Cafe, 916 West Fourteenth Street, 1; Herman Yancey, Chris Cafe, 902 Main Street.

North Little Rock

Mrs. Faye Barker, Barker's Restaurant, U. S. Highway 67 East, 1; B. R. Emberton, Jake's Cafe, 106 East Second Street, 2; William T. Fisher, Fisher's Grill, MacArthur Boulevard and Conway Pike, 1; Roy Fowler and Willie Booth, West Sandwich Shop, 411 East Thirteenth Street, 1; James M. Fryar, Green Door, U. S. Highway 67 three miles south of Jacksonville, 2; Mrs. E. L. Gassoway, Terminal Cafe, 624 East Twelfth Street, 1; R. H. Glover Esso Station, 1600 East Broadway, 1; R. H. Glover, Esso Station, 100 Jacksonville Highway, 1; Charlene W. Graham, Wendy's Drive Inn, 498 MacArthur Boulevard, 1; S. P. Hammons, Hob Nob Drive Inn, 3805 New Conway Pike, 1; Josephine A. Jenkins, Chicken Shack, 700 East Broadway, 1; L. O. Jobe and Robert Kirspell, Wonder Grill, 100 East Thirteenth Street, 2; Eldore Johnson, Johnson Diner, 4410 East Broadway, 1; Moose Lodge No. 942, 113 North Maple Street, 3; Salvadore A. Marchese, Southern Grill, 321 West Eighteenth Street, 1; Ralph E. Miller, Millers' Truck Stop, Route 5, 1; Annis Mugley, Coffee House, 415 Main Street, 2; North Hills Country Club, Highway 5, 4; Elks Lodge No. 1004, 123 East Broadway, 5; Mrs. Frank Nowell, Star Cafe, 119 East Second Street, 2; Albert L. Paladino, Bo Bird Sandwich Shop, 1733 Pike Avenue, 1; Frank W. Schafer, Catter Box, U. S. Highway 67 East, 1; F. H. Sharp, Jack's Place, 121 East Second Street, 2; Sam Stephens, Sam Stephens Cafe, 5007 East Broadway, 3; Ned R. Thomas, Ned's Restaurant, 402 Main Street, 2; Mathew Walters, Walters' Drive Inn and Motel, Route 5, 1; Lois Williams, Second Street Cafe, 105 East Second Street, 1; M. R. Williams, The Chief, Route 5, 1; Herman Yancey, Griddle Shop, 234 McArthur Drive, 1.

Fort Smith

R. E. Adams, Pastime Parlor, 1; V. B. Blankenship, Riverside Bar and Grill, 1; Herbert E. Bornitzke, Jumbo's Cafe, 1; Arnold Brasch, Arnie Brasch Deep Rock Station, 2; W. T. Bromley, Dub's 22 Tavern, 2; C. H. Carnal, Square Deal Cafe, [illegible] Rowena Carnal, Swing [illegible] 3; J. D. Nation, Little Buckhorn, 1; Edward Neumler, Dinty Moore's Cafe, 2; Elmer Nye, Elmer's Snooker Parolr, 1; Hugh Oglesby, Mildred's Cafe, 1; Sidney Parker, Cisco Bar, 1; Mary Peluso, Pagliacci, 1; Albert Porta, Albert's Malt Shop, 3; Ralph Roberts, Roberts Service Station, 3; W. H. Rounsaville, 4000 Club, 1; Mary Schwartz and John H. Smith, Oasis, 2; Arthur J. Sharum, Pete's Place, 2; Sophie Smith, Sophie's Place, 1; Juanita Stanley, Melody Lounge, 1; C. R. Thompson, Thompson's Tap Room, 2; W. E. Thompson, 1206½ Garrison Avenue, 2; A. J. Odouj, Sportsmen's Ice House, 1; Coy M. Veach, Western Club, 1; Arthur Vervack, Vervack Brothers, 2; Curley Vervack, Curley's, 3; Mrs. N. G. Walraven, Walraven's Cafe, 2; Mrs. Zedia Ma[illegible] Watkins, Bar B Que Grand, 2[illegible] Robert Floyd White, 71 Cafe, 2[illegible] Chet Wilcox, Brass Rail, 1; Terry Williams, Corral Bar, 1; Gussi[illegible] Wilson, My Place Drive In, 1[illegible] Wintergarden Bowling Lanes Inc., 2; W. W. Womble, 100 North Greenwood Avenue, 2[illegible] Gene Wood, Gene's Barbecu[illegible] Lounge, 1; Mary Louise Wright[illegible] Charles and Mary's Bar, 1.

Hot Springs

Ellis Agre, Old South, 2; Ga[illegible] Agre, Gorge Road Tavern, 1[illegible] Truman Agre, Truman's Tavern[illegible] 2; Lewis P. Allen, Dug Out In[illegible] 1; American Legion Club, [illegible] Fred S. Austin, H. Dane Harr[illegible] and Gordon Henderson, Ne[illegible] Tower Club, 3; George L. Bach[illegible]lor, Hot Springs Golf and Coun[illegible]try Club, 2; Eugene Bailey, Mu[illegible]ray's Landing, 1; Addie Baxte[illegible] Baxter Hotel, 1; Belvedere Coun[illegible]try Club, Inc., 4; C. J. and J. [illegible] Brooks, Cliff's Drive Inn, 4; B[illegible] M. Bryant, Bob's Drive Inn, [illegible] Mrs. J. B. Buck, Buck's Cafe, [illegible] Marion Bush, Joe's Red Rose, [illegible] M. L. Butler, Butler's Bar B[illegible] 1; Timothy Cain, Oakland Gri[illegible] 1; Gilbert Caldwell, Windy's Ta[illegible]ern, 7; Earl O. Carmical, Top H[illegible] Lounge, 2; L. E. Carmicha[illegible] Rondevoo Cafe, 4; [illegible] man, Peacock Club, 1; [illegible] Cook, Hoosier Bar, 2; J. [illegible] Tulsa Club, 2; W. M. [illegible] White Cafe, 1; Arthur [illegible] L Cafe, 2; [illegible] Jena's Bar B-Q, 2; Frank [illegible] Frank's Dairy Treat, 1; Wal[illegible] Ebel Jr., Harry [illegible] Dane Harris, [illegible] Robert Gooden, Rock Court, [illegible] Wilbur Green, [illegible] 3; Mae Halligan, [illegible] Dane Harris, Gordon [illegible] Walter Ebel Jr., Harry [illegible]los, Fred Austin, [illegible] Bowman, [illegible] ter, Belvedere [illegible] Haskell [illegible] history indicates that we will fall flat on our faces, but we plan to change that outcome; we just don't know when or exactly how. I had set my mind to it knowing that no matter how tough, there would be some guidance if I asked for it. It had to be divine.

"They" were out there, we just had to find them and figure out a way to shortstop the mob, or the "Little Combination" and the related gangsters, and the local law enforcement. They were out there and had been there in one way or another for at least a hundred years. And that is no exaggeration. Casinos, crooked cops, "bust-out joints", shootouts on main street by the bad guys against the bad guys, as well as the good guys against the good guys, *i.e.* Deputy Sheriffs vs. Hot Springs policemen and other events that have been reported happening on the streets of Hot Springs since the early 1880's.

The real world jumped up and replaced my smoking fantasy when an Undercover Officer (UC) shows up at our command car. The police radio had been silent for quite a long time. We were monitoring the Garland County Police Radio but had heard nothing but 10-7's (Off Duty) and 10-8's (On Duty). Our own Arkansas State Police Radio, out of Little Rock has been silent for about an hour except for routine traffic.

The Undercover Officers and Agents began reporting, some through coded messages over the ASP Radio and some, by orders, came directly to the Safeway store to report the results of their efforts. Notwithstanding their efforts, the news was not good. About fifteen of our officers were on the city streets and in about three unmarked patrol cars waiting just outside the city on isolated parking lots and other places where they would not particularly stand out.

The first perimeter of Undercover Officers, like tourists, was cruising the downtown streets and sidewalks. They could hear the activity in the clubs; dice shooters yelling, slot machines clunking and activity in general, but found that the clubs were admitting only couples, man and woman, and only those with out-of-state driver's licenses. These undercover officers knew their business.

They would fit right in a party. They were professionals and were dressed the part of partygoers, but the news was still not good. The mob evidently believed my threats of raids but not enough to completely shut down.

It seemed that tonight was going to be a wash, simply a feint rather than a real honest to God raid of the gambling casinos and joints running in Hot Springs. We had determined one thing though; they had not taken my threats of a close down seriously.

Any broadcast radio signal from ASP Radio located at headquarters on Roosevelt Road in Little Rock was strong enough to reach the entire state and the closer the monitoring county/city radio was, the stronger the reception. Garland County Radio which monitored our ASP radio frequency could pick up any message broadcast in the clear. We had to make our message from ASP, Little Rock, appear to be broadcast to another county radio in the clear.

The Little Rock ASP Headquarters radio operator called for Car C- 77 (a fictitious patrol car number), for example, and sent a particular message, in the clear and blind. This meant that the radio message being sent did not require a reply or a comeback. Not hearing a reply or answer would indicate that Car C-77 had been out of range or, maybe, out of car when the message was sent.

"Little Rock ASP - C-Seven Seven be advised that the attempt to contact subject in Forrest City was negative." This coded message, which had been set up in advance, meant that efforts in Hot Springs had been bad or negative. The amplification of the County radio in Hot Springs should not have changed that much. We hoped the radio ruse worked, but it looked like this was just the beginning of the bad news. Close and yet so far.

I admire these guys who have the guts to walk right up to a casino entrance, an illegal operation run by some sort of mob or Syndicate, gangsters all, which they called, in Hot Springs, the "Little Combination". In the twelve days I have been on the job, I have not had the good fortune of knowing an official name for the Hot Springs mob, but everyone seemed to know that "They" were known by that name, the "Little Combination."

The operations were guarded by armed over-grown Neanderthals just looking for someone trying to get into the casino by using a phony driver's license, or by using a cooked-up story meant to get an undercover state police officer into the club of interest to put it out of operation. We had threatened "them" and "they" were obviously cautious; not knowing whether we were serious or not. "They" had faced threats before and even a few legitimate threats! (But not that many)

WHAT ARE THE CHOICES? ARE THERE ALTERNATIVES?

I reasoned, three choices, Lynn: (1) Go back home with nothing; (2) Hit a black crap game and go back home (with nothing); or (3) Do something else, but what else?

The "go back home" and the crap game argument never had a chance even though it had been recommended by one who had survived these shows for years. It's either now or never and, within the scope of minutes, between the door of the command car and the telephone booth outside the Safeway Store, the idea came to me and the decision was made. A decision destined to change the history of Arkansas. (And I had to borrow a dime to make the call to LRASP Headquarters to start the process of the raid.)

Why had I not thought of it before? I had decided weeks before that we are not after people but equipment, but that was easier said than done. How do you pin the equipment down physically and bide your time in gaining whatever legal authorization you need to search and seize it? If you can't get in and see the equipment, you can't get a search warrant. However, with the gambling equipment nailed down, you get the search warrant in hand, and, then, you take the sequestered equipment. The illegal slots, tables and other paraphernalia will be there waiting.

But how do we make sure it is there and will be there? It has a habit of sneaking away. Like a bolt out of the blue, it came to me. Because we will have uniformed troopers at the front and the back of all the operating clubs nailing the equipment down.

I had momentarily lost sight of the objective and that was to take the equipment! Once we took the equipment, we could then destroy it at our leisure. I had completely forgotten that there are more ways than one to skin a cat. Our mission was to enforce "all" the laws of Arkansas, and closing down casino gambling in the State of Arkansas was the first thing on my agenda; not to arrest every person who took part in those activities. If we arrested people, we could wind up arresting more than our jails would hold and, historically, those people would beat us home. However, if we had control of the equipment, we would have closed down the games, at least in Hot Springs. If the past was any guide, "they" would simply be fined $100.00 or less, as usual, and, then, just walk down the street returning to their casino or bookie operations.

WHAT IS OUR JURISDICTION? HOW FAR CAN WE GO?

Like an open book, oral question and answer test, I would ask the question and the answer would come, quicker than I thought. Come to think of it, we had jurisdiction right up to the casino door, as "up to the door" is public property. We can stay on the sidewalk here forever or at least longer than they can publicly stand. The tug of war would then become clear; us against what we would later learn was called the "Little Combination", according to Mark Palmer, local historian. It would become a contest of wills, us against all the political and enforcement types in Garland County and state government in Little Rock; but the contest would be carried out in the public, rather than in the courthouse or police station where in Hot Springs the odds were against us. I knew from that August day that it would take more than luck to pull this caper off. I knew that it had to happen fast before reaction could be brought down on us. It was obvious to anyone who thought about it, they had the resources and based on the past had the ability to see that our efforts could be stopped in a number of ways, legal and otherwise.

For 12 years Governor Faubus used his powers of persuasion to convince everyone (or almost everyone) that he had closed down gambling in Hot Springs—especially at election time.

Today, it is just the printed word, but can you imagine what a thrill it was that day when we had found their weakness and our strength. The speed with which we could act and the pressure and support of the "agginers", the people of Arkansas.

Thankfully, the security perimeter lights of the closed Safeway Store on Central Avenue did not shine as brightly on the telephone booth located on the East Side of the building. If you looked closely, you would see one or two unmarked state police cars at the side of the building as well as several other unmarked vehicles parked around the corner.

This night or rather morning, turned out to be a "hit" rather than a "feint." We found though, that "they" were smarter than we were. At least for a while; about thirty minutes.

Intelligence gathered earlier by the ASP Criminal Investigation Division (CID) had indicated that some of the casinos in Hot Springs were opening up. Opening up meant that "they" were either not convinced of the crackdown promised, or thought "they" could operate as before. It was a test for us. After all, even the Rockefeller Administration, in its first six or so months, had not been able to really put a dent in their operations, but through no fault of their own. Neither the Governor nor others had convinced the State that, *it could be done.* Governor Rockefeller, of course, thought it could be done with the right people and attitude. He never once mentioned Hot Springs or gambling, but I made sure he knew of my stance for enforcement of the law, all the laws and, obviously, that including gambling and prostitution. I knew from his response, he was for that stance.

The Criminal Investigation Division (CID) has been mildly successful in past years and years hitting the Clubs, getting one or two machines (or none) and going back home knowing that the system had stacked the cards against them, yet the politicians made it seem a victory against the mob.

They took what the gangsters would give them. The ASP/CID had to alert their targets, the clubs, of a pending raid, because they had to go through the city officials to get search warrants and that meant the city police, sheriff's department, and, practically, the whole city knew that ASP was coming. ASP would be forced to take whatever was chosen to be left, which was usually some decks of cards, some dice, and if "lucky," some old slot machine parts.

It seemed absurd that pictures of the ASP beating up a few old discarded slot machine parts was enough to show that the gambling laws were being enforced. However, it seemed to do the trick; Orval Faubus and a number of other governors made it seem routine. Convince everyone that it was a local matter, or it couldn't be done, and at the same time, "passing the plate," getting maximum political contributions and political favors from the "Little Combination."

If that wasn't enough, there was always intimidation. The targets owned the police department personnel; the Sheriff's Office, the judges, the mayor, and just about everybody and everything official in Garland County plus the City of Hot Springs. This wasn't the beginning of the mantra, "They Said It Couldn't Be Done." We had been told that so many times some of us Arkansans believed them. And if we didn't believe it we thought there was nothing we could do to change it.

That piece of information had been drilled into nearly every Arkansan's mind. This had been the prevailing view for over 100 years. Don't believe for a minute "The Valley of the Vapors" had not come under the scrutiny of the Mafioso, La Cosa Nostra, the Blackhand Society or whatever moniker the mob was known as during that particular time, from the mid 30's to present and before. The city was so well known in mob circles that it even gained another common name or names, "Bubbles" or "Hot Town."

"Wanted" gangsters were so welcomed by the Hot Springs mob that Arkansas Attorney General and later Governor Carl Bailey said publicly that it seemed that every wanted criminal in America went to Hot Springs to hideout. That wasn't far from the truth. The Department of Justice agreed with them, but was unable to do anything about it.

For years, "Bubbles," as the Mafia back east called it, drew varied types and numbers of gangsters because of its wide open gambling and prostitution activities. They came from Chicago, New York, New Orleans, and points West and East and even South and found a perfect atmosphere, for either pursuits of pleasure or to split the take or checking their holdings.

However, whichever way you looked at it, the activities they practiced and relied upon was illegal and 100 years and more didn't legalize it. It was the one thing, supposedly, the police had not been able to control for over 100 years. Of course, seldom had they tried, and seldom had the State demanded that they stop. The state leaders lacked the will not the way.

You can "bet the farm" that Hot Springs enjoyed the protection of the Italian Mafia, but when did the Mafia take an interest? Anyone who knows how the Mafia operated knew that there was always tribute to be paid to the Italians and only Sicilian Italians. In the case of Hot Springs, "they" wanted control so "they" could dictate who could operate and who could not; and charge tribute for the franchise. The System as the local operation was and had been in place but out of official sight, and "they" meant to keep it that way even though no one, insofar as I know, ever admitted that the Mafia directly dictated the operation of the rackets at Hot Springs. It requires little mental gymnastics, however, to assume that this had to be a fact of life.

Go back East and tell them that it was estimated that over 200 million dollars gross and 30 million net in 1946, was coming from a small town of some 30,000 population while Frank Costello, the gambling czar of the Mafia, La Casa Nostra, or the mob, and his bunch weren't getting a franchise fee. "They" would laugh you out of town.

Frank Costello, "Capo" or the "Boss of the Underworld" was a regular visitor to Hot Springs, as a guest of Owney "The Killer" Madden. Incidentally, Costello controlled organized gambling nationwide, from coast to coast, border to border. (Remember the admonition that there was an agreement between the Italian Mafia

Alphonso Capone, his brother, Bottles, and Al's driver (on his ass in front) at Happy Valley Amusement Park which was reached by a trolley pulled by mules who rode down the mountain on the back of the trolley.

Years earlier, Frank James had a side show at Happy Valley telling about his and Jessie's lives and exploits. Here is Al Capone and a friend enjoying Hot Springs hospitality.

and other ethnic groups that the others could operate illegal rackets, but they had to pay "tribute" to the mob. (Do you think they overlooked Hot Springs?)

The Chief of Detectives, "Dutch" Akers of the Hot Springs Police Department might have said it best when he said that he was an honest person before joining the Hot Springs Police Department, but when he couldn't get a share of the big money, he would take what he could. That was just before he went to the penitentiary for harboring Alvin "Creepy" Karpis, a FBI Top Ten Wanted criminal, prosecuted by a reform Prosecuting Attorney, Sid McMath in about 1946.

Millions of dollars came out of Hot Springs and some stayed, but the money that stayed was limited to certain movers and shakers as well as the local gambling czars of the "Little Combination," the name taken by the racketeers in Hot Springs. All this, except the amounts and to whom it was paid, was more or less out in the open. Payment came in many forms, some just as simple as getting and keeping a job. How did this system operate?

Everyone knew that the prostitutes, for example, put on their finery every month and trooped down to the Courthouse, went before the judge, pleaded guilty to prostitution, paid a fine which was split with the mayor, the Chief of Police and several other movers and shakers. The same procedure went for the gamblers.

The "Ladies of the Evening" (or actually morning, noon, afternoon, or night) pleaded guilty under their own names until they started to build up such a criminal record that they could be viewed as habitual criminals, a crime in itself. They started then to plead under fictitious names, selecting a different species of names to use each month. For example, this month they would use tree names: Opal Pine, Delores Oak and next month flowers: Lamonte Rose, and Milly Chrysanthemum. (I'll wager this name threw the judge for a flip, trying to spell it.)

The public seemed to view this form of graft as a contribution from the rackets, a patriotic chore, rather than an obligation, like paying taxes.

'They're Playing Our Song . . .'

This scene changed when the Little Combination found that WR wasn't going to sign the casino bill giving a gambling franchise to four (4) unnamed clubs, and then they blamed WR for not signing the bill.

There are those in Hot Springs who still credit the "contributional" income from the "Little Combination" to the building of the events center, the two swimming pools and a fire station and such, rather than taxes. *Contributions by the rackets rather than taxes* were an attempt to legitimize the rackets, giving the mob the chance to brag that their contributions were keeping the city afloat.

Out of millions of dollars coming out of Hot Springs or Garland County, the Legislature made part of the Arkansas State Police state budget depend upon the amount of income wagered at the Oaklawn race track, a legitimate operation.

NO PROMISES HAVE BEEN MADE... (Have they?)

These heroes, these troopers who take chances with their lives every day have to go back and face themselves as well as their families and their neighbors after a supposed raid. Again, going back in defeat due to no fault of their own. That's just the way the game was played.

We came here to follow through on a promise. A promise made to nobody in particular, but we know that no matter how we cut it, or what we call it, we will have failed ourselves most of all if we don't do what we came to do. We will have been unable to enforce "that" particular law. A promise believed by thousands of people to have been made in all the braggadocios statements made by me, their leader.

Everybody believed it couldn't be done until we could show differently. They said it couldn't be done, but we had to do it. We had to make an even bigger decision. Even without a Lucky Strike, we had to make a decision, to somehow win in spite of all the odds. (I had already made the decision to quit smoking, so closing down casino gambling in the State of Arkansas can't be that much harder, or can it?)

The traffic on Central Avenue, Hot Springs' main thoroughfare, is getting heavier and the element of surprise lessens with

ARKANSAS DEMOCRAT

NINETY-SIXTH YEAR

Published Daily and Sunday by the

ARKANSAS DEMOCRAT COMPANY

Capitol Avenue and Scott Street, Little Rock, Arkansas

Telephone—All Departments—FR 4-0321

SUBSCRIPTION RATES—Daily and Sunday—By carrier, 45c per week, $1.95 per month. By mail in Arkansas, payable in advance. $22.00 per year; $11.25 for six months; $5.75 for three months; $1.95 for one month.

Single copy price: Daily 5c, Sunday 15c.

Member of The Associated Press. The Associated Press is entitled exclusively to the use for publication of all local news printed in this newspaper as well as all AP news dispatches.

Sunday, March 5, 1967 

Vicious Gambling Proposal

Gov. Rockefeller's action on the legislature's move to legalize gambling in Garland County is a mandate to the right-thinking citizens to stand up and be counted.

The governor, in announcing that he would not sign the bill under any circumstances, called on the people to let their representatives and senators know their reactions to the ill-advised legislative action.

"The people overwhelmingly defeated such a proposal in 1964, and I cannot believe they have changed their minds since," Rockefeller recalled in his public announcement, calling for grass-roots action to encourage reconsideration of hasty action of Thursday and Friday.

Some political observers have seen in the action an attempt by some legislators to put Rockefeller on the spot. If this be their motive—and no one can know the true motive except the individual—they are more despicable than those who see in the legalized gambling an economic windfall.

Like most such vicious proposals, the Garland County gambling bill appears safe and simple. Just four "regulated" gambling spots in Garland, says the bill. But who guarantees that, as gamblers gain power, the number won't be expanded to more in the future? Who guarantees that "regulated" gambling spots won't spread to your county, too? It is the very nature of gambling greed and vice to grow.

[illegible]galized gambling spreads its corruption, as d[illegible] illegal gambling, to affect low and high public officials. Surely Arkansas has seen enough to every passing minute. You could cut the tension with a knife and the smoke coming from the back seat didn't make it any easier.

Who could blame us for going back to Little Rock and admitting at an inevitable press conference that we had been outsmarted; that it couldn't be done? Based on the reports we were getting, success tonight did look slim. Reports came in fast and furious. You could, according to reports of our Undercover Agents, hear the activity of a casino in the background, guarded by an off duty police officer, but couldn't get in.

Every time one of our UC's tried an entry, whether they were fresh faced or not, to the man, they were turned away. These reports came by way of coded messages from the State Police radio at Little Rock as well as verbal reports by the UC's. So close and yet so far. (No time to worry about smoking now, for sure.)

How easy it would be to simply back off into the shadows, give an excuse, go home with a crap game under our belt, and at least imply that the political machine was right when they said enforcing the laws against illegal casino gambling couldn't be done. After all, we never promised anyone that we would do it, did we? We had simply told the Governor that we would enforce all the laws. For years no one had been successful in closing down casino gambling in the State of Arkansas or take away the hundreds of slot machines operating in the State. So maybe we, too, had just failed. Failure was sometimes inevitable, right? This scenario kept reverberating in my mind. Could we do it? Sure, *if we set our mind to it.*

My wife has no idea as to where I am, but some of these older troopers have surely told their loved ones where we were going, and what we were planning to do. Now, they must ease back home with a very negative feeling. The same feeling they had gone home with so many times before. I can only waffle for so long and, in this case, not more than a few minutes. Do you take a black crap game down, as has been suggested and as has been done on quite a few occasions in prior "raids," or do you go back home facing an inevitable, "I told you it couldn't be done."

Snake-Eyes

We had to make them roll a snake eyes ... but how?

The ultimate intimidation, giving ASP only old slot machines and parts, then having Governor Faubus announcing that he had closed down casino gambling.

BLESS ORVAL'S HEART ... Notice the calendar, "November" — election time. Notice the surprise. Obviously he didn't know who was dropping the ball or money at the capitol broom closet, a political contribution.

Obviously, WR, after his election, used some pretty strong hints to get ASP director Lindsey moving toward Hot Springs. The ASP found in March, 1967, eight casinos operating in Garland County. By the time they got search warrants from the local judge mandating the ASP take along the policy, they found only two decks of cards and a pair of dice — out of 85 slot machines and related paraphernalia.

I fought off the notion that I never made any promises, only threats. We might have stepped into it when we told Governor Rockefeller that we would enforce all the laws. We didn't have sense enough to put in some qualifiers, to set up some conditions, to set out disclaimers. (Words or excuses I later learned when I got my law degree!!!) No amount of rationalizing will set off the sun rising. It will take place in a matter of an hour or so. The sun will be rising when all these UC's are called off, and I order our retreat from the field. *No, I have set my mind to it, but we must hurry!*

The Governor obviously put the monkey on Colonel Lindsey's back months before.

Evidently, at the insistence of Governor Rockefeller, ASP/ Criminal Investigation Division went undercover in about March, 1967, to find whether casinos were operating after his election and promise to close down gambling in the state. In Hot Springs, they found an interesting array of equipment, all laid out like a Christmas party and more than an ample array of equipment for a hometown poker game? (Surely, the Racketeers thought nothing had changed.)

This is what ASP found in March, 1967, about four months before I became Director:

Citizens Club: Poker table, bingo games, slot machines, dice table, "21" table;

Bridge Street Club: Three dice tables, three Blackjack tables, 30 slot machines, one roulette wheel;

Oasis Club: Five slots, one dice table;

Palms Club: Poker table, three "21" tables;

White Front: 30 slot machines, four dice tables, four Blackjack tables;

Cliff's Club: One poker table, one Blackjack table, one Keno table, seven slot machines;

Ohio Club: 11 slot machines, one dice table, three Blackjack tables;

Cameo Club: 4 slot machines, three dice tables;

Arkansas Gazett

148th Year—No. 103 LITTLE ROCK, THURSDAY, MARCH 2, 196[illegible] [illegible] Pages

courts ... (The entire Arkansas dele- ... committee. He said that to exclude the member-elect ... (See POWELL on Page 2A)

8 Raids Made At Hot Springs

Gaming Equipment Found at 1 Place

Gazette State News Service

HOT SPRINGS — Seven clubs and a drive-in were raided here Wednesday night by state troopers, Hot Springs policemen and officers of the Garland County sheriff's office after search warrants were issued on the basis of State Police affidavits alleging that there was gambling equipment in the places.

At only one—the Cameo Club at 508 Malvern Avenue — was any gambling equipment found. Officers said they found one dismantled dice table, two check racks, two boxes of cards and two gross of dice on the third floor of a vacant hotel over the club.

The proprietor of the Club, identified as Thelma Page, was arrested on a charge of exhibiting gambling equipment, according to Sheriff Eugene (Bud) Canada. She was released on $500 bond.

All eight places were raided simultaneously about 9:15 p.m. by 25 state policemen, Canada and three of his deputies and five members of the Hot Springs Police Department including Chief John Ermey.

The other places were the Ohio Club at 336 Central Avenue, the White Front Club at 310½ Central, Bridge Street Club at 801½ Central, Palms Club at 2806 Central, the Oasis at 431 Malvern, Cliff's Drive-in at 1212 Malvern and the Citizens Club at 740½ Central.

The investigators said that they found no gambling equipment at any of those places but they said all were crowded with customers.

The affidavits were brought from Little Rock and signed by Maj. William C. Struebing, commander of the Criminal Investigation Division of the State Police. They were taken to Hot Springs Municipal Judge Earl Mazander, who issued search warrants late Wednesday afternoon.

The affidavits alleged that the places had gambling equipment as follows: Citizens Club—poker table, bingo game, slot machines, dice table, "21" table; Bridge Street Club — three dice tables, three blackjack or "21" tables, 30 slot machines, one roulette table; Oasis—five slot machines, one dice table; Palms—poker table, three "21" tables; White Front — 30 slot ma-

Lindsey at press conference on gambling plans

Lindsey Outlines ASP Attack on Gambling: Warrants, Then Raids

By BILL LEWIS
Of the Gazette Staff

The State Police will move against illegal gambling in Arkansas only after obtaining warrants from local authorities, State Police director Col. Herman Lindsey said Wednesday.

Lindsey called a news conference at his office to announce that he had delegated Maj. Bill Struebing, head of the Criminal Investigation Division, and Capt. Kenneth McKee, commander of the uniformed Highway Patrol Division, "to act at will" in enforcing gambling laws "without any further contact from this office."

He also urged news media to co-operate by notifying the State Police when they send their representatives to establishments "where gambling is alleged to be taking place" before publishing their reports so that the troopers can take possible legal action."

Publication in advance, said Lindsey, "makes it very difficult, if not impossible, for this Department to carry out its instructions and to do the job that is expected of us."

He said any such information furnished the State Police would be "given the proper attention and, if there is any question in our minds as to whether or not the information furnished is legal, we will then consult our legal counsel"—meaning Attor-

... secure warrants, where needed and necessary, and to take action at will in their respective districts without any further contact from this office, but to immediately notify this office after any action is taken and be prepared to furnish a detailed verbal report by public service on the action taken."

On the basis of these verbal reports, Lindsey said he then would issue press releases from his headquarters at Little Rock, after which the local officers would be at liberty to notify the local press. Then the officers would make a detailed written report.

Every officer in the State Police Department, Lindsey said, would be guided by these instructions.

Lindsey also laid down the ground rules for press coverage of State Police gambling activities. First, he said, news media would not be notified in advance of any raids, just as the State Police would do "our dead-level best not to let anyone know what, where or how we're going to do it." After the action, whatever it was, the news media would be informed and supplied—in all probability, he said—both still pictures and movie films of the action.

Asked whether he had any legal evidence now on which to base a raid, in light of an explicit listing of slots, crap tables, operators and customers given newsmen by Governor Rockefeller, Lindsey replied, "That's classified information."

Mr. Rockefeller said his source for the information was the State Police.

What About Private Clubs?

Was there some question of legality about raiding private clubs that has delayed State Police action to stop gambling? "That," said Lindsey, "is a very broad question." He replied that his men had received specific instructions about what to do and that he wanted the State Police to be "legal in every move that we make." He said he had checked with Purcell to be sure of this.

How soon, Lindsey was asked, would the State Police act after they had discovered gambling? It depends on "how soon we can file information and get a warrant."

Did this mean that the State Police could not act without first obtaining warrants from local authorities? In a variety of replies, Lindsey said that it did.

Why did the State Police find it so difficult to locate illegal gambling when newsmen could spot it with consummate ease? Well, said Lindsey, the State Police have other things to do and they can't be everywhere at once.

Wouldn't his news conference serve to tip off the gamblers that they faced raids? Lindsey replied that the State Police's intention was not new because the governor already had said the same thing.

Would Destroy Gambling Devices

Would he destroy gambling equipment found in raids, if any are made? "If and when we ask for a warrant," Lindsey said, "it would be to enter, search, seize and destroy, by publicly burning, all contraband gambling equipment found in a raid."

Would his officers arrest only the immediate operators of gambling devices, or would ... "We will arrest every man or lady in the establishment that has anything to do with the operation of it," Lindsey replied. He said if he was not satisfied that the State Police had arrested the person owning the establishment they would ascertain the owner through investigation and would go to the prosecuting attorney with the information.

And what about the patrons? Lindsey said that as in the past their names and addresses would be taken so that they could be subpoenaed as witnesses. Prosecution of them, he said, would be up to the prosecuting attorney.

Would State Police concentrate their anti-gambling efforts in Pulaski and Garland Counties? "We wouldn't concentrate on any county," Lindsey replied.

CUAG Head Hits New Try To Make Gambling Legal

Legalizing gambling in Hot Springs would make a bad situation "infinitely worse," according to James B. Gannaway of Little Rock, a lawyer and chairman of the Churches United Against Gambling.

CUAG successfully fought ...

8 raids made on those clubs ... two decks of cards and one pair of dice! Do you think the deck was stacked?

That comes to about 83 slot machines, 11 dice tables and about 25 other tables, all personally observed by ASP/UC's in operation in the space of probably an hour or so in Hot Springs. What a difference a few hours make!

Surely it is coincidental that all of the equipment above was in place and in operation with apparent customers; customers who stood around waiting for the "coming" raid, signaled by the moving of all the contraband equipment, waiting for the action to again begin. (That wouldn't be long, based on past experience.)

When the undercover officers (UC's) "worked the town" in March, before I was appointed, and found all the equipment, as above, they listed it on an affidavit swearing as to its existence and its operation and took it to the local judge for his signature. Hours later when the (UC's) conducted their raid on the eight clubs, they found: *Two packs of cards, some dice and little more.*

Mayflower Moving couldn't have done it any faster. The cards and dice they found just happened to be in a black club, and it all happened in a matter of an hour or so. It doesn't take a mental giant or even a great amount of deductive reasoning to know that between the time of the warrants being signed by the Hot Springs official, the local judge, and the actual raid, the balance between the good guys and the bad guys had shifted. It's not there if you don't find it, right?

The *raiding* party consisted of *25 state policemen, Sheriff Bud Canada and three of his deputies and five members of the Hot Springs Police Department including Chief of Police John Ermey.* (Emphasis added). Just having the Chief of Police and Sheriff's Office forewarned of the raid was a guarantee of finding nothing except a pack of cards or such—just so that the "aginners" could read in the newspapers that the State Police had been successful in closing down casino gambling in Arkansas.

The election of Rockefeller had evidently made no difference. (What a mistake!) The Affidavit for the search warrant had been signed by ASP Major William Struebing, who was simply act-

'I'm Confused, Doc . . . Who's My Boss?'

The Attorney General order the ASP to hold the machines. A Little Rock judge ordered the machines held in Little Rock and the Hot Springs judge ordered all the machines returned to Hot Springs. Could this be intimidation?

ing on orders issued by Judge Mazander. Guess what happened to Major Streubing? Let me tell you.

On March 19, 1967, before the above described raid, ASP had "found" four slot machines making a total of 40 machines seized in prior raids in a purported effort to crack down on casino gambling again. (The number of 40 machines total seized is surprising in itself. Could it be that they counted old parts and scraps, too?) The owner of the Carousel Club from which the last four machines were seized was released on a $500 bond on the *misdemeanor charge* and the Municipal Judge ordered the contraband machines returned to the custody of the Hot Springs officials.

However, all the machines seized here and there in Hot Springs over the years had been ordered by Circuit Judge Digby in Little Rock to be held for a trial in that jurisdiction, a suit to determine if the clubs could operate as private clubs. ASP, in view of Hot Springs' Municipal Judge Mazander's order to return the machines, returned only seven machines, one for each trial which was to be held in Hot Springs. (The Attorney General had advised the ASP to hold the machines from all the raids, the Carousel Club and the others.) These are three different orders regarding what to do with the same machines. As the Major had not returned all the machines to Hot Springs, only seven, Mazander held Major Struebing in contempt of court. (What an opportunity for a Hot Springs judge to show that the seizure had been a local matter and still in his jurisdiction.)

Judge Digby, Circuit Judge in Little Rock, had ordered all the equipment held for a hearing on another case which was to decide the question of whether private clubs had such a status that being private, they could conduct gambling operations in the club safe from the state prohibition on gambling. It was just another attempt to bypass the constitution. (I wonder why Judge Mazander of Hot Springs issued his order to the head of the CID, Streubing, rather than to the head of the State Police, Herman Lindsey?)

Could this have been an effort to harass and intimidate Major Streubing who was simply acting on orders? (Remember my admonition about intimidation?)

This little scenario brought in the major players: Municipal Judge Mazander, ASP Major Streubing, ASP Colonel Lindsay, Former Governor Orval Faubus and Governor Rockefeller as well as "*non-innocent*" by-standers: Chief of Police Ermey, the "Little Combination," the Civil Service Commission and dozens of others who played bit rolls, but important bit rolls, nonetheless.

"WE" AND NOT "I"

"I" means "we," a reference you will find a number of times in this book. This is not a highlighted "I" or "we" because there are hundreds of thousands of people who could and should bc included in those terms, people who for one reason or another decided to adopt a cause bigger than any one of them or a group of us, but many of whom had been crusading for years to meet the problem and do away with it. 1967 was a memorable year.

The year 1967 just happened to be a time when it all came together, a man of principle who could disregard the blandishments of political contributions for illegal favors, who could have been any place in the world, doing just about any thing he wanted to be doing with whom he wanted to be. Yet, he adopted the State of Arkansas not for what he could gain, but what he could give. He was guided by his training and God-given talents in selecting his goals—Winthrop Rockefeller. (That was my assessment of the man, and I never had reason to believe otherwise.)

Little did I know that his plans included finding me, Lynn Davis, who agreed with his quest for strict, honest law enforcement. Since I already had the training in law enforcement, FBI, I was ready and anxious to return to my home state and lucky enough to find a home at the Arkansas State Police, even if for only 120 days. Even though I was the acting Director of the Arkansas State Police for only 120 days and nights, I learned the level of devotion of hundreds of state policemen and women who adopted those goals and provided every ounce of effort they had to help achieve

The battle over my appointment and others was still raging. We had to saddle up and <u>move</u> as there was a chance we would lose out to the gangsters one way or another!

those goals. I learned too, that we were not alone. So, as they say, we saddled up and remembered that we had to "Cut them off at the pass," and do it quickly. The ten year residency requirement standing in the way of my appointment was hard on our heels.

THE 10 YEAR RESIDENCY REQUIREMENT

There was a lot of "back seat driving" by the Democratic Senate bogging down Win's executive appointments, obviously based on politics. That was true in my case.

The ten year residency law, passed in the late forties, dictated that the Director of the Arkansas State Police had to have been a resident of the State ten years next preceding his appointment. Of course, I had been employed out of the state six or seven years. The question was whether the "residence" meant "physical residence" or as "residence is where the heart is" as in voting residence. I always meant to move back to Arkansas as soon as I could and, as a matter of fact, had gone to see Mr. Hoover on two occasions asking that I be transferred to the Little Rock FBI Office.

Sid McMath, World War II hero, wasn't a qualified physical resident… (or so they hoped). He had been in Europe helping protect this country. The Legislature evidently took note of the fact that veterans returning from the War were getting plum appointments and getting elected to political positions. Could they take a chance on their Governor or any other Governor taking out the old ASP Director and putting in an appointee who thought it could be done? (Especially, a crusader like Sid McMath, who as the Prosecuting Attorney for Garland County had, in 1946, prosecuted most of the police force, Maxine Jones, the Madam, the Mayor and assorted other people for bribes and payoffs, sending some of them to the penitentiary.)

Mr. Hoover, during my last "visit" told me that he would "do what he could to get me transferred due to my mother's illness." Old time agents assured me that the words, "do what he could" meant that my transfer was most likely to be "in the bag." Little

4A • ARKANSAS GAZETTE, Thurs., July 6, 1967.

Davis Appointed; Suit to Decide Residency Issue

7-6-67

—Staff Photo

LYNN A. DAVIS

Governor Rockefeller said Wednesday that he would go ahead and appoint Lynn A. Davis, an FBI agent who is a native of Texarkana, as director of the State Police. He said that a friendly suit would be filed so the courts could decide whether Davis meets the residency requirement in the law.

A 1945 act says that the State Police director must have lived in Arkansas for 10 years "next preceding" his appointment. Mr. Rockefeller said over the week end that his lawyers advised him that Davis, a native of Texarkana, was eligible to serve.

Davis, who will be 34 Friday, resigned as an FBI agent at Anaheim, Cal. to accept the $12,000-a-year state job. Davis said he earned more as an FBI agent, when overtime and other benefits were figured in, but that he regarded the State Police appointment as a challenge and an opportunity to return to Arkansas.

The announcement came after the governor met with the State Police Commission and later with Davis. Mr. Rockefeller said that the appointment, had the support of the Commission. All of the members but Mike Berg of Camden were present.

Commision Says That It Approves

The Commission adopted a resolution in which it pointed to the "exclusive authority" of the governor in making the appointment. Not even the Senate has confirmation power over the appointment, the resolution said. The members expressed their appreciation to Mr. Rockefeller for consulting with them before formally naming Davis. This showed the governor's desire to co-operate with them, they said.

"We move that we thank Governor Rockefeller for the courtesy he has shown us; * * * we concur in his selection of the new director; and, * * * we pledge to the new director our co-operation and assistance in the administration of his many duties as such director * * *," the resolution concluded. It was signed by Clark H. (Rusty) Ralston, the chairman and the governor's first appointee to the Commission, and the other five Maj. Kenneth McKee for the job.

Ralston told newsmen after the governor's announcement that McKee's name had been offered on the assumption that Mr. Rockefeller would look to the Department to furnish a successor to Lindsey.

"The governor has seen fit to make the appointment and we concur," Ralston said of Davis' selection. Mr. Rockefeller said that he wanted professionalism and that was why he settled on Davis. Mr. Rockefeller said that a mutual friend had told him about Davis and that his office checked Davis' record and background and then he decided to pick Davis.

Mr. Rockefeller later confirmed that the recommendation came from B. Bryan Larey of Texarkana, the state revenue commissioner. Davis said that he and Larey are friends.

Davis Says Job Not Political

Davis said that he didn't look on the job as political. He said that neither did he believe that detailed knowledge of the state was essential. Law enforcement is fairly general, Davis said, and this is why FBI agents are rotated periodically and assigned to different sections of the nation.

Davis said he believed he can handle the responsibility. He said that he had the desire to "do my part to make Arkansas an even greater state."

He said he anticipated no major shakeup within the Department after he takes over. one could seriously question his residency.

"Four generations of my family have lived in Arkansas," W. E. Davis of Texarkana, served as Miller County sheriff for 18 years. Davis said that he always considered Texarkana and Arkansas his home.

'Might Call Me A Gambler'

He agreed that his leaving the FBI for a job which will be involved in a lawsuit has an element of risk. "It could be that you can call me a gambler," Davis said. "But, I resigned without hesitation at the chance. Security doesn't mean that much to me."

Davis said that he had no doubt but that he would be able to get along with sheriffs and local law enforcement officials. He said they all had a mutual interest in law enforcement and a desire to serve the public.

He saw no problems in this area or public relations in general. Davis said that he had experience as a teacher, salesman and as public relations man for the Texarkana Chamber of Commerce.

did they or I know that instead of transferring agents out of Los Angeles, in 1967, they transferred in about 200 new agents.

Two border patrolmen had been ambushed by drug runners and later brutally executed in the Mountains of California. The runners handcuffed the two Patrolmen with their hands together through a pot bellied stove and took turns seeing who could shoot closest to their ears without shooting them in the head. After shot after shot, according to the informant, (one of their girlfriends) reluctantly told us that one of the bad guys, tired of the game, shot each of the patrolmen in one ear and out the other.

Another investigation, FBI code named "Youngnap" involved the kidnapping of an 11 year old male child from Beverly Hills for whom a ransom of $250,000 was paid. We recovered Kenny Young, the victim, after paying the money, but the ransom was never recovered, which was, at that time, the highest ransom ever paid for the safe return of a victim. About a hundred and fifty FBI cars were on the streets of Los Angeles and Southern California the night of the payoff. Agents met the kidnapper (on his demand) at a freeway turnaround on the Orange County Freeway. After the kidnapper took the gym bag with $250,000 cash he told Kenny's father that he could see Kenny shortly.

After about three hours we despaired of recovering Kenny when Kenny called his dad. He had been dumped in an abandoned car in an apartment underground parking lot close to the beach in Santa Monica, after being given a knockout pill.

I enjoyed my time with the Bureau, but the call from WR was not "*like*" an answer to a prayer but *was* the answer to a prayer. (A daily three hour round trip commute and a 9 to 10 hour per day seven days per week schedule was not easy, but necessary.)

H. D. Thoreau wrote:

> "In most books the, "I" or first person, is omitted, in this it will be retained; that in respect to egotism, is the main difference. We commonly do not remember that it is, after all, always the first person that is speaking. I should

1946

CITY UNHURT AS GAMBLING ENDS IN HOT SPRINGS

Ark. Gaz. 2-13-47

No Loss of Popularity Seen.

By JOHN L. FLETCHER.
Day City Editor of the Gazette.

Hot Springs, Feb. 12.—Gambling houses have been closed for six weeks but no grass was growing on Central avenue today.

National Park Service records will show, when they are released in a few days, that more persons registered for the baths last month than during any January in Hot Springs history.

These figures tend to refute Mayor Leo P. McLaughlin's prediction that "Grass will grow in the streets" if visitors are not provided with a chance to gamble. He did everything he could to keep the handbooks and dice games going but the operators closed shop before victorious war veterans assumed all county offices January 1.

Col. Thomas Boles, superintendent of the Hot Springs National park, said 90,672 bath sales were made last month. This was a 10 per cent increase over the 82,730 in January, 1946. The greatest number of sales in any month, 114,000, occured in April, 1946.

Massage sales increased from $33,299 to $40,060, or more than 20 per cent.

Colonel Boles said 18,626 visitors toured the park last month compared to 18,497 in January, 1946. He said last year's abnormal figure could be attributed to the big army distribution system that was operated in Hot Springs then.

He said 287,895 visitors registered as park tourists in the 1946 calendar year and predicted that 350,000 will walk on the trails this year.

Business Men See No Harmful Effects of Ban.

Colonel Boles' figures were corroborated by "Mickey" Callahan, operator of the Quapaw Bathhouse and president of the Hot Springs Bathhouse Association.

No additional reservations are being accepted at the Arlington hotel until the second week in March. A similar situation exists at the Majestic. It is almost impossible to obtain a room at most other hotels and tourist courts.

W. E. Chester, manager of the Arlington, said his business never had been affected by the presence or absence of gambling. He said visitors don't come to Hot Springs to gamble, although some frequent the bookmaking establishments when they are open.

Several store owners said their afternoon business has increased because customers don't spend their afternoons in gambling joints.

R. Walls, owner of a Central avenue barber shop, said his income is not affected by gambling.

"Business in general is off slightly this year," he said. "I'll be satisfied with a small decrease in rev-

NO PLACE FOR SUCKERS TO GO IN HOT SPRINGS

Gaz. D 31 '46

Gamblers Hang On To Telephones.

By JOHN L. FLETCHER.
(Day City Editor of the Gazette.)

Hot Springs, Dec. 30. — Like the fellow who quit drinking when the liquor ran out, Garland county gamblers took the veil today.

They had no place to go.

Cecil Parker's decision to shut off his horse racing news service to the 10 handbooks was an accomplished fact. His teletype machine in an office over Bill Muncrief's print shop, where running accounts of races had been received from New Orleans, was silent.

Gambling rooms were empty in contrast to Saturday's big crowds. Floors had been swept and chairs stacked in corners. Except for the blackboards on which remained remnants of Saturday's wall sheets, the rooms resembled a chapel in a funeral home.

Although they had been informed that the books would not be open today, many horse players congregated at the clubs soon after noon, apparently not convinced the show was over. They drank beer at the bars up front or downstairs. Some studied copies of the Racing Form just in case they should discover they had been dreaming.

Most gamblers seem to believe the shutdown is temporary. Yesterday's demand for today's Racing Form was as brisk as ever, dealers said.

Hopeful Gamblers Retain Their Telephones.

Club owners have not removed their telephones. Parker's private telephone lines leading to each handbook have not been disconnected. These leased wires have been used for years. Formerly, the teletype receiving machine was in the Southern Club building. The headquarters operator described the progress of races through loud speakers at each book.

In those days, everybookmaker had four to 12 telephones. When the then Governor Adkins sent State Police to raid the clubs and take out the telephones, the operators were lucky to get back one phone and an extension because of the war shortage of equipment. Until Saturday, the headquarters operator called the races over all private lines at one time. An employe at each handbook, equipped with a headset, relayed the information to the customers.

Since the telephone shortage remains acute, the operators are reluctant to relinquish their service. Probably they will continue to pay for service they won't need when Prosecuting Attorney-elect Sidney S. McMath and other war veterans assume office Wednesday.

Hotel Owners Expect No Loss of Business.

Mayor McLaughlin's followers . . . at ouort an.

---

tion proceedings, subject to the mayor's approval. The city did not, though, continue with its condemnation proceedings. The city, represented by the mayor, the water committee and the acting city attorney, agreed upon a purchase price with Gus Walton of $1,900,000. This agreed purchase price exceeded by $400,000 the original valuation placed on the property by the bond company, Lewis W. Cherry and associates.

"Lewis W. Cherry and associates employed Jay Rowland, then acting city attorney, as local counsel. The city attorney, as local counsel. The sale of the bonds and purchase of the water company was completed in December, 1943. The bonds were sold to Lewis W. Cherry and Associates without competitive bidding. The city sold to Lewis W. Cherry $1,900,000 worth of bonds, bearing interest at the rate of 3 1-2 per cent.

"Later Lewis W. Cherry & Co. converted the bonds to a $2,075,000 issue, bearing interest at the rate of three per cent. The grand jury finds from all evidence that the interest rate of the bonds was excessive. It is believed that these non-taxable bonds could have been sold at an interest rate of 2 1-2 per cent."

High Fees Paid.

The report then went into further detail and asserted that Attorney Jay Rowland received $15,000 as a "finder's fee," and another check for $35,000 for "attorney's fees." It further stated that Alderman Moody and Alderman Smith each received $11,500.

In conclusion, the report stated that "the irregularities of the transaction indicate that other officials may have received bribes."

The special grand jury called on the incoming grand jury—which takes over tomorrow—to continue the investigation on the water works matter. The statute of limitations prevented the special grand jury from returning indictments, the report said.

Page Five of the report deals with the alleged use by McLaughlin of city equipment and employes to construct buildings and bridle paths on his estate. The mayor is a great lover of horses and his legendary trips down Central Avenue behind his matched buggy team of "Scotch and Soda" attracted the attention of the thousands of visitors.

The report also charged that city employes engaged in private deals with city equipment; that several ... trucks were sold for $50 each; there were election irregularities and termed the state election "inadequate." The report said ... state election setup made ...ed irregularities possible.

...sled.

...ing paragraph, the grand ... landed ...

terday climaxed an investigation of several days by special agents of the Thoroughbred Protective Association into the alleged "doping" of the horse Dashaway early in the week. He was arrested by Deputy Sheriff Ted Kilgore and released under $2,500 bond. Bond for the trainer, Mr. McLellan, also was set at $2,500.

Resignation Rumored.

Judge Ledgerwood's anticipated resignation had been "rumored" for several days and is expected to be forthcoming by tomorrow.

The indictments returned against Mayor McLaughlin yesterday accused him of:

Four for accepting bribery.

One as accessory to illegal voting.

Two for indirectly being interested in conducting and operating a gambling house.

The mayor was arrested at the Oaklawn race track just as the third race was completed by Sheriff Brown and Deputy Sheriff Walt McLavey.

Taken to the sheriff's office, McLaughlin was booked for the second time and placed under bonds amounting to $19,000. Three of the bonds were signed by John Wolfe, retired Hot Springs business man, and the remainder by Ed B. Mooney, Hot Springs contractor.

Afterward, the mayor was taken to the city jail, where he was "mugged" and fingerprinted. The fingerprinting office is not too many steps from the mayor's office.

Mayor McLaughlin withdrew from the coming city elections April 1 in face of the grand jury investigation. His withdrawal leaves the way open to five candidates, four business men and one attorney.

The mayor declined to make a statement while being booked, except to say later that "My friend are astounded at the amount of these bonds."

COURT

(Continued From Page 1.)

000 and the power to serve as executrix without bond.

The opinion today said:

"Elaine attempts to make a reasonable explanation of everything that was done and to show that the will was not made because of any undue influence on her part, and that there was no fraud in failing to fully inform Alice Love" about details of the trust left by George R. Love.

"Both sides offer expert and lay testimony as to the mental capacity of Alice Love. But this is a case where actions speak louder than words. Undue influence may be inferred from facts and circumstances."

The opinion, by Associate Justice Sam Robinson, pointed out the relationship between Elaine and Mrs. Love was not a close one, and that the May 30 will Mrs. Love "did the natural thing * * * the large bulk of her estate was left to her two sisters" and other relatives.

Elaine argued that if the June

Previous shutdowns, even though temporary, had not proved to be detrimental to Hot Springs' businesses.

not talk so much about myself if there were anybody else whom I know as well. Unfortunately, I am confined to this theme by the narrowness of my experience."

I, the author, taking Thoreau's advice to heart, find that even though my efforts are to diminish the personal pronoun, I can find no one who can consistently and fairly present the events of those 120 days in 1967. For that reason, I rely upon published reports and opinions of those whom I trust. Who else could recount all the scrapes and bruises of my 6½ years in Washington, D.C; Springfield, Champaign-Urbana and Rock Island, Illinois; Denver, Colorado; Rock Springs, Wyoming, and Los Angeles, California, serving as a Special Agent in the Federal Bureau of Investigation?

The Arkansas Legislature, after a protracted fight reluctantly reduced the ten years residency so that I would be eligible for appointment to the Directorship within a few months, but I felt that we had proven our point by that time some 120 days after we had started our mission to show that it could be done.

What I found upon my return from the FBI?

Illegal casinos were still in a wide open mode, hoping that Governor Rockefeller was going to allow the clubs to operate as private clubs or otherwise.

Chances are good that the guard or bouncer at any one of the Hot Springs casinos was an off duty cop or deputy sheriff and carried a badge to prove it. He had the power to arrest anyone he chose and to take that person before *his* judge; handpicked by the Mayor or the other powers that be, the "Little Combination."

There is no question that the ASP Undercover Agents understood the importance of getting into the clubs. We not only needed to know and show which casinos were operating, but also to get inside so we can use personal observation to warrant a search warrant. (Even though the observations and search warrants have not worked all these years, hope remains eternal.) Other than their giving ASP some "junk" so that the raid could look to be legitimate, ASP had gone home empty handed.

Gambling at Hot Springs

Gaz. June 17, '62

These pictures made during the 1960 racing s are typical of today except for the horse p

One of the big clubs with a big crowd during the 1960 Oaklawn season.

A horse race betting parlor in operation before the McClellan committee exposed the syndicate's rac. De

Of course, I know that getting this information about their being active is only the beginning. Seventy-six angels swearing that the clubs are in operation would not change a fact of life. We still have to find some way to overcome the time lapse; the time between getting the information about the casino operating and with what and our getting the search warrant which we have to have signed by the Municipal Judge and, of course, as in the past, taking along the police and the sheriff's deputies.

This is something Arkansas State Policemen have wanted to do for years, maybc cvcn close to fifty years, since they were formed, but they had to make half-hearted efforts look like they had tried and failed again. They have suffered mostly in silence the taunts of others that gambling can run rampant all over Arkansas; slot machines in private clubs, casinos, convenience stores and honky-tonks and some even across the street from the Hot Springs Police Station, but the police couldn't find them. They could, though, find a person going ten miles over the speed limit and issue that person a "ticket," even when that person is going to Hot Springs or elsewhere in Arkansas to gamble.

Little comfort is taken in a fact that we all know—we are fighting a fight, not only with our hands tied, but also with the opposition having a blueprint of every punch we are going to throw. The referee is the opposition's brother and the judges are his uncles. (And that is not far from the truth!)

I ran over, in my mind, the usual procedure—locate the illegal casino operation, get a search warrant signed by a judge, serve the warrant on someone at the location and seize the illegal equipment before the gangsters have a chance to move it. (Impossible!) The delays could and usually were enough to give the "Little Combination" time to move the gambling equipment and certainly enough when they had the City Police and the County Sheriff's helping them move. Within that extra time lapse the gangsters could move the gambling paraphernalia to a safe place.

The "Little Combination" sometimes found it was enough to slow down the process by getting the judge to be otherwise occupied, unable to sign the warrants needed, or, in some cases, using their power to threaten the very officers who were meant to uphold the law. Fear and intimidation ran rampant in Hot Springs and Garland County, and there seemed little that could be done about it, especially since the "Little Combination," and the city and county officials acting together to protect the rackets, made the rackets seem almost legitimate and accepted as complete, almost official authority with implied permission to run them; gambling, prostitution and related rackets. The "Little Combination" could very well do as "they" liked especially when implied permission came from Governor Faubus on down. Hot Springs had what was termed an "open city." Very few tactics were out of bounds, and selected members of the "Little Combination" could operate until they got orders to shut down. This was nearly always only a temporary shutdown, an order which nearly always came from the Governor depending upon the political situation—campaign contributions, etc.

The "Little Combination" controlled the "who" that called the shots and the "who" shared in the proceeds and "how" the money was delivered to those people. Their interest was in keeping control. They were considered the elite as opposed to those who did not have the political clout to get a "permit" to operate, and it appeared the clout came from the National Syndicate, a group of thugs who ran the rackets all over the country.

One of the arguments used to keep the selected clubs open was that if there was no control, there would be a lot more "bustout joints," cheapening the Hot Springs mystique. The Hot Springs situation was almost an afterthought until political season rolled around, and then it became a political issue. During the campaign, invariably gambling and prostitution became a "hot potato," and Garland County was the prize. There was an argument that lack of gambling would hurt the City. It didn't seem to hurt the City in 1946.

The "Open City" crowd claimed it could be no other way. Closing the illegal activities had been tried and failed; there was not enough money to run the city without taxes on the casinos, and the business they brought to the city. Besides that, there was no way it could be done, closing down the biggest illegal casino operation in America, a description given to "Bubbles" by the United States Department of Justice. That had been tried many times and failed. Why not take the manna from heaven (the rackets) and spend it on roads and streets?

J. Edgar Hoover, Director of the Federal Bureau of Investigation, could not close it down, even though Mr. Hoover put forth maximum effort to "get the goods" on Owney "The Killer" Madden, the Boss Gambler in Garland County. Hoover declared that Madden was the number one or two criminal in the United States and ordered his file to be upgraded to "Top Hoodlum" status, and ordered him kept under almost constant surveillance.

When Carl Bailey, Arkansas Attorney General, and later Governor of Arkansas, said it seemed that every time someone was "wanted" they came to Hot Springs, Arkansas to hideout, I would have told him, you can't have one without the other. The rackets and their progenitors, the Racketeers went hand in hand with "wanted" men. He should have known that. (It should also be noted that, as attorney General, it would seen that he could have done more to close down the rackets in Arkansas.)

Maxine Jones, the "Two House" Madam, who operated her houses of prostitution with impunity, said that she never sent any money to the Syndicate. She said "they" had told her she had to contribute. "They must think I am crazy to do such a thing." The owner of two houses of prostitution, when she got new girls in town, posed them on the back of the cover on her Cadillac convertible top. They sat there in their finest, most revealing outfits and drove around town. (Advertising, don't you know?) (I wonder if she paraded them through the casinos and other joints?) I doubt that Maxine failed to pay her franchise fee to the mob. Anything less could have put her out of business ... permanently!

That's history though, a lot of which I did not know that night in August, 1967.

I did know, though, we either do it tonight or maybe never. I have only told two or three ASP Officers about the raid planned.

Arkansas

118th Year—No. 271  LITTLE ROCK.

Breaking into the Bridge Street Club — What a beautiful door!

(Loose lips sink ships.) I have set my mind to it, and there is no wiggle room. Halfway doing it doesn't count. We knew it was there and that it had to be done. The worry though was, we just didn't know exactly how. Everyone else carrying an ASP badge is on board for the general proposition, but they had no idea that it would be this soon.

Today is the day. Let's "Head 'em up, and move 'em out."

BREAKING INTO THE BRIDGE STREET CLUB

The first "real" raid on gambling establishments in modern Arkansas history was about to take place. That, in itself, should be enough to sharpen the memory and get my attention.

In fairness, I should point out that the Hot Springs Municipal Judge Earl Mazander and the prosecuting or city attorney, did call us back, just before the first raid to add to the first search warrant that it could be served at nighttime. (Thanks.)

We had the original search warrant in hand standing about one block from the city hall ready to go when we heard someone yelling, "Wait!" while they were fast walking toward us. I tucked the warrant in my pocket to preserve it not knowing what they had in mind. We were all in a defensive posture when the judge said they had made a mistake and had not included on the warrant that it could be served during "nighttime," a requirement of law.

Standing in front of the Bridge Street Club, I could have been angry, but I wasn't. I could have become angry, but I didn't. Probably, I should have been angry, but looking at it from a different point of view, it was actually amusing. Here is the head of the Arkansas State Police who has just put state troopers in the front of "Your" Bridge Street Club and four others to seize their illegal gambling equipment, possibly to put "you" out of a job. These troopers, who now guarded the Clubs, decked out in class A uniforms, armed and maybe even dangerous, would not let anyone in, only out. They stood at parade rest, which seemed to fit what they had been told to do, to make certain that no one brought out any gambling equipment from the club. Let people out, keep gambling equipment in.

We, the Arkansas State Police, are about to do what one would expect, since we have a Search and Seizure Warrant, get into the Bridge Street Club even if we have to break down the door. Sure enough, it was locked. That door was probably the only casino door ever locked at the time of a raid. Before, on any other day, the door obviously, would be left open so the raiders could get in without any damage. No need to lose a pack of cards and a dice table or two and have the door smashed down, too.

This is the amusing part. Appearing from the crowd of about fifty people a nondescript man stepped forward and had some great news. He thought he could find the "key keeper" making it unnecessary to break down the front door and save the decorative trim on the door and the side windows. (That descriptive assessment, was mine not his.)

It seemed a reasonable solution. I had broken a number of doors open before but never a big, commercial type door such as this. I feel sure, too, that "they" didn't expect us to get this far, a search and seizure warrant on the outside of a casino filled with slots and other gear, since we got there before they could be moved.

This individual who was going to find "the" key, however, seemed to have something more nefarious in mind. Wouldn't it be hilarious to keep Davis waiting a little bit, if only five minutes, to show that the Director was not in complete control? (Well, evidently someone thinks it would be amusing, I suppose.) The "volunteer" searcher appears and talks as if he knows something about the club. He is standing there in the night, or, rather the morning, fairly well dressed; too well dressed to have come downtown just to see the excitement. If I were to guess, I would say he had something to do with the Bridge Street Club, at least enough to know who might have "the key" to the front door.

My confidence had been misplaced. For thirty minutes or more we stood on the sidewalk, sometimes chatting with the crowd while looking around for our helpful key search volunteer. After another thirty minutes, or so, I spy him, and then reality sets in: He, the volunteer, is leaned against a parking meter with a sly grin on his face.

Well, I have been snookered again, but not for the first time. I figure these infernal little machines which have dashed many dreams while supporting others have escaped the bonfire for about another hour. However, that was a bonfire that was not to be, at least for a while. I didn't know it at the time but the "powers that be" were going to make me wait even longer. I had to turn the entire lot of machines and other devices over to the city police which gave them another chance at life. This is what the Attorney General, Joe Purcell, told us to do.

The "Key Looker" seemed surprised to see that I wasn't upset. I gave him a knowing nod of the head and a smile that acknowledged that he slowed me down, but, it should have seemed to him that it was not going to slow me down that much. There are times to leave big footprints and times to leave smaller footprints or none. I felt this was a time to leave the smaller type, to tear up as little legal stuff as possible, but they had made it impossible to save the door.

"Beartracks" Chandler was and is one of the premier Questioned Document Examiners in this part of the country. He could have been a national authority in that calling, but instead he chose to do that very thing for the Criminal Investigation Division of the Arkansas State Police. He was good at identifying document forgeries and identifying and matching handwriting, but to his everlasting credit, that night he gave me the first swing at the side window on the door. The crash of glass could be heard for blocks since the hush of the crowd was deafening.

Wouldn't you know it! After breaking the window, I reached in and found that the lock was a two-way and needed an inside key as well as an outside key to open. I must admit to some feelings of vindication when I drop-kicked the door open.

Finally, we found the light switch. It wasn't a dream! "They" hadn't outsmarted us! It was even more than I had imagined. Slots were lined up ready to gobble up nickels, dimes and quarters. Blackjack tables, roulette wheels, poker tables, well stocked bars and all the accoutrements of a gambling Mecca was there before us. Unbelievable! We had legally made it in and hit the jackpot for the first time ever! If we had beads, we could have declared Mardi Gras right there on the shortest street in the world—less than one block long. The crowd was in an investigative rather than

a raucous mood, though. It seemed that they expected to come into the club and look around, but, of course, we couldn't let them do that.

I was not sure what to expect. But nobody else could claim to know because they had never been on a "real" raid either, only staged ones. Nobody claimed to know exactly how this scenario was going to play out. Especially, we did not plan on taking equipment like crap tables downstairs.

Maybe it was retribution for "hiding the key" to the Bridge Street Club. Trooper Mickey Smith and another trooper at the Ohio Casino were trying to wrestle a crap table downstairs but had trouble getting it down. Smith just shoved the table down the stairs, declaring to his follow trooper that, "This is the way." It not only went downstairs, it took out two of the front doors. About the time it took out the doors and landed, spread out on the sidewalk, I walked by from where the table had come. I had seen the action and remarked to the two young troopers that, "those things are sometimes hard to hold." Mickey replied, "They sure are." All three of us felt vindicated. — *The Big Hat Law, Michael Lindsey, 2008.*

Little did I know that this was just the beginning!

Why was this the first "real raid"?

The twelve year Governor Orval Faubus was generally recognized as encouraging raids on Hot Springs shortly before any Election Day, when he would come under fire to enforce the laws of Arkansas, but, after the election, no one seemed to know or really care when or whether raids would be or had taken place. That is, no one except the better number of citizens of the city, including the Arkansas Baptist Association, Churches United Against Gambling, (CUAG), a number of pastors of churches in the city, the Ministerial Alliance and many other people and organizations including Father McVeigh and Rev. John Miles and thousands more.

Remember, politics makes strange bedfellows. Now you take the Governor of a small Southern state, (Arkansas) and hook him up with a person whose nickname is, "The Killer," like Owney "The Killer" Madden, once and maybe even until his death in 1965, the biggest bootlegger in the country who J. Edgar Hoover declared #1 or #2 thug in America, with the son of a preacher, an attorney, Q. Byrum Hurst, with at least one madam, Maxine Jones, who was known throughout this part of the country, and a lot of other people who "Know what is right for the economy of the city", and you have an unpredictable crowd of folks.

Some of the other actors in this "Book of History," Jesse James, Frank James, Frank "Jelly" Nash, "Bottles" Capone, Al Capone, "Charles" Lucky Luciano, Alvin "Creepy Karpis," Curly Slaughter, Frank Costello and assorted others gangsters had been gone, from my perspective, only a short period of time and some, of like ilk, were likely still there.

Al Capone, bootlegging king of the Prohibition era, at least in the Chicago area, came to rest and relax in comfort while also doing business. According to old timers he used barrels labeled, "Mountain Valley Spring Water" to ship some of his bootleg whiskey to Chicago and beyond. Owney Madden was the *king of the New York City bootleggers* until he moved to take over Hot Springs' rackets in the middle 1930's. (Even today many people vie to stay in the "Al Capone Suite" in the Arlington Hotel.) It was reported that even rival gangs came to Hot Springs at the same time as Al and yet Al and the others kept the peace waiting to go back home (supposedly) to "shoot it out" or worse. (Make reservations for Al Capone's Suite early and visit Hot Springs often … a beautiful town and a great place to visit; five lakes, two rivers, a diamond field and crystal mines within a few miles, hundreds of rooms in motels, cabins, boats, yachts and campgrounds. An editorial comment about one of my favorite towns.)

Al wasn't around in 1967, but there was always some other hoodlum or deranged person who would like to strike the blow that would, hopefully, take away this threat to a way of life, an "Open City," but that threat was to come later and be a little more orchestrated. I knew this was coming, just not when and by whom.

LITTLE ROCK, THURSDAY EVENING, AUGUST 17, 1967 ★ ★ 40 PAGES—3 SECTIONS PRICE 5¢

Troopers Seal Off, Raid 4 Spa Casinos

Warehouse by State Troopers

Democrat/Glen Moon

Gaming Items Fill 3 Trucks

By BOB SALLEE
Democrat Staff Writer

HOT SPRINGS — State Police moved in on four Hot Springs night clubs early today after information was received that casino type gambling had been resumed openly, State Police Director Lynn A. Davis announced.

Three big truck loads of gambling paraphernalia were unloaded at a private storage firm here after State Police turned the seized equipment over to Hot Springs city police.

That was the extent of local law enforcement participation, Davis said. He explained that there was not enough room for the array of crap tables, roulette tables and slot machines at city hall or the police station.

No arrests had been made by mid-morning, but Davis indicated that further action would be forthcoming.

ONE-ARM BANDITS AMONG CONTRABAND
. . . Confiscated from Hot Springs casinos

Democrat

It takes a lot of experience and much more luck to pull off a successful "whacking" against the Director of the State Police and the Governor. (Remember moving targets are harder to hit, but maybe not faster than a speeding bullet?) I had enough experiences with law enforcement and its dangers to be wary at all times. (The scotch tape taped to my car hood wasn't to hold my hood down but to make sure that no one had been "checking my coolant" during the night.)

My uncle, W. E. "Elvy" Davis, a 16-year Sheriff of Miller County, Arkansas, whose thumb was shot off by a couple of bank robbers at the bridge on Highway 67 at the Red River near Fulton, Arkansas in the early 1940's gave me some good advice, and he and that advice were always remembered by me when a dangerous situation presented itself. And too, just to prove that a shootout doesn't necessarily come when expected, Uncle Elvy was shot once by a wife beater who had been arrested a number of times in Texarkana and had never shown any indication that he would shoot an arresting officer, but this time he did. When my uncle died, thirty years later, he still had the shell lying just below his heart. The shell, fired by that husband, had hit a rib and ricocheted off the lining of his heart. He recovered, but made sure that I always understood the mistake he made, of assuming that past conditions dictated present behavior.

A great uncle, Hence Giles, a Texarkana, Arkansas Police Detective, was killed on Broad Street in Texarkana by a bootlegger. Shot in the head through the right temple while checking the back seat of the bootlegger's car, and the killer was never identified.

My great uncle, Marlin Giles was Chief of Police for Texarkana, Arkansas. He had his share of shootouts and somehow survived with a few scars here and there. (I didn't get to be 34 years [1967] old by luck.)

The thought ran through my head, thinking, you know, if my mother knew where I was and what I was doing right now, she would probably come over here and take me home by the scruff of the neck!

Gaming Machines Thrive

Arkansas cafes, night clubs and other establishments have paid federal taxes of $150,500 in order to operate 602 coin - operated gambling devices during the fiscal year 1960-61, according to records of the Internal Revenue Service at Little Rock.

The devices—pin ball machines equipped for gambling and slot machines—operate despite a state law which prohibits their use. The $250 federal tax on each machine applies regardless of whether the state law is enforced.

Altogether 321 establishments have paid the gambling tax. They operate anywhere from one to dozens of machines. The Southern Club at Hot Springs sets the pace with 31, and its affiliated firms, the Southern Bar and New Southern Grill, account for eight more. Their tax bill: $9,750.

The tax is reduced proportionately when machines are placed in operation later in the fiscal year, which ends June 30. Many [illegible] the Hot Springs cafes and [illegible]ubs place additional machines [illegible]n operation in February just in time for the horse racing season at Oaklawn Park.

The Belvedere Club at Hot Springs began the 1959-60 fiscal year by paying $3,000 in taxes to operate 12 machines, but on February 13 installed 74 more and paid taxes of $7,703.21 on [illegible]em for the balance of the fiscal [illegible]ar.

The Southern Club, Southern [illegible]ar and New Southern Grill start[illegible] last year with 21 machines [illegible]d completed it with 44. Their [illegible] bill came to about $8,000.

[illegible]y the end of the 1959-60 fiscal [illegible] 846 coin-operated gambling [illegible]ces were operating in Arkan[illegible]. They could be found in 450 [illegible]aces of business, which shelled out a total of $189,139.75 for tax st[illegible].

[illegible] Leads

Hot Springs, with its casinos, perennially leads the Arkansas [illegible]es in the number of coin-ope[illegible] gambling devices. Slot machines, also known as "one-arm bandits," are the most popu[illegible] there.

[illegible]his year tax stamps have been issued for 234 gambling machines at Hot Springs, 101 at Little Rock, 88 at Fort Smith, and 4[illegible] at North Little Rock. Next comes Springdale with 19, a large number considering its size, Texarkana 18 and Fayetteville 17. The remaining 81 are divided among many cities and towns.

Pine Bluff, the state's fourth largest city, has no gambling machines, according to IRS tax stamp records. Neither does [illegible]

number of machines at each place:

Little Rock

James E. Allen, Community Club House, 114 West Capitol Avenue, 2; James L. Angel, Angel's Cafe, 614 West Ninth Street, 6; James L. Angel, Burger Bar, 514 West Ninth Street, 6; Lola Martin Baker, Lola's Steak House, New Benton Highway, 1; B. F. Bennett, Main Recreation Parlor, 117 Main Street, 2; Jack Braswell, Braswell's Diner, 824 West Ninth Street. 2; Rose Brinkley, 106 Louisiana Street, 3; Cecil Burks, Burk's Mobile Service, 2524 West Twelfth Street, 1; Thelma W. Campbell, Thema's Cafe, 2230 Arch Street, 1; A. B. Cassinei, Brunswick Billard, 118 Main Street 3; L. C. Cassinelli Harlem Bar, 600 West Ninth Street, 2; Donald D. Cummins, Center Bowling Lanes, 415 Center Street, 3; Columbus Club Association, Inc., 215 East Ninth Street, 3; Roy and Pat Cook, Cook's Cafe, 119 East Third Street, 2; R. C. Coulter, Blue Bowl Cafe, 814 Main Street, 1; Ex-Serviceman's Club, 120½ West Markham Street, 2; Max H. Ezell, Ship Ahoy, 1108 Battery Street, 2; H. C. Faucett, Citizens Cigar Store, 316 West Capitol Avenue, 3; 3; Phillip F. Geller, The Purple Cow, 714 Broadway, 1; Dorothy C. Graves, Stifft Station Recreation, 3015 West Markham Street, 1; T. J. Graves, Pastime Pool Hall, 1204 West Seventh Street, 2; J. O. Hale, Jim's Place, 1207 West Thirty-third Street, 1; C. L. Hendricks, Lowber's Billiards, 5302 Asher Avenue, 4; Coy L. Hively, Circle B, 2001 East Roosevelt Road, 2; Gurley Javada and Frances M. Sullivan, Sully's Cafe, 5308 Asher Avenue, 2; Carl William Knoedl, Joe's Grill, 6322 West Twelfth Street, 1; Ralph M. Kuykendall, 3100 West Roosevelt Road, 2; J. W. Land, Courthouse Cafe, 323 West Second Street, 1; H. A. McMurry, Mac's Drive Inn, 2520 West Twelfth Street, 2; Marie Maher, Bismark Cafe, 1210 West Seventh Street, 2; Thomas V. Marbut, The Band Box, 1623 Main Street, 1; Paul M. Maus, American Grill, 113 Main Street, 1; Mrs. Mike Miller, Miller's Coffee Shop, 212 Main Street, 1; Gene O'Kelley, Red Gate Inn, 1437 Stagecoach Road, 1; W. T. Parks, Amoco Service Station, Roosevelt Road and Arch Street, 1; Freddie Perciful, Freddie's Drive Inn, 515 West Eighth Street, 1; George Peters, Majestice Confection, 800 Main Street, 1; Pla-Mor Bowling Lanes, Inc., 901 West Seventh Street, 1; Cleon L. Rogers, Anchor Cafe, 2727 Arch [illegible] Country Club, Hot Springs Highway, 2; Gladys Williams, Summerfield's Restaurant, 1123 Main Street, 2; J. P. Willis, Jimmy's Billiard Parlor, 1105 Main Street, 3; E. E. Wycott, Pitcher Cafe, 916 West Fourteenth Street, 1; Herman Yancey, Chris Cafe, 902 Main Street.

North Little Rock

Mrs. Faye Barker, Barker's Restaurant, U. S. Highway 67 East, 1; B. R. Emberton, Jake's Cafe, 106 East Second Street, 2; William T. Fisher, Fisher's Grill, MacArthur Boulevard and Conway Pike, 1; Roy Fowler and Willie Booth, West Sandwich Shop, 411 East Thirteenth Street, 1; James M. Fryar, Green Door, U. S. Highway 67 three miles south of Jacksonville, 2; Mrs. E. L. Gassoway, Terminal Cafe, 624 East Twelfth Street, 1; R. H. Glover Esso Station, 1600 East Broadway, 1; R. H. Glover, Esso Station, 100 Jacksonville Highway, 1; Charlene W. Graham, Wendy's Drive Inn, 498 MacArthur Boulevard, 1; S. P. Hammons, Hob Nob Drive Inn, 3805 New Conway Pike, 1; Josephine A. Jenkins, Chicken Shack, 700 East Broadway, 1; L. O. Jobe and Robert Kirspell, Wonder Grill, 100 East Thirteenth Street, 2; Eldore Johnson, Johnson Diner, 4410 East Broadway, 1; Moose Lodge No. 942, 113 North Maple Street, 3; Salvadore A. Marchese, Southern Grill, 321 West Eighteenth Street, 1; Ralph E. Miller, Millers' Truck Stop, Route 5, 1; Annis Mugley, Coffee House, 415 Main Street, 2; North Hills Country Club, Highway 5, 4; Elks Lodge No. 1004, 123 East Broadway, 5; Mrs. Frank Nowell, Star Cafe, 119 East Second Street, 2; Albert L. Paladino, Bo Bird Sandwich Shop, 1733 Pike Avenue, 1; Frank W. Schafer, Catter Box, U. S. Highway 67 East, 1; F. H. Sharp, Jack's Place, 12[illegible] Second Street, 2; Sam St[illegible] Sam Stephens Cafe, 5007 [illegible] Broadway, 3; Ned R. Thomas, Ned's Restaurant, 402 Main Street, 2; Mathew Walters, Walters' Drive Inn and Motel, Route 5, 1; Lois Williams, Second Street Cafe, 105 East Second Street, 1; M. R. Williams, The Chief, Route 5, 1; Herman Yancey, Griddle Shop, 234 McArthur Drive, 1.

Fort Smith

R. E. Adams, Pastime Parlor, 1; V. B. Blankenship, Riverside Bar and Grill, 1; Herbert E. Bornitzke, Jumbo's Cafe, 1; Arnold Brasch, Arnie Brasch Deep Rock Station, 2; W. T. Bromley, Dub's 22 Tavern, 2; C. H. Carnal, Square Deal Cafe, [illegible] Rowena Carnal, Swing [illegible] 3; J. D. Nation, Little Buckhorn, 1; Edward Neumler, Dinty Moore's Cafe, 2; Elmer Nye, Elmer's Snooker Parolr, 1; Hugh Oglesby, Mildred's Cafe, 1; Sidney Parker, Cisco Bar, 1; Mary Peluso, Pagliacci, 1; Albert Porta, Albert's Malt Shop, 3; Ralph Roberts, Roberts Service Station, 3; W. H. Rounsaville, 4000 Club, 1; Mary Schwartz and John H. Smith, Oasis, 2; Arthur J. Sharum, Pete's Place, 2; Sophie Smith, Sophie's Place, 1; Juanita Stanley, Melody Lounge, 1; C. R. Thompson, Thompson's Tap Room, 2; W. E. Thompson, 1206½ Garrison Avenue, 2; A. J. Odouj, Sportsmen's Ice House, 1; Coy M. Veach, Western Club, 1; Arthur Vervack, Vervack Brothers, 2; Curley Vervack, Curley's 3; Mrs. N. G. Walraven, Walraven's Cafe, 2; Mrs. Zedia Ma[illegible] Watkins, Bar B Que Grand, 2 Robert Floyd White, 71 Cafe, 2 Chet Wilcox, Brass Rail, 1; Terr[illegible] Williams, Corral Bar, 1; Guss[illegible] Wilson, My Place Drive In, 1 Wintergarden Bowling Lanes Inc., 2; W. W. Womble, 100 North Greenwood Avenue, 2 Gene Wood, Gene's Barbecu[illegible] Lounge, 1; Mary Louise Wrigh[illegible] Charles and Mary's Bar, 1.

Hot Springs

Ellis Agre, Old South, 2; Ga[illegible] Agre, Gorge Road Tavern, 1 Truman Agre, Truman's Tavern 2; Lewis P. Allen, Dug Out In[illegible] 1; American Legion Club, [illegible] Fred S. Austin, H. Dane Harr[illegible] and Gordon Henderson, Ne[illegible] Tower Club, 3; George L. Bach[illegible]lor, Hot Springs Golf and Country Club, 2; Eugene Bailey, Murray's Landing, 1; Addie Baxte[illegible] Baxter Hotel, 1; Belvedere Country Club, Inc., 4; C. J. and J. [illegible] Brooks, Cliff's Drive Inn, 4; B[illegible] M. Bryant, Bob's Drive Inn, [illegible] Mrs. J. B. Buck, Buck's Cafe, [illegible] Marion Bush, Joe's Red Rose, [illegible] M. L. Butler, Butler's Bar B[illegible] [illegible] Timothy Cafe, [illegible] Gr[illegible] [illegible] Gilbert Caldwell, [illegible] T[illegible] [illegible] 7; Earl O. Carmical, Top H[illegible] Lounge, 2; L. E. Carmicha[illegible] Rondevoo Cafe, 4; Velma C[illegible] man, Peacock Club, 1; [illegible] Cook, Hoosier Bar, 3; J. K. C[illegible] Tulsa Club, 2; W. M. Da[illegible] White Cafe, 1; Arthur Dill, C[illegible] L Cafe, 2; [illegible] Jena's Bar B-Q, 2; Frank [illegible] Frank's Dairy Treat, 1; Wal[illegible] Ebel Jr., Harry [illegible] Dane Harris, Ohio Cigar Store, [illegible] Robert Gooden, Rock Court, [illegible] Wilbur Green, Perky Drive [illegible] 3; Mae Halligan, [illegible] Dane Harris, Garden [illegible] Walter Ebel Jr., Harry L[illegible] los, Fred A[illegible] Bowman, [illegible] ter, Belvedere Club, [illegible] Haskell, [illegible] Club, [illegible]

Angry about the key deal at the Bridge Street Club? Naw, just received a radio message from the raiding party at the Ohio Club. They had found a "jackpot" there, too. Major McKee, Highway Patrol Commander, had just reported that the Sheriff of Garland County was there. Well, I'll go see what his story is.

As I walked up the wooden steps to the Ohio Club just south of the Southern Club on Central Avenue I passed the troopers carrying out crap tables and such.

Even though I had been told that the Sheriff was there, I was still surprised to find him leaning on a crap table. The red headed young man stated:

"Colonel, my name is Bud Canada; I'm the Sheriff of Garland County. If you had told me this was here I would have taken care of it." Of all rehearsed lines he could have used this had to be the lamest.

My reply was:

"It would seem that a blind man could find several casinos, some within hollering distance from here to the jail and/or the police department, and if you didn't know they were here, I'd be afraid to take you with me on a raid."

I don't think there was any miscommunication between us. We were on opposite sides, "Open City" vs. the law. He seemed to understand that I wasn't angry, just wanted him to know that hopefully this was a new day. (I knew for sure that this event wouldn't go unnoticed, that this was just the beginning).

The last serious convictions in that city had been the Chief of Police Ermey, Chief of Detectives "Dutch" Akers and Maxine Jones, among other highlights of society in Garland County, about twenty years or so ago. Some time later more arrests and more convictions; (1946-47) Sid McMath, once the prosecuting attorney, then a new Governor, had made some waves in the political structure, but a fight like that never ends … vigilance is called for.)

"-BET'S OFF ON THE NEW STATE POLICE DIRECTOR!"
GRAHAM

ounty Affairs.

ices at the Garland county house also were closed today. oing officials were bringing records up to date before they Wednesday.

unty Collector Mack Wilson County Clerk Roy C. Raef are happy about the new deal. It id that both blame their de- on their association with or, McLaughlin. Both were ilar personally. Mr. Wilson his office 14 years ago from a aughlin candidate, George P. therman.

is reported that Mayor Mc- ghlin turned against Mr. Wil- last fall because the latter per- ted GI lawyers to inspect the nty's poll tax records. At any , Mr. Wilson received nearly 0 fewer votes than some of the chine candidates.

heriff Marion Anderson, who l relinquish his office to I. G. own Wednesday, has announced plans. He and Circuit Judge rl Witt, who will give way to de H. Brown, own a beautiful odivision on Lake Hamilton, 10 les from Hot Springs. The sher- also owns a fine home on a ce peninsula in addition to his y property. He won't starve. Judge Witt owns a farm six miles om Mount Ida, Montgomery coun- , where he formerly lived. He so has a home in Oaklawn just itside the Hot Springs City lim- s. He is eligible for a state pen- ion by virtue of his 24 years on ne bench.

Prosecuting Attorney Curtis Ridg- vay will practice law with Earl ane in the Citizens Bank build- ng.

Mr. Raef, a certified public ac- countant, has been offered several obs, but has told friends that he will hunt rabbits for several months with his packs of beagle and basset hounds.

County Judge Elza T. Housley has been employed at the court- house 34 years. Treasurer Henry Murphy and Circuit Clerk John E. Jones have made no commitments.

Will Attack Remnant Of McLaughlin Machine.

The GI's are ready to go to work on Mayor McLaughlin, City Attor- ney Jay Rowland and other mem- bers of what once was the strong- est political organization in Ar- kansas. Nathan Schoenfeld, life- long friend of Mr. McMath and his law partner, will be appointed special prosecutor to handle com- plaints against the mayor and his followers.

Capt. Jerry Watkins, popular po- lice officer who was fired by the mayor without explanation last week, will become a special in- vestigator for the prosecutor's of- fice. Even the mayor's friends can't understand why Captain Watkins was discharged on the eve of a scheduled grand jury in- vestigation of the mayor's activi- ties.

One of the mayor's strongest supporters said: "That's the dumb- est thing I ever saw. If there is an apple cart to spill, Jerry is the fellow who can do it."

M'LAUGHLIN IS ARRESTED, WILL FACE 32 COUNTS

Gaz 3-18-47

Brother And Secre- tary Indicted.

By JOHN L. FLETCHER.
Day City Editor of the Gazette.

Hot Springs, March 17 (Spl).—Mayor Leo P. McLaughlin, his brother George and his long-time private secretary, Mrs. Hazel Marsh, were arrested here tonight as the result of indictments return- ed by the special Garland county Grand Jury that has been investi- gating the Hot Springs city govern- ment.

Mrs. Marsh is accused of first degree perjury as the result of her testimony before the Grand Jury.

George McLaughlin is accused of having wrongfully received city funds.

The Grand Jury literally "threw the book" at the mayor.

He faces seven indictments con- taining a total of 32 counts. Most of them charge him with having accepted bribes.

It is expected that other persons connected with Mayor McLaugh- lin's administration will be indicted.

The Grand Jury has not com- pleted its report. It will meet again Wednesday and Saturday.

Whether Mayor McLaughlin will be suspended from office pending trial is not known tonight.

Circuit Judge Clyde H. Brown and Prosecuting Attorney Sidney S. Math were in Little Rock to- night but before they left they said that the law is not clear on the subject. They said that it provides for suspension from office of coun- ty officials who are indicted but they have been unable to find any law on the subject concerning city officials.

Arrested at his office by Sheriff I. G. Brown and Deputy Earl Ful- ton, Mayor McLaughlin notified his attorney, C. Floyd Huff, and then he and Mrs. Marsh accompanied the officers to the sheriff's office.

Bond of $40,500 was made for the mayor by his two sisters, the Misses Elizabeth and Stella McLaughlin.

Mayor McLaughlin made bond for Mrs. Marsh.

Officers are looking for Elmer Walters, an associate of the mayor, who has been indicted on a charge of wrongfully receiving city funds.

First Indictment Deals With Poll Tax Receipts.

The first indictment against Mayor McLaughlin contains 20 counts. It deals with the "block poll tax" system, under which it has been charged that the mayor managed to keep himself in office

This was in 1947. Charges being brought by the crusading prosecutor and later, Governor Sid McMath.

Leo P. McLaughlin, Mayor of Hot Springs for over twenty years, was arrested March 18, 1947, on a seven count indictment, 32 counts of accepting bribes from gamblers;

George McLaughlin, the Mayor's brother, arrested on charges of wrongfully receiving city funds;

Hazel Marsh, part-time secretary to Mayor McLaughlin, was charged with perjury before grand jury;

City Attorney Dickey was charged with accepting bribes from Associated Auction Galleries at the rate of $200.00 per month from April 1944, to November, 1945, bribes from Esskay Art Gallery, Saad's Galleries, Garris Galleries, Edwards Galleries as well as accepting bribes from taxi companies.

Samuel Kirsch, Sr., proprietor of Esskay Galleries was indicted for perjury.

Elmer Walters, Associate of Mayor McLaughlin was charged with wrongfully receiving funds.

This is not a history book, but a book of history. I have tried to simply report what the press said during that period, and to point out the particular newspaper articles that were published, and hopefully some interesting sidelights. This was in 1947.

There is a time and place for everything, and 1967 seemed to be the time; a reform-minded Governor, Winthrop Rockefeller, who believed in enforcing the laws of the State and people, who for years, had been attempting to find the right combination to rid Hot Springs, Arkansas, of the label, "biggest illegal casino operation in America" a label placed on that city specifically by the United States Justice Department, J. Edgar Hoover, Director of the FBI and United States Attorney General Bobby Kennedy. They could have added several other cities too: Lake Village, North Little Rock, Little Rock, Newport, and hundreds of restaurants, clubs and honky-tonks, except they didn't seem to have the same background of mafia control. (Notice I said "didn't seem.")

In the grand scheme of things, it probably doesn't matter a whit what I think or what I say. On the other hand, my experiences

'Say When–'

may, in my humble opinion, shed light on some truths, one being that you can do what you set your mind to do.

Modesty has never been a virtue of mine, but I believe honesty has been. I believe reality can be tempered by humor and that tall tales can embellish life as we know it. However, when I tell you that throughout this piece, when I say "I," I mean "we." When I say "us," I mean myself and hundreds and thousands of others; Arkansas State Police Troopers, Ranking Officers, and other personnel, Governor Rockefeller, his people, my lawyers (which I affectionately call my "mouthpieces"), Lieutenant Governor "Footsie" Britt, G. Thomas Eisele and thousands of other supporters who opted to join the effort begun by the Governor, not a moral crusade, but one simply meant to point out that, "*It could be done*"—the fair enforcement of all the laws. Enforce them or change them.

No matter how you slice it, as "they" say, no matter how many times you, the citizens of Arkansas have heard, "It couldn't be done" the truth simply requires that you set your mind to do it and, hopefully, get other people to join your efforts. (And I'll be immodest for myself and you, and say to anyone who will listen … We fought the good fight and *won*, fair and square!) We destroyed nothing except some illegal equipment and a few reputations, or so we thought, and seemed to have gained the confidence of many people.

Neither I nor anyone else knew exactly when it was going to end or how, but we were soon to find out.

After I went to jail for two days and a night and appeared before the Arkansas Supreme Court twice, it was courtesy of Pulaski County, Arkansas, which includes Little Rock, Arkansas, not Hot Springs, Arkansas. It seemed that they couldn't get rid of me before we ruined the games.

I never wanted to be the one that caused Hot Springs to close down for any reason and I stated so on several occasions. However, that wasn't in my job description, to determine whether Hot Springs could do without the games. It should be noted that Hot Springs, notwithstanding the lack of the rackets, set a record for sales taxes paid the year after the raids, 1968. Somehow that, in my mind, was another bit of vindication for what we did.

I am not sure how many residents of Hot Springs knew or appreciated the shady past of their city, but they would have been deaf, voiceless, and blind to not have known what was happening in their city. The question is how much had others paid attempting to change the system when they had to have known it had not changed appreciably during the last century, that the Mayor and

Garland Sheriff Is 'Incensed,' Claims Davis 'Bypassed' Him

From the Associated Press

HOT SPRINGS—Garland County Sheriff Eugene (Bud) Canada complained Thursday that State Police Director Lynn A. Davis bypassed his office by leading state troopers in raids on Hot Springs gambling establishments earlier in the day.

"I'm highly incensed," the sheriff said. "It's a sad state of affairs when the highest elected law enforcement officer of any county is not consulted or asked to co-operate with the State Police."

"This co-operation has always been the policy in the past," Canada said, "but it looks to me as though with the advent of a new director, there has been an entirely new policy."

He said that he always had co-operated "100 per cent" when called on to help in State Police investigations and the serving of warrants.

"But now, under an apparently new policy, the State Police are going to disregard any and all local enforcement officials—especially those who have to be elected and must answer to the people," the sheriff said.

his minions, the Mafia was, at least in modern times, in control and that opponents were run out of town either ceremoniously or otherwise. Many paid dearly…let's hope not in vain.

It seemed, though, that Hot Springs could rightly point out that Little Rock and North Little Rock should take care of the rackets in its midst; bookmaking, prostitution, The Westwood Club, The Checkmate Club, and other casinos, dives and honky tonks running almost wide open.

Mayor Leo McLaughlin predicted, "Grass will grow in the streets if visitors are not provided with a chance to gamble." Massage sales, a Hot Springs staple, however, notwithstanding Leo's admonition, increased more than twenty percent. After another earlier attempt at closing down the rackets, W. E. Chester, manager of the Arlington Hotel, earlier said at one time that his business never had been affected by the presence or absence of gambling and that visitors didn't come to Hot Springs to gamble.

Of course, Leo's statement about the grass growing in the streets without gambling was self serving as he had been Mayor for about 20 years and if impressions count, his bragging about his non-work all his life closely matched Owney Madden's as far as work. Owney, when asked what line of work he did, answered, "I've never worked a day in my life." (I guess he didn't count being the biggest bootlegger in New York and, maybe, the world counted as work.)

Mayor McLaughlin once said, when asked about his not taking a salary from one of the city projects, said,

"Don't worry about ole Leo, he'll get his."

He didn't explain where he was going to get it but he evidently knew. His standard of living, while not working, certainly proved that you could do it, live without working, and especially if you had a cash cow, like Hot Springs, based on a cornerstone of gambling, prostitution and a gangster protection operation.

Bloodletting

Readers' Views

HOT SPRINGS NUMBER ONE NATURAL

Hot Springs is nestled in the foothills of the Ouachita Mountains, but this, in itself, is not what is unique. It is a bavarianesque type of town, and, so much so, that walking the streets of Hot Springs you could very well expect to hear someone yodeling in the background. There is even more, much more, like three mountains in the city, West Mountain, North Mountain, and Hot Springs Mountain.

Hot Springs, in addition to the scenery, is even more unique for its bubbling hot waters from 47 springs, which percolate out of the ground at 143 degrees Fahrenheit, day and night, 24 hours a day at 365 days per year, evidently flowing at the same rate for thousands of years.

Hydrologists tell us that the water coming to the surface in the Valley of the Vapors today drained into the earth about four thousand years ago as rainwater and is heated by unseen volcanoes, pushed to the surface of the earth by pressures within those geographical features. This water has been coming to the surface at Hot Springs for thousands upon thousands of years. It has been celebrated as healing waters and, as a matter of fact, was the first National Park designated by the United States Government by President Andrew Jackson in 1832. President Jackson, told of the hot springs flowing out of hundreds of fissures on Hot Springs' mountains and all over the valleys between those mountains, declared it "protected" even before Yellowstone and any of the other national parks. It was so unique that the federal government recognized the healing waters and built the Army Navy Hospital there to attend to the ailments and wounds of servicemen.

Legends tell us that the hot springs were declared "sacred" before being declared "protected" by the federal government. It was neutral territory for all the Indian tribes who populated the area and beyond. The Indians came for the medicinal healing baths, even hundreds of years before Hernando Desoto came there in about 1541.

Desoto came hunting for gold and found it. He found a treasure. Not the kind of treasure he could put in his pocket and take with him but the kind of treasure one can only find in very few places. More precious than gold, water flowing to the surface of the earth, century after century, even before written history, bubbling to the surface, pure unadulterated, and untouched by the human hand. So pure, that for decades upon decades, the water has been bottled and sold to those unfortunate enough to not have the time to come to the springs and fill their own containers with this elixir. It is free to those who come, whether they come with a paper cup or a ten gallon jug. Free to all that need the water of the gods to quench their thirst. On the other hand, to not recognize the other, more human side of Hot Springs, telling of the city would be like trying to describe the buttercup flower without recognizing the color yellow.

From the years before and after the 1870's, the City of Hot Springs was like a magnet. It inexorably drew those who had the wherewithal to come to take the hot baths. The good and the bad. Those who were wealthy enough to leave their lives behind and come to take the baths sometimes brought a lot of wherewithal. According to the Indian lore and to what is believed by some, even today, the waters could cure whatever ailed you. Even the federal government obviously believed in the healing aspect of the hot springs; they built bathhouses or allowed them to be build on the East side of the City's main street, Central Avenue.

Come one, come all to be immersed in the healing 143 degree water, to be wrapped in swaddling clothes until, as they say, you felt like you were cooked well done and then have a massage of rough cloth to abrade the skin making way for the healing elements to enter the body.

These who came with the "wherewithal" (*money*) sometimes brought quite a bit of it with them. Before the days of national banks, ATM's and the credit card, you could only spend what you carried with you. Those who did not have the "wherewithal" recognized this opportunity to profit by that fact. If you could only identify those who might have what you wanted, money, it would be easier pickings than being a flea in a dog pound. These people, including Jesse and Frank James and numerous others, too plentiful to name, soon came to recognize that people riding the stage coach into the City of Vapors from Malvern, Arkansas, in all likelihood had brought enough money with them to sustain life until they were either healed or had run out of the "wherewithal" which in some cases was all too soon and then run out of town.

Frank and Jesse and these others stopped these travelers on the rough road to the city and relieved them of their money and, fortunately, usually spared them their lives. Not too long after Jesse was ambushed and killed, Frank retired, came to Hot Springs, opened a sideshow at "Happy Hollow Amusement Park" and made his living telling about himself and his brother Jesse and their hard riding days.

Some of the bad guys of modern times, like Al Capone and his brother "Bottles" Capone and hundreds of Capone's compatriots known then as the National Crime Syndicate came to "Bubbles" to make plans and develop strategies and divide territories, as well as share "dividends."

The traveler, who came through these mountainous, piney woods, crossing rivers, creeks, streams and all manner of impediments, years before modern transportation found they were not spared. So long as they had the means, there were those who ran what was later called the "rackets", who, in a somewhat more genteel manner, would try to take what was left without the specific use of a gun and violence, but dice tables and slot machines. These were the recognized rackets considered by some as legitimate businesses, although no more legal than holdups, bunco games and other nefarious activities.

Less recognized were those known as "drummers," "docs," purveyors of medicinals, lawyers, doctors, merchants and whatever other descriptions they might choose, whether they were licensed practitioners or not.

These purveyors of health "caught" the sick and the lame on the trails and trains coming to Hot Springs for the healing waters. Of course, they were told by the drummers they would need a "doctor" and that they, the "drummer" had heard of a miracle working "*doctor*" who had healed many people. The drummer furnished the weary, traveler the name and address of the miracle worker and if enough money was involved would take them to the flim flam, conscienceless artist for "treatment."

Cards, dice, roulette wheels, booze, women, and just about whatever you wanted, (even some illegal!), were available for the asking, so long as you had the "wherewithal" to afford it. The early pioneers recognized that the hot springs valley had much to offer for what bothered them, but what would these people, who came by droves, the sick, the lame and those that simply wanted a vacation, do in their spare time? This was before the entertainment tax, before the sales tax, before the airport landing fees, and varied and sundry other methods to raise money to keep the City afloat.

What, indeed, could be provided to keep the city afloat?

Then, in the 1880's, in steps the likes of Frank Flynn, Boss Gambler and his "progeny" promoting a legacy of activity, providing "entertainment" for the visitor, attempting to satisfy a number of urges, illegal in other cities, as well as Hot Springs, but tolerated by the unique city in the Foothills of the Ouachita Mountains. It was the opinion of the "city fathers" (mostly in the category of "Drummers") that these activities, even though illegal, were a part of life in Garland County, Arkansas, and that they were a necessary part of the equation, especially if they, the city fathers were running them. It didn't seem to matter that the town was lawless and one that did not have the fortitude to resist the lawless atmosphere.

Frank Flynn, seems to have figured out how the money could be made and who should be able to keep it and he, therefore, became the "controller of commerce," or by a better name "Boss Gambler." Those loyal to him were allowed to run the rackets and tax their gambling equipment and their prostitutes just enough to convince the city dwellers that the rackets income was indeed a necessity for the city. Just enough to convince the City, one way or the other, that the rackets were a necessity if the City was to survive.

It is not surprising that the City catered to the impression that it was a "party town." It took in, in season and out, some of the most notorious ne'er do wells, hoodlums, bunko artists, prostitutes and successful gangsters in the country. Of course, there were the usual naysayers, like preachers and priests and parishioners who fought tooth and toenail against the rackets, but they seemed to be outnumbered by those in support of this "necessity" if the city was to survive. In order to placate or to attempt to placate these "do-gooders," the "City Fathers" and the bad guys, knew every trick in the book and then some.

Tax records recall heyda

BY SCOTT CHARTON
Associated Press Writer

HOT SPRINGS – More than two decades ago, in this resort spa's heyday, illegal gambling was hotter than the much-touted healing water bubbling below the Ouachita Mountains.

Throngs of tourists and townspeople took chances, in violation of state law, on at least 350 slot machines, card games, bingo and bookmaking.

And local government winked, according to records rediscovered last fall that show the city reaped revenues from taxes on the lawless activity.

Police looked the other way, except to collect the municipal "amusement" tax, until 1967, when a crackdown initiated during the administration of the late Gov. Winthrop Rockefeller sent tons of betting devices to dumps to be demolished and torched.

Gambling tax records turned up during a City Hall housecleaning two decades after collection ceased.

"It was probably the only illegal tax in this country collected by a city," recalls state Sen. Eugene "Bud" Canada, who was Garland County sheriff in 1967.

But Canada, like other longtime Hot Springs residents interviewed recently, says he isn't sure how much was collected.

"They built a city auditorium, where the Miss Arkansas Pageant is held, a beautiful place, and a City Hall, and the main firehouse downtown – all on an illegal tax," he said.

"I think this is a record of the history of Hot Springs," said Hot Springs Finance Director Jim Scott, who found the dust-covered documents.

The city levied $10 monthly for each slot machine, making it affordable for any business to offer action.

'... All of the clubs could be found by tourists. They could have been found by a blind man. And if the sheriff didn't know they were there, then I was afraid to take him with me on a raid.'

The Baxter Hotel, Butler's Barbecue, Harlem Chicken Shack and the Eatmore Cafe had one slot each. More adventurous were the J.D. Jackson Fish Market, VFW Club and Hot Springs Country Club, with two slots apiece.

At Coy's Steak House these days, the best bet might be the fork-tender prime cuts. But in 1967, diners could wager on the restaurant's eight slot machines while waiting for a table.

Tax rates ran $100 monthly for bingo and cards, $500 for large casinos – more than five gaming tables – and $300 for five or fewer tables, called small casinos. The Ohio Clu Southern Club and The Va pors casino, all defunct, fel into both categories, depend ing on the season.

The Elks Club refused t pay the difference when ta rates were raised in 1964. Re cords show club officials sen payments on their five slots a the old rate until documenta tion stops in early fall 1967 when the raids began.

"The cornerstone of publi morality is respect for th law," Rockefeller remarke that year, when he hired ex FBI agent Lynn A. Davis to b chief of the State Police an lead enforcer.

Davis says he told Rockefel ler he wanted to concentrat on law enforcement, not poli tics, and specifically on clos ing casinos. He says Rockefel ler "slapped his knee and said 'That's exactly what I want.' "

Early on Aug. 17, 1967. Davi and about two dozen officer converged on the Bridge Stree Club in downtown Hot Springs

The door was locked. Pa trons had left. The owner was summoned, according to news paper accounts. When he didn't show after an hour Davis broke a glass panel in the door with a tire tool as photographers captured the scene. Troopers then knocked in the door.

Newspapers reported that searches of the club and several other gambling operations produced three truckloads of

Where else could you find that an illegal activity was taxed voluntarily? Who decided how much each of the 350 machines would bear? The movers and shakers, of course. Each slot had a number marked on the case. The tax collector surveyed each to determine how many machines were in a business, a convenience store, a barbershop or elsewhere, made a list, decided how much money was needed that particular year, divided that amount by the number of machines collected that and paid the bills.

WHY NOT CASINOS SUPPORTING PHILLIPS COUNTY'S "CHARITY" DRIVE?

Did we, in 120 days in 1967, reform the rackets?

It seems that where there is a will, there is a way and this maxim even prevailed in 1991 in Phillips County, Arkansas, about 25 years after our casino crunch in 1967.

The cities of Helena and West Helena in Phillips County "suddenly" discovered about 200 slot machines within the city and county, all still illegal according to state law, and in operation even in 1991.

The city survey of the machines found that a number of them, privately owned would pay the player absolutely nothing while some machines were making small returns to the player. (So nothing had changed the ratio of money in - money out, *but much left behind!* (So what else is new?)

The county, found, too, that only about 200 people in the community were able to support the welfare needs in the county without some other support.

City and county officials put two and two together, confiscated the machines and put them in operation to benefit the county. (So much for private enterprise!) In a thirty-month period they brought in $326,276.74 or almost $11,000 per month, which they used to build an airfield, pay for a police car and do other charitable things. They had formed a committee to expend the money.

(*Arkansas Gazette*, July 7, 1991). It is not clear from the article how the balance of the funds was spent and who spent them and with whom, and who got the administrative fees.

WHY NOT LEGALIZE GAMBLING?

Why not have legalized gambling? It didn't seem to matter to the people that the machines and the gambling were illegal. Phillips County seemed to ignore the fact that making the playing of the slots a civic obligation would seem to be a high price to pay for disrespect of the law. (There's that "law" again.)

Many people use Las Vegas as a poster child for legalized gambling, pointing out the glitter and the gold of Las Vegas. This is somewhat inaccurate because Las Vegas, in one respect is almost the single city in Nevada to draw tourists and it can draw crowds and share the proceeds with the rest of the state. The "System" doesn't rely on visitors to the other less desirable spots in Nevada. They don't have to have crowds in Tonopah, or "Sunshine," Nevada, for example. Being known as a gambling state does not hurt them in drawing industry, because industry is not likely to choose a desert location for its expansion.

If we could figure out how to get out of state customers to come to Prescott or Nashville or Harrisburg, Arkansas to gamble, we might be able to support such a spot as Las Vegas in Hot Springs.

It has been proposed, but to make those cities or others "party towns" would, in my opinion, be what we might call a bust or a losing proposition. Arkansas would become known as a party state, but most of the State would not attract gambling customers and industry afraid of all the bad vibes of gambling would not come to these other cities.

Compare this situation with Hot Springs. Even though the games weren't charitable and not owned by the city, the city did tax the machines, the tables, the clubs (small and large), and still in 1947, after a temporary close down, the *Arkansas Gazette* reported under headlines that the National Park Service reported that more persons registered for the hot baths in January than during any January in Hot Springs history. The McMath regime had closed the games down that year after prosecuting a number of Hot Springs City officials and yet tourism didn't suffer.

No history of such a fantastic place as the Valley of the Vapors, or what the gangsters called "Bubbles" would be complete without an in depth description of some of the people who frequented Bubbles and/or hid out there when they were "wanted," wanted by the law and usually for really good reasons!

THE RACKETS, THE RACKETEERS AND THEIR PROTECTION

Historically, the racketeers from the earliest days controlled law enforcement in Garland County, Arkansas. From the earliest days to 1967, as far as I and others could determine, law enforcement was "simply around" to enforce the law if it agreed with the dictates of the boss gambler or whoever was sitting in that catbird seat and his minions. Officers were there to protect the clubs and those who had a stake in the status quo. They, the police officers and their superiors, did a good job of providing that protection as well as seeing that no one else came in to take care of the lawlessness.

How great is it when you carry a badge and a gun, and when you give an order the "ordered" either obeys or goes to jail? The order, legal or not, is good until it reaches a person that has more control. The person who did the ordering has the key to your jail cell, unless you know somebody higher on the totem poll than he is. (Unbelievable but true!) Can you imagine what that means if you are not even on the totem poll and don't know anyone who is? Several options present themselves; get a protector or leave town. Who does that leave? Obviously it leaves those who carry guns and are willing to use them and those with the power to maintain the status quo, without too many questions if any asked.

The modus operandi (The mode of operation or in this case "as the play was written" because that is what it was) for the State Police had been to always locate the casinos, establish that "They" were in operation, then go to the municipal judge, get a search warrant, go back to the casinos, confiscate the gambling paraphernalia and destroy it. That was the theory anyway. That is the way it would happen in a perfect world, but not how it was done in Hot Springs, and a lot of other places in Arkansas. In the imperfect world of Hot Springs and other parts of Arkansas, the application for a search warrant made the news "hotline". In other words the gambling fraternity learned about the up-coming raid before the ink had even dried on the search warrant.

The racketeers were smart enough, though, that when they needed results for political reasons they sacrificed a few old machines and/or parts to be destroyed by the Arkansas State Police to make it appear that the politicians were making their promises good, closing down casino gambling.

When it came time to make good on hiding the equipment, when in a "closedown" mode the perfect hideout proved to be under Central Avenue, the main street, under which the Hot Springs Creek ran. The City simply constructed a street, Central, over the creek. The creek is still there under the Avenue but not open to the public or "traffic."

You can bet the racketeers and the raiders, had worlds of evidence to prove that this time the politicos had scored a touchdown. They, in the name of politics, tried to prove that it could be done after all these years, by allowing the State Police to "find" some old machines or parts which they could beat up, take pictures for public consumption and then declare that they had crushed gambling while the machines would be in hiding, possibly even under Central Avenue. This was the attitude Winthrop Rockefeller found when he took office.

For the twelve years Orval Faubus had been Governor, and his Director of State Police, conducted the State Police "raids" and helped the powers that be, including Faubus, claim the "victory."

Governor Rockefeller had run for the Governor's Office on the promise to close casino gambling. In March, 1967, Colonel Lindsey ordered another raid as a result of one of the Little Rock newspapers having pictures of gambling casinos operating in Hot Springs. Lindsey laid out how it was going to be.

Lindsey implied that their lack of success, in discussing the difference between pictures newspaper photographers had in hand, showing casinos in full operation, and what the State Police had found on that particular raid was the result of publicity, implying that if the newspapers published the results of their investigation and their findings of casino operations rather than first taking that information to the ASP no raid could be successful. Imagine the difference between those newspaper pictures and an accounting of what was found by the police; a few cards and dice.

Lindsey urged the media to cooperate by notifying the State Police of any gambling activity. He said any such information furnished the State Police:

> "would be given the proper attention, and if there is question in our minds as to whether or not the information furnished is legal, we will then consult our legal counsel."

He then said that when the newspaper reporters went to establishments where gambling is alleged to be taking place, before publishing their reports, they should furnish their reports to the ASP so that the troopers could take "*possible legal action.*"

This statement might have been misconstrued as being a signal from the Rockefeller Administration that he, too, was going to view the situation of gambling and prostitution in Arkansas as a "local" matter. (What a beautiful way to blame the newspapers for "spilling the beans.")

In other words, you boys don't be sending any reporters over there to discover anything that is not there, and if we slip up and let you find something that's not there you absolutely cannot publish stories or pictures of what's not there in your newspapers. *For goodness sakes, give us a chance!!!* (How do you say unbelievable?)

"The State Police will move against illegal gambling in Arkansas *only after obtaining warrants from local authorities...*"

This was pretty plain talk, nothing was going to be done without going through "local" authorities; (sheriff, police, municipal judge, etc., etc.) and only then after getting legal advice from the Attorney General who was the ASP legal authority. In other words, gambling and prostitution and other rackets were to remain a 'local' matter to be handled as always, that is in the hands of those hand-picked people, "authorized" to operate the rackets. This sounded like Faubus speak. Gambling wasn't there but if it was it would be handled as a local matter. (Even though patently illegal!)

This piece of information must have given the mob hope because they opened up again while the newspapers published cartoons spoofing the situation. Ala, the gangsters threw "snake eyes" while music played from the "WR" jukebox.

True to form, the supporters of gambling passed legislation that would give four unnamed casinos in Hot Springs rights to the entire action. They claimed the Governor said he would sign a gambling bill. The governor denied this and even if he had done so, surely he wouldn't sign a bill giving the rights to four unnamed casinos without even knowing who would own and operate the casinos. If he had promised to sign a bill, he certainly shouldn't have signed one giving four clubs licenses without some more restrictions. He shouldn't have signed the one they passed. He denied that he ever promised to sign any bill anyway and he didn't.

Passage of the bill was obviously a dare. Evidently the Legislature, thinking that the operation had been around for a hundred years or more and that nearly everyone said and believed or thought or expressed an opinion when it came to closing the Rackets down, "It couldn't be done", that they could pass whatever legislation they wanted. And yet, it had to leave the gangsters in control.

They were saying in effect, either sign the bill or close the rackets down. (A reasonable dare.)

The legal counsel at that time was Attorney General Joe Purcell. This was the same Joe Purcell who advised us, the Arkansas State Police, in August, 1967, to return our first haul of slot machines and other paraphernalia to the Hot Springs Police Department even though this had been the disposition of the paraphernalia for years; seize it, turn it back to the police department who would then turn it back to the Rackets..

The (Big) Combination, Frank Costello, the Gambinos, and the other Mafioso types from back East, must have laughed themselves silly thinking how stupid Arkansas authorities must be to evidently believe the old shell game applied to this and other scams in Hot Springs and other parts of Arkansas for all these years and never becoming wise to it.

Gambling was nothing new in Hot Springs in the early 1900's almost as it was in 1967. One can follow illegal, wide open gambling, illegal whiskey and prostitution even before the 1870's. You can probably still find "bust-out" crap games going on in Garland County, the "Valley of the Vapors" aka Hot Springs, but not as it once was. (One thing for sure is that there are hundreds of slot machines and assorted equipment that won't be available for use.) You can also place more dependence upon your city and county leaders including your law enforcement agencies.

FRANK FLYNN, HOT SPRINGS' "BOSS GAMBLER" MEETS THE MAJOR

Was It Better in the Distant Past?

Frank didn't get his title, "Boss Gambler," by perfect attendance at Sunday School.

Frank took umbrage at anyone trying to open a saloon or gambling club without his explicit approval and blessings, which he bestowed on certain people while denying others. The rein of the "Boss Gambler" would prove to be more apparent during the time when it seemed that everyone was armed and willing to risk it all on the draw of a gun or the flip of a card. Don't count out the success of a good ambush, and there were plenty of those in the 1880's.

These conditions permeated not only the gamblers, card sharks, and bunko artists, but also most of the Garland County law establishment, if not all, during most of those years. Some will undoubtedly claim that they were honest and law abiding and simply trying to get along. (You be the judge.)

An example of just how serious Ole' Frank took a violation of this unwritten rule, to get his approval, is the Jim Lane affair. Jim, Frank's sworn enemy, owned the Monarch and the Palace saloons and gambling clubs. The news that Lane was going to open these clubs was disturbing to Frank. Especially disturbing when Frank found that Lane was going to use subterfuge to get the clubs open after Frank had ruled against such openings. The new operator was going to be Major S. A. Doran, but it was going to take some shenanigans to pull that off.

Major Doran had left a trail of dead men from the Civil War, to Kentucky, to Tennessee and, maybe, Arkansas. Doran was a Confederate veteran but not all of his kills were the Yankees, enemies of the South.

Doran shot and killed three men in Kentucky. Unfortunately, the details have been lost in history. It is documented, however, that in 1868, Doran shot and killed his landlord who had come to collect the rent. According to accounts, the landlord found the good Major in bed with "lewd" women. The landlord seemed ready for the violence, having his gun drawn before he entered the bedroom, but Doran managed to shoot faster and straighter than the landlord. The landlord was just listed as another victim.

Flynn nearly always got his way and he had no intention of yielding any of this power and prestige to any person who might be as ruthless as he was. Jim Lane, a pretender to the throne, had employed Doran because of that reputation. Lane even told Doran that "certain leading citizens had raised $6,000 to have Frank Flynn murdered."

Flynn was known to be not only stubborn, but had, likewise, killed his own share of men in gunfights. He did not have the reputation of backing down. He had killed another gambler in Austin, Texas, as well as Hot Springs' Hornet newspaper editor Charles Matthews; and two years earlier in 1886, he had shot and killed ex-deputy James Kinnehan when Kinnehan had attempted to shakedown Flynn's gambling operation. (An account of this entire incident, before and after, is dealt with in *Hot Springs Gunsmoke*, by Orval Albritton.)

Come with me back to 1884. This era and this particular case are well documented in the newspapers of that day.

Flynn sent word to Doran after hearing that he was going to defy Frank's orders and open the Palace and the Monarch Saloons, that he was calling him out, one on one to settle the matter man to man. While Flynn making preparations, was surprised, thinking it would be some time before he met up with Doran. It was, however, sooner than later, minutes really, when the two met. Flynn was wearing a shoulder holster, but it was under his suit coat, which was under his topcoat. Enough to keep Flynn dry and warm but sure stood in his way of a quick draw.

Meeting on the street, Doran told Flynn to draw, but before Flynn could unbutton his garb and draw his long barrel pistol, Doran pulled his .44 caliber pistol from his belt, aimed and pulled the trigger twice without firing a single round. (So much for the maintenance of your sidearm, which can mean life or death.) Having these misfires, Doran dropped the first gun, drew his long barreled Colt pistol and fired three quick shots. They had to be quick shots as Frank was digging through his coats trying to draw his gun.

Witnesses to the shootout reported that they saw puffs of dust coming from Flynn's chest. He then staggered, bleeding, into the doorway of the barbershop there on Central Avenue. It was learned that he had worn metal plate under his coats, this amounting to a "bullet-proof vest." These same witnesses say Flynn called out to Doran, "Give me a chance," to which Doran replied, "Take one." (*Arkansas Gazette*, 19 February, 1884) Flynn took his best shot, but there was not much chance of hitting Doran as Doran had stepped behind a post. (He wasn't known for his street smarts for nothing.)

Two policemen rushed in to stop the melee. Surprisingly, Flynn survived as did Doran. This was the first time in Garland County, Arkansas, or maybe in the United States, or anywhere else that a "bullet-proof vest" was used in a gunfight. It proved to be very effective, as Flynn was staggered but survived to fight another day. A description given by witnesses makes it sound like Flynn was hit by a metal door to a cook stove. Flynn spit up blood for several days while Doran and his boys laid low. Oh well, they both survived to fight another day. Flynn was reportedly wearing a cook-stove door on his chest, possibly the first bullet-proof vest in America.

Both men were arrested. Flynn paid a fine of $25.00 for carrying a weapon and $5.00 for disturbing the peace. On the next day, Doran and one of his henchmen, one David Pruitt, paid a $23.50 fine for operating a gaming house. (How did Doran escape the charge of carrying a weapon? (*City Records*, Page 450, 28 December, 1883)

(Just days later, Lane told Flynn that he did not want to be on bad terms with him. They shook hands on it like gentlemen—which they weren't.)

After the fight, Jim Lane met with Doran, and planned to sign over the gaming operations, leave town until things cooled off, then come back and take over the operation of the Palace and Monarch Saloons, lock, stock and gun barrel. Maybe in this way, they hoped, Flynn could be flim-flammed into believing that he had won. Far from it. There was no prediction as to what the situation might be when Lane came back but he was planning to be in control when he did.

In this one gunfight, so many shots were fired on Central Avenue that a haze of gunsmoke, according to witnesses, hung over a block of that street. Doran obviously had not forgotten about Frank's intentions to ambush him.

The Flynn's, Frank, Billy and Jack were so apprehensive about an ambush that every morning and night they took a closed carriage from Frank's house to the Office Saloon, their headquarters, and on the return to his house.

Doran was apparently just as apprehensive expecting that the feud between himself and Flynn might erupt into even more action. Each was wary of the other, what one might call a deep personality clash. Doran did not take this potential confrontation lightly. He lived in one of the rooms at the Palace Saloon, but took his meals at the Arlington Hotel at precisely the same time each day. Flynn noticed this habit, but he should have also noticed when Doran stopped these trips to the Arlington.

Flynn and some of his men, one who registered as a Mr. Wilson from Winnipeg, Canada, took a front room on the second floor of the Arlington Hotel. (*Arkansas Gazette*, 17 February, 1884, Interview with A. E. Dow)

On this particularly cold and blustery day, Doran noticed a couple of Flynn's cohorts standing outside the second floor of Billy McTeague's Saloon looking South down Central Avenue. He decided he would have his sandwich at the Palace, choosing to not go outside. Doran had lived long enough to recognize a potential ambush from a mile off. In this case it was on the same block. That same evening he noticed the same two men standing outside in the blustery cold in the same position, so he sent someone for his dinner.

Believe it or not, Frank Flynn made a near fatal mistake. Frank was ready for Doran to show himself but when a maid was denied entry into the room rented by Frank and his boys at the Arlington Hotel, she went to Colonel S. H. Stitt, who was part owner and manager of the hotel. Highly incensed, she reported that three men in a second story room had refused her admittance. She just wanted to clean the room, but they wouldn't let her in. Stitt went to the room to confront Mr. Wilson from Canada. (An alias for one of Flynn's men.)

Stitt demanded entrance and finally pushed his way through the door. The sight of a stack of guns on beds in the room was not unusual for that day, but so many? Stitt, upon seeing Frank Flynn and the small arsenal, realized what they must be planning, especially when the half-raised window looked right out on Central Avenue and Dorans' place. He realized what Flynn was up to and ordered Flynn and his men to vacate the room or he would report them to Tom Toler, the 28 year old Chief of Police.

The very idea, an *ambush* from the Arlington Hotel!

The men left the room taking their arsenal with them and soon word spread like a runaway .44 slug about the *ambush* that was about to take place. (*Ibid*, 19 January, 1884 and *Gunsmoke, Hot Springs*.)

This planned *ambush* did not set well with Doran. He didn't care to be the guest of honor. He decided he would set up his own *ambush*, from his own place, his own saloon with several of his gang.

Frank and his brothers, Billy and Jack, boarded, as usual, the closed carriage on their way home but didn't plan for Doran and his gang jumping them. They should have known that someone was keeping tabs on them and reporting the results to Major Doran. They surely knew that the bad blood between them would come out soon and not knowing when and from where wasn't very smart. They had, though, taken the precaution of putting a shotgun and several rifles in the carriage, in addition to carrying their own firearms, but that would prove to be not enough. (Close counts in horseshoes, but not as much as accuracy in gunfights.)

Naturally, there was a dispute as to which one of the factions fired the first shot. Some spectators said that Frank, as they were passing Doran's Saloon, pulled up the back curtain on the hack and fired into the saloon. This controversy was of little help for Jack Flynn and his neck. He was the first casualty suffered. Jack, Frank's brother, slid forward and lay dying on the seat of the carriage. The hack driver was shot through the upper body by buckshot, but would live for a few days before he expired, cursing his luck, saying he should have known better. (*Gunsmoke, Hot Springs*, Page 54).

Frank took a round of buckshot deep into his thigh but notwithstanding the hole in his leg he jumped to the ground and hobbled over to join his brother, Billy. The two were both firing back at those at the saloon. Frank emptied his pistol in the direction of the assailants in the saloon while Billy ran from the street toward the bank to find a firing position. He was shot through the breast. He fell to the sidewalk and was helped into the stairway of the Commercial.

When Frank ran out of ammunition for his pistol, he pulled out a Winchester rifle from the carriage in which they had been riding. Sprinting toward the doorway of the Owl Club ready to do battle, Frank took another round in his hand.

By this time “Brave” Tom Toler, the Chief of Police was reported to have yelled for the shooting to stop and it did. *(Arkansas Gazette*, 10 Feb, 1884).

Tom Toler, now there was a Chief of Police. He obviously knew the characters involved as he also worked in and around many of the clubs when he wasn’t denominated the Chief of Police or some other law enforcement position. It seemed accepted that a sufficient number of Hot Springs “Cops”, of both the city, as well as the county sheriff types, were always on hand to lend support to the gambling industry. There were even “turf wars” where city law enforcement vied with the county officers to see who could be cozier with that element. In this case it seems that the Chief of Police meant to keep the peace, somewhat unusual over the years.

One gambler dead, two innocent men dying, and three seriously wounded. This seemed to be a little much for even Hot Springs so there was a gasp of shock and awe when Chief Toler got the shooting stopped. He obviously knew the characters involved and must have known of their reputations as thugs, ready and willing shooters, but he still took charge of the crime scene where there were dead and dying men still intent on killing each other. He stood his ground right in the middle of the mess.

Flynn’s faction as well as the Doran faction, or at least those still surviving, went to trial on various charges, pleading “self defense” and all were found “Not Guilty.” (That could probably only happen with those characters involved and only in Hot Springs.)

When he wasn’t Chief of Police, Tom worked at some of the various saloons and gambling halls around town. (They must have known good ole’ Tom and must have been convinced that he would, even at his tender age of 28, do just that … *kill the next man that fires a shot*.)

All the firing stopped. This could have been because six men had been shot on a street populated by hundreds of people: one gambler dead, two innocent men dying, and three seriously wounded, but most likely they stopped shooting because of Tom's threat.

Now this was too much. Businesses seemed to pay attention—visitors were fleeing the city in droves. The town folks had maybe had too much, or at least the tourists had.

The fire bell began to ring on Sumpter Square. It banged away until a fairly good crowd flocked to the grassy knoll to learn the cause for the bell. Some reported with rifles, others with shot guns, and pistols and assorted weapons we assume. The bell had been rung by the Mayor as was always done in an emergency.

"Mounted upon a large goods box and frantically waving his arms with hat held in one hand," the Mayor started a chant. (The Record – 1973, eyewitness account of "Omaha" Frank Borland, p. 50)

The chant rang up and down the valley and got louder as more men gathered. The chorus of voices struck fear into the "sporting men," (pimps, gamblers, bunco artists, etc.) of the town as an even larger crowd gathered that evening chanting,

> *"Hang every gambler in Hot Springs ... hang every gambler in Hot Springs." Up and down the street, clubs and saloons locked their doors.* — (Ibid)

(This was an excellent way to close the saloons, houses of prostitution and gambling halls, but not quite legal.) A resolution was later presented by the City Attorney and adopted by the citizens:

"Resolved, that a committee of twelve be appointed by the Chair to investigate the recent killing and also matters connected therewith, and to call upon the other citizens for such assistance as they might need to enforce the laws, with powers to act."

The mayor was called upon to take steps to close up all gambling houses but houses of prostitution were not mentioned, unless they were counted in the addendum, "and all matters connected therewith." *(Arkansas Gazette* 12 February 1884)

Tom Toler requested the Committee to give notice to three "toughs" known to be imported desperadoes and also three members of the Flynn gang to leave the city at once. When the Committee started to run them out of town, however, the sheriff interfered and took the men under his protection. (Before he did much he better find what Frank wanted and would agree to.)

The Committee though, evidently without asking, organized a militia company of "100 Men", while petitioning the governor for commissions for the militia. As a result of that request, the Committee was sent "one hundred stand of arms". (Actually, only seventy men were organized into the militia rather than one hundred. This was not the first time the city had been shorted by the State.)

But Judge J. B. Wood, by court order, ruled all six prisoners be placed under control of the sheriff. (This should be a hint as to who was in control of the city.) Even a mob, much of the citizenry of the city, and a militia company of either 70 or 100 men were overruled by a local judge.

There were periods within that time frame when the clubrooms were dark and closed, and the general population was under the belief that gambling was completely and absolutely shutdown. One such period immediately followed the Flynn-Doran conflict in 1884, (described herein) and several other short periods, but even in the "closed periods," there was some illegal gambling taking place. There would be evidence of bust-out crap games and back-room card games or dice rooms. The gamblers were a long way from being run out of town.

Wide open or closed it would seem that during the time everyone, or at least the ones seemingly in charge were armed and willing to risk it all on the draw of a gun, the draw of a card or the success of an ambush. These conditions permeated the gang of gamblers, card sharks and bunko artists, and, believe it or not, that included, of course, most of the law enforcement officers as well. Judging from that era, it seems that if you did not have a gun when walking the streets in "Bubbles", the gang comprised of the latest desperados would issue you one just to make things even.

Frank Flynn seemed to be the embodiment of the spirit of that day, at least in Hot Springs: you wouldn't be "Boss of Gambling" if you let a person with the reputation of a Major Doran come to your town without any attempt to keep him out. Not likely if you were the boss gambler. You only become the boss gambler if you are willing to use whatever force is necessary; even a few killin's to maintain control over not only the competition, but also the enforcers of the law. You only maintain control through the pocketbook or violence or the threat of violence. Historically, to stay in power you must have the ability to, in effect, compel the police authority not only to "look the other way," but act affirmatively to help you put competition out of action. (You don't maintain that kind of control by sending Christmas turkeys to your local police.)

Then a logical question is, "How did the "Little Combination" and its members, in the 1930's, the 40's, 50's and 60's, whose names are scattered throughout Hot Springs history, maintain order and exclusivity? How did those members keep other people from moving into their territory?" The obvious answer is, you buy everybody you can, and you intimidate those you can't buy. Sometimes it would appear to be the Mayor who had the upper hand, but history will record that usually it was the boss gambler, and in this period, 1930's through 1960's, it was surely true. The "Boss" was not an elected position but one gained by power, influence and control over the ballot box as well as fear and intimidation. This was a tailor made opportunity for the mob aka Owney "The Killer" Madden, J. Edgar Hoovers #1 nemesis, who held the title of the biggest bootlegger in America. He was even reputed to be bigger than Jack Kennedy's daddy, who Madden claimed was his partner in the bootlegging business.

Our story would not be complete without describing a few of the thugs, gangsters and killers who came to Hot Springs to relax, to hang out or to hide. For any of this they found open arms, dependent, of course, upon how much clout or how much money they had.

FRANK "JELLY" NASH: LEAVENWORTH'S LOSS, HOT SPRINGS' GAIN?

A perfect example of protection by the law "enforcement" fraternity of that day was the story of Frank "Jelly" Nash. He had been serving time in the Leavenworth, Kansas Federal Penitentiary, when he decided to leave. He just decided to go and found a way.

Frank was a member of the Harvey Bailey gang, a bunch of thugs who went around the country robbing the rich and giving to themselves. Nash was captured at Hot Springs, but, of course, not by local police authorities. There was so much distrust in the law enforcement system in Hot Springs and Garland County that the federal government, when they heard that Nash was in Hot Springs, dared not "notify" the locals, but, instead, sent a Chief of Police from McAlister, Oklahoma with two Special Agents of the FBI to nab Nash to take him back to Leavenworth from whence he came.

Oh, yes, he didn't go out the front gate of the pen. It didn't matter to him that he had been sentenced to spend a good part of his lifetime behind bars. He was so openly contemptuous of the law that after his own escape he later came back and helped seven other "lads" escape from the minions of the law. The warden and his guys thought they had the only keys to the cell doors of the prison, but it turned out that they didn't.

Nash made one or more mistakes while freeing the other prisoners. One of those that he had helped escape somehow knew or found out where Frank was holed up and was convinced that it would be in his best interest to tell the FBI where that place was. (Hot Springs, of course.) It could save the "rat" several years from his lifetime behind bars.

Sure enough, Nash, according to the escapee informant who Nash had helped escape, had learned through the grapevine that Nash was in Hot Springs under the fellowship provided by the "Law," meaning, evidently, anyone carrying a badge and a gun in that county.

The Chief from McAlister and two FBI Agents came to Hot Springs. Almost before they got checked into their motel, they had staked out "Jelly's" favorite club. Looking over the Clubs' dance floor they thought they had missed him when he suddenly appeared coming out of the restroom. Before he realized he had been identified his pursuers shoved a couple of pistols in his side, threatened to kill him if he raised an alarm. Before he could fully react, they had taken him into custody, quickly threw him in their car, and hustled him off to Fort Smith, Arkansas. There, within a few hours, under fairly heavy guard, the Chief, the two agents and "Jelly" boarded a fast moving Missouri Pacific passenger train, Kansas City bound.

"Jelly" was on his way back to Leavenworth, Kansas, but little did he know he wouldn't make it. (His well-meaning friends made that happen whether by mistake or on purpose.)

This mission was quite secret so the Hot Springs authorities had no idea the feds were closing in on one of their protectees, but Nash's girlfriend had been told that her boyfriend Nash had been snatched. No one knew for sure whether he had been kidnapped or arrested, but taking no chances she did as she had been told. She contacted certain people as instructed. Sure enough, she called the "friend," Richard "Tallman" Galatas, a known thug, who lined up the rescue of his buddy.

Galatas contacted "Pretty Boy" Floyd, and Floyd enlisted his running buddy, Adam Richetti, to help out. (To his dying day Floyd, although he freely admitted most of his crimes, including the killing of a sheriff, always maintained that he had nothing to do with the attempted escape of Nash and the killing of the police officers in Kansas City.)

Galatas, a Hot Springs resident, had been earlier sentenced to four years confinement and a fine of $10,000. After serving 14 months of his four-year sentence in the federal penitentiary he was returned from Alcatraz to the Leavenworth Federal Penitentiary for release. He took a pauper's oath and served an extra month in prison, as he could not pay the $10,000 fine imposed.

He returned to Hot Springs where he and his wife Elizabeth, also known as "Betty," bought a car. Being an ex-con and having no visible means of support he couldn't finance a car. No problem. None other than Mayor Leo P. McLaughlin and his brother George signed a note pledging that they would pay for the car if Galatas didn't. And believe it or not, the Chief of Police took the license off his wife's car and put it on Galatas' new car. (Isn't that sweet? Anything for an old friend.) (*Public Opinion*, 25 August 1933, p.3.)

THE KANSAS CITY MASSACRE AND "JELLY": THE FINAL GO-ROUND, MISTAKE?

The Missouri Pacific passenger train had not even come to a complete stop at the Kansas City train station before one of the officers jumped down from the train. History has not designated who stepped first from the slow moving train, but all those waiting officers who were to meet the train knew of the possibility that their "cargo" might have warranted a reception committee, like some associates from the underworld, who stood to gain something from the removal of their "most wanted cargo." That "cargo" was no less than Frank "Jelly" Nash. Frank was known, not only in the underworld where he traveled, but recognized by respected citizens. He was known for and had proven his ruthlessness many times meriting his picture on wanted posters throughout the Southwest.

In 1913, Frank was sentenced to life at the state penitentiary at McAlister, Oklahoma, for murder. After he was pardoned, he left the prison certain to go "straight" or so the prison officials thought. Frank, though, had other ideas.

In 1920, Ole' Frank was sentenced to twenty years for burglary with explosives. Frank had learned one sure way to open a safe—dynamite. Some people are slow learners, but not Frank. He was later pardoned again. Surely, this time he could take the hint ... go "straight." Maybe, he still had the best of intentions, but you know how that goes. He, again, went "almost straight." At least, he was finally caught and on March 3, 1924, to be exact, Frank began another twenty year sentence. This time it was for a federal offense, so Frank was sent to the United States Penitentiary at Leavenworth, Kansas. He had been convicted of assaulting a mail custodian, namely, a post office job, robbery of a post office. (Somebody up there liked "Jelly.") He just kept assaulting people and blowing things up.

After six years of breaking rocks at Leavenworth or doing what they do there, Frank had all he could take. The rocks got bigger and the hammer got heavier. So on October 19, 1930, using crafty methods known only to Frank, he left the joint.

He probably had an almost perfect chance to go "straight," but it is hard to break old bad habits. (His mother would probably say he fell in with the wrong crowd.) Of course, he, himself, might have constituted the wrong crowd. Whatever the reason, he chose to take the lower road. A little more than a year passed, and then on December 11, 1931, Frank went back to Leavenworth, not as a resident, but helping the seven of his friend's escape. Misery loves company.

Proving there is no honor among thieves, Francis L. Keating, Thomas Holden and several other well known gangsters, known at least throughout the Southwest during the depression ridden thirties, were arrested for various violations of the law. Like so many thugs facing serious charges and sure time in the joint "informed" or as they would say, "ratted out," Nash. To curry favor with the G-Men, they told the FBI Agents that Frank Nash, who was hotter than a firecracker on the 4th of July of that year, was holed up in Hot Springs, Arkansas.

That was a perfect place for him given the reputation of the law there. This information furnished by these wise guys was believable and true to form. The G-Men wanted Frank to send him back to the rock pile, but they knew enough about the law in Hot Springs to not give any hint to them that they were coming for Frank. Sure, the law already knew Frank was there. And the law, that is the legitimate "law" knew that Frank was living "in the open" under the protection of the law in Hot Springs. It was plain to see that the "law" in Hot Springs cared about keeping ole' Frank free. It was about money, don't you know?

The Special Agent in Charge (SAC) of the Oklahoma City FBI Field Office decided they would go over there, to Hot Springs, themselves, get Frank, and take him back to Leavenworth. (It seemed the only decent thing to do, don't you see?)

They took seriously their need to put ole' Frank back in the slammer. Due to past experience and because of the mistrust of the locals, two FBI Agents, Frank Smith and F. Joseph Lackey, from the Oklahoma FBI Field Office along with McAlister, Oklahoma, Police Chief Otto Reed, went to Hot Springs. Chief Reed knew what "Jelly" looked like. They found him, sure enough, in the bowels of the "Valley of the Vapors."

Nash had developed a tight relationship with Chief of Police Wakelin and Chief of Detectives Dutch Akers, a thing called "bribes." As a matter of fact, Wakelin and Akers served as trip wires for Nash. Whenever someone came looking for him, the police were usually the first to know. This was perfect for the Hot Springs law enforcement. When they were alerted, Nash was told so he could take to ground, get lost, or change hideouts but not have to leave town. He had it too good and safe in the "Valley" to leave town.

Nash had some cosmetic surgery done to his nose, grew a mustache and began to wear a wig, presumably to alter his appearance, which had been widely circulated by the FBI and the United States Marshals Service. He had no idea this misidentification might lead to his being shot … dead. His buddies had no idea he had tried the old disguise trick!

FBI Agents Lackey and Smith, accompanied by Chief Reed registered at the Hot Springs Como Hotel. Nash's car had been spotted near the White Front Club on Central Avenue not far from the Como Hotel. Neither of the agents, Lackey nor Smith, had ever seen "Jelly," but Otto Reed had, and he could identify him for sure. The Bureau normally works with the local authorities in cases like this, but these Hot Springs local authorities had burned them too many times.

The Agents and Reed pulled up in front of the White Front Club and left the motor of their Buick sedan running. At first, they did not see Nash, but then, while they waited, he came from the poolroom. He had been in the bathroom. Nash walked directly into their arms. They grabbed him right in front of many people in the Club, jammed their guns in his ribs, rushed him outside, put him in their Buick and headed for Fort Smith, where they planned to catch the Missouri Pacific Passenger Train for Kansas City. The handcuffed Frank must have known by this time that he was headed back to Leavenworth to break some more rocks for an even longer time with an even heavier hammer.

Anyone who knows Hot Springs would not find it hard to believe that there were a few places where one could hide, since Hot Springs is built between the mountains in the foothills of the Ouachita Mountain Range. The rear of nearly all of the buildings on Central Avenue back up to one of Hot Spring's Mountains whether it is on the state side or the federal side. Even now, Hot Springs is not that big, and for a town of nearly always less than 30,000 souls, it would not be a prize hiding place, except for the people who were supposed to be looking for you were instead hiding you. They didn't always get away with it, ala "Lucky" Luciano, Alvin "Creepy" Karpis and other thugs, though no thanks to law enforcement in Garland County and Hot Springs authorities.

Matt Picchi, a friend of any thug who would claim him and always faithful to the code, saw the two men flank Nash in the club and hustle him into the waiting car. As quickly as he could, he grabbed a phone and notified "Tallman" Galatas and probably Betty, Nash's girlfriend. "Tallman" served as a go-between Hot Springs' "finest" and the Chicago bad guys. Galatas, not certain whether Nash had been kidnapped or captured, contacted the Chief of Detectives, Herbert "Dutch" Akers, who supposedly could not understand why he and his associates had not been contacted by the feds regarding the presence of "Jelly" in the Spa City, as well as why they had not been notified of the hunt for Nash. "Dutch" had some 'splainin' to do. *It was a black mark against his reputation and he just wasn't going to stand for it*. He was in a snit. The black mark would be his letting a person under his protection get collared and sent back to breaking rocks.

Imagine that ... In a city of less than 30,000 folks, a well known hoodlum like Frank "Jelly" Nash was in town and "Dutch," the Chief of Detectives didn't know about it? This is the same man, "Dutch," who finally went to prison over just such criminal activity, harboring a top ten fugitive, Alvin "Creepy" Karpis. That was his modus operandi (MO), getting money from any and all sources where he could, just like he said he would when he later talked to an FBI Special Agent when he was on trial for the harboring charge.

"Dutch" dutifully sent a car after the fleeing Buick carrying Nash, the two agents and Chief Reed and at the same time sent out radio messages to the Benton, Arkansas Police: BOLO (*Be on the lookout*) with a description of the car and its occupants. He sent the same BOLO to the Little Rock police. (Later, the police admitted they did stop the car in Benton, but, being satisfied as to the identity of the occupants, the three officers and Nash, police officers let the car proceed.) (Do you suspect that the Benton officers knew the score?)

Nash's girlfriend said that Nash had instructed her that if anything ever happened to him, she should contact an individual in Chicago. Supposedly, this was Doc Stacci. Galatas contacted Stacci, who got in touch with Verne Miller. Vern was an ex-sheriff turned hoodlum who had some ideas as to how Nash could be freed.

Galatas was so concerned that he chartered an airplane, piloted by one John Stover, the manager of the Hot Springs Airport, to fly Elizabeth or "Betty", Nash's girlfriend, her eight year old daughter and himself to Kansas City.

The *Sentinel-Record* on 18 June, 1933, noted that Stover did take charter flights for some very dangerous and wanted underworld gangsters. As a matter of fact they later reported that Stover was charged and tried for harboring and aiding Alvin "Creepy" Karpis, a well known top 10 hoodlum, on the FBI Most Wanted list, on a couple of his trips. (Stover was exonerated at trial, not an unusual result.)

The Agents and the Chief intended to keep "Jelly" for a while, hopefully for a lifetime, so they kept a sharp eye out for anything or anyone suspicious. At 8:30 p.m. sharp, after nightfall and as dark as blue blazes, they boarded a fast moving Missouri Pacific passenger train from Fort Smith, Arkansas bound for Kansas City, Missouri, a sister city to Kansas City, Kansas. It was just a short trip from there to Leavenworth, Kansas and the rock pile.

These officers knew of "Jelly's" reputation, which was that he was dangerous and a definite escape risk. They were taking no chances. Little did these officers know they had a date with destiny. Keeping a close eye on Frank and everyone else that came within spitting distance, they felt fairly secure, but also knew that an ambush could come from anywhere at any time. The agents might have even had a premonition that Nash would be wanted by the Chicago thugs, dead.

Their next exposure to any thugs who might want to rescue "Jelly" Nash would probably be at Kansas City. It was not for the lack of careful planning by the officers that their destiny had been set. At 7:15 the next morning on June 17, 1933, at the Kansas

City Train Station, the gunplay and shootout, later known as the Kansas City Massacre, was foreordained to take place. The best laid plans of mice and men often go awry and destiny had a surprise for the officers. Their plan did not include preparations for a suicide attack.

Frank had made friends with a great number of thugs of like ilk who operated in that part of the country during the roaring thirties. Some of them, for one reason or another thought they would just spring ole' "Jelly" by ambushing his captors. (That should be a lot of fun.) Possibly others, for some reason or another, might want Frank dead. After all, dead men tell no tales and if dead, "Jelly" could not tell the authorities about Hot Springs' open secret, their hide and seek operation. Supposedly, his rescuers were not to kill him, however, they did!

History records that before leaving Fort Smith, Arkansas one of the FBI Special Agents made a telephone call to the Special Agent in Charge (SAC) of the Kansas City FBI Field Office, R. E. Vetterli. Vetterli rounded up some of his top Agents and armed them to the teeth. He knew of the possibility of a rescue attempt. He called the Kansas City Police Department. The KCPD assigned two detectives to this caper. It was simple enough. They made plans to meet the Oklahoma Agents and Chief Reed and put "Jelly" in a car and to return him to Leavenworth, where he would get a hammer and some rocks assigned to him as his very own.

A major consideration, however, was getting Frank off the train, through the station, out to the car, and then delivering him to Leavenworth where they were not expecting him but would make room for him anyway.

How and why Frank Nash commanded such respect from his brethren? No one is sure, but obviously his being removed from the minions of the law appealed to a few of his precious associates and others. He had, after all, put himself in jeopardy in springing the seven cons from Leavenworth earlier in his career. Maybe he was just a likeable felon, but not too likeable to be turned over to the law to save the skin of one of those he had helped escape.

Frank's friends in Hot Springs got the arrival time of the KC bound train from Ft. Smith and passed the word along,

"They got 'Jelly.' What are we going to do about it?"

Being told when the Missouri Pacific passenger train was to arrive, Verne Miller, a no-account thug, got on the telephone and made a number of long distance phone calls seeking help in springing Frank from the bad (good) guys.

Verne had little trouble in his solicitations. Joining with him were other "engineers" of the escape/rescue plan; taking Frank from the clutches of the law:

Richard "Tallman" Galatas, Herbert Farmer, "Doc" Louis Stacci, and Frank B. Mulloy, outlaws all were only too happy to help spring ole' Frank, who would do the same for them. (?)

"Pretty Boy" Floyd and Adam Richetti, both known throughout the Midwest and beyond for their ruthlessness and willingness to do whatever was necessary to take, as they called it, from the rich to give to the poor, were late getting to the party. (History, however, does not record any charitable contributions made by these ruthless killers during their rampage through the middle ground of this country.)

They had no compunctions about taking what they wanted by the use of force and God help anyone who dared to stand in the way. Machine guns (Chicago Typewriters) have a certain effect on a person, causing him to make some earth shaking snap decisions, like, "Take anything you want."

"Pretty Boy's" adventure to Kansas City was not without suspense.

Just happening upon the scene in Missouri, on the way to Kansas City, Sheriff Jack Killingsworth, a country law enforcement officer, didn't have a chance. Unsuspectingly, he found Adam Richetti and "Pretty Boy" Floyd waiting for a mechanic to patch up their touring car that had "taken out" on them just outside a little wide-spot Missouri town. They were on a short deadline to make Kansas City before morning to meet the train. Richetti recognized Sheriff Killingsworth, but, evidently, the sheriff did not recognize

Richetti. They caught Killingsworth by surprise and before he could react, Richetti and "Pretty Boy" got the drop on him.

They held the Sheriff at gunpoint while they transferred their guns and thug related paraphernalia to another car. The 'stuff' transferred were things any self-respecting bad guy would not be caught dead without. With the sheriff at gunpoint, Floyd and Richetti took the Sheriff captive and hightailed it to Deepwater, Missouri, where they, for some reason, unnoted by history, dropped that car and took another one. If history recorded anything, it probably came to the conclusion that each and every car they set foot in that day was stolen. (In those days, before police channel radios, the old saw about, "You can't outrun a radio" didn't hold true. Back in those days even if the cop had a radio, he had to find a high hill to send signals.)

Fortunately, these two known killers had become, for some reason, acquainted with Sheriff Jack, and they spared his life. They released him, stole another car, and met up with Vernon, the architect of the escape plan. Vernon had been successful in getting their enlistment in freeing Frank. They hardly had time to turn the motor off before heading for the MoPac Train Station to meet the passenger train.

Verne had the perfect plan. They would hide and ambush the officers when they came through the station. Simple, direct and to the point. Three associates (thugs) armed with Thompson Submachine Guns would grab Nash and put him in a waiting car. This seemed, at least to these dummies, a perfect plan. There was one problem, though, which they had not foreseen. Frank, who had undergone plastic surgery (as it is known now), would be in the midst of the officers and might take a bullet or two. Maybe, they did not recognize him or *maybe*, they were afraid he might "rat out" other associates, or maybe, "Dutch" Akers had put the finger on "Jelly" afraid that he might blow the whistle on the operations in Hot Springs if he was again captured. How prophetic!

The good guys were looking (and surely expecting) that there might be gunplay at the train station. Agent Lackey, taking no chances that they would be ambushed, jumped from the moving train and hit the ground running. This left Smith, Reed, and Nash still on the train awaiting the all clear signal.

Stepping out of the shadows, SAC Vetterli saw Lackey on the station platform. They quickly made plans for the transfer of Nash to one of the two vehicles that Vetterli had brought to the Station. A long look around the loading platform revealed no obvious bad guys. They were absent from that scene. The reason for that must have been that the bad guys were on the other side of the Station waiting for the Agents to bring Frank to them.

SAC Vetterli, Special Agent Lackey, McAlister Police Chief Reed, and Special Agent Smith along with Kansas City Detectives Hermanson and Grooms took the handcuffed Nash through the Station to the street outside. It was obvious to anyone who cared to look that this was serious business. Lackey and Reed carried, in plain sight, pump shotguns, each loaded with six Double Ought buckshot shells (nine .22 caliber slugs in each shell meant to be man stoppers, and would do just that.)

It seems though that they had no chance to stop any man during the up coming shootout. The surprise was so great that the officers and agents had no chance to get off a shot.

Agents are trained that action is faster than reaction. This time it worked for the thugs. These seven law men, slowly and cautiously, expecting trouble, checked out every nook and cranny for anything suspicious, say bad guys with submachine guns. Even the restrooms were cleared. Not seeing anyone, they walked right into the trap.

Parked about six feet away on the right side of Kansas City Agent Caffrey's Bureau car was a stranger, a green Plymouth. Caffrey's car was going to be used to transport Nash to the Leavenworth Pen. Before Agent Lackey, who saw one of the thugs rushing in, could sound the alarm, three men armed with Thompson Submachine guns rushed the officers from behind the stranger car. (Bear in mind, the action reaction theorem can work for the bad guys, too.) Agent Lackey clearly saw the plan coming together, if you could call the rescue a "plan", but, too late. The slugs from the submachine guns clattered on the street, and the business end of the rounds buzzed like angry bees, dropping officers right and left.

The cops didn't stand a chance. Not one round from any of their guns was fired. The good guys were caught flatfooted. SAC Vetterli took a round to his left arm from a second hood that was crouching behind another car. He fell to the pavement. There he saw Special Agent Caffrey dying, shot in the head.

Nash, the subject of the rescue attempt, and Chief Reed were killed inside Caffrey's Chevrolet Bureau car in the front seat while Lackey and Smith fell forward in the back seat of the car and survived the hale of bullets. Both Lackey and Smith were lucky. Lackey took three bullets and lived to tell the tale. Smith was unscathed. Detectives Hermanson and Grooms lay in puddles of blood, dead. This meant four cops and at least one bad guy had died, Frank Nash. (Hermanson and Grooms are memorialized as Kansas City Police Department fallen officers.)

This whole scenario seemed to be sound police work except upon closer scrutiny. (Each incident requires a report indicating what went right and what went wrong.) Evidently, there was some uncertainty about the car seats each was to take. Nash started to get in the back seat but was told to sit in the front seat. Nash had obviously ridden in a car while in custody before. He must have known that the arrestee always sits in the back just behind the passenger's seat. This could have confused the thugs or maybe they didn't know that Nash had tried to alter his appearance … or … maybe they meant to kill Nash. Nash was supposed to be in the seat just behind the passengers seat, but wasn't. In any event the bad guys cleared out without determining if "Jelly" was alive.

After the gang got away we are not sure where they went or why, but we do know that Verne Millers' bullet riddled body, too hot to hide, was later found near Detroit, Michigan. Why his body was riddled, we don't know. (If he was taken out to take the heat off others, it wouldn't be the first time, proving once again that there is no honor among thieves … and these guys sure met any definition of that word.)

Adam Richetti, another rescuer was apprehended in the State of Ohio, tried by his peers, convicted of murder and executed by the State of Missouri in 1938.

"Pretty Boy" was hunted down by the FBI in Ohio, and I am proud to report was gunned down in a hail of bullets on 22 October 1934.

Lucky Luciano

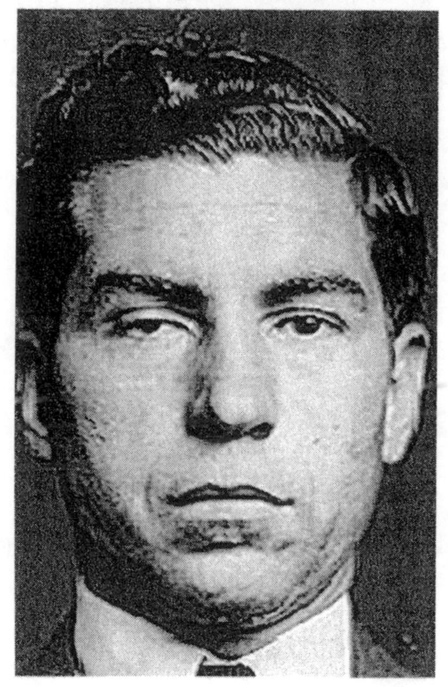

CHARLES "LUCKY" LUCIANO, TOP TEN FUGITIVE, GUEST OF OWNEY "THE KILLER" MADDEN

Charles "Lucky" Luciano has always been considered by most law enforcement agencies to be the father of modern organized crime. At age ten he was arrested for the first time for shoplifting; at age fourteen, he served four months in a youth correctional facility for truancy; at eighteen, he was sentenced to six months in the reformatory for selling heroin and morphine; and at age twenty-eight, he was grossing over a million dollars a year. Much of the money was being used to pay off politicians and cops.

"Lucky" was adept at gambling, loan sharking, procuring and pimping young women, and extortion. (Isn't it strange that "Lucky" ran to Hot Springs, Arkansas, directly from his suite in New York City, just ahead of the authorities who were enroute to his suite in his hotel?) They were Thomas Dewey's guys armed with an arrest warrant for Luciano on charges of white slavery, ninety counts. Dewey was a Special Prosecutor for New York, known to be a hardnosed racket buster and later a presidential candidate against Franklin D. Roosevelt.

Was it just luck that "Lucky" chose Hot Springs as his hideout. Not really! Remember Carl Bailey, Arkansas' Attorney General, soon to be Governor, made it clear that if you were "wanted" it seemed you always came to Hot Springs. No wonder! This is exactly what "Lucky" did. He evidently underestimated the fact that the Chief of Detectives as well as the Chief of Police, and Owney Madden and other thugs were in charge of Hot Springs, but not in charge of the whole United States and not above the laws of other states if Tom Dewey was involved. (Only an idiot would believe that the Chief of Detectives, Akers and Chief Ermey, *et al* were that powerful.)

Guess who had been one of the top gangsters in New York who was now a respected gentleman in the city of Hot Springs and who must have introduced "Lucky" around? Guess who was the owner of the Hot Springs' Southern Club, one of the ritziest "joints" outside Las Vegas? Guess who had, at one time, a major interest in the Cotton Club in New York, before being given the option of being "rubbed out" or "whacked" or being banished to Hot Springs, Arkansas? Guess who was or had been the biggest bootlegger in the country? If you guessed Owney "The Killer" Madden you would have been right.

It would be hard to believe that Owney, as the scuttlebutt of that day held, had retired from the rackets. If he did, he was one of the few, especially seeing how he went to Hot Springs in retirement and yet wound up as the "Boss Gambler", overseeing a racket which netted, according to the records presented to the 1946 Grand Jury, thirty million dollars. Not a bad retirement fund especially when you consider the protection he was afforded by the local law as well as his thuggy buddies.

"Lucky," according to accounts of that day, was extremely wealthy and feared. He frequented the most exclusive clubs in New York City, such as the Cotton Club, and usually, with a different woman every night, so he just naturally knew Owney Madden, the owner of the Club.

Some background would help:

Luciano was eventually known as the capo of capos, or the boss of bosses after he set up the rules that five Italian families would split up the United States, in an effort to make sure that there would be no turf wars like there had been in the past.

Thomas E. Dewey, the Special Prosecutor for New York City, dubbed Luciano "Public Enemy Number 1 in New York."

Reportedly, there was an unwritten rule that the National Crime Syndicate (as it was known then) would not kill anyone who was "straight". This sealed the fate of "Dutch" Schultz who tried to set up a hit on Tom Dewey. Dewey aspired to be racket buster number one, an entrée to his planning a campaign for the presidency of the United States against Franklin D. Roosevelt. (A low level hoodlum remarked that this "no killing rule" must mean that they could only kill each other!)

Needless to say, there was no love lost between "Dutch" Schultz and Dewey. Nothing personal, you understand, but Schultz was not going to stand by while a short, mustachioed mouthpiece got points to use in his fight against Franklin D. Roosevelt for the presidency of the United States. Other thugs, finding out about Shultz's plan to whack Dewey, called upon the rule that they had established that all the capos or leaders of the families had to agree on a hit. They knew that a hit on Dewey was sure to bring a lot of heat on the bootlegging and other rackets and Shultz's plan to kill Dewey was vetoed.

Luciano, in order to keep a mob war from starting, was the principal actor dividing the country up into areas and assigning an Italian family to be the "Boss" of that area. This "rub-out" plan against Dewey by Shultz did not meet with Luciano's approval. Dewey, we can assume, went about doing his job, which was knocking a hole in New York racketeering, but instead of taking Schultz out he evidently decided to jump on Luciano, one of the biggest pimps in the country and the founder of the Sicilian Mob, The National Crime Syndicate, La Casa Nostra and other names.

Luciano was a friend of Meyer Lansky, Vito Genovese, and Frank Costello, all hoodlums, among others. Luciano joined forces with Joe "The Boss" Maranzano, but one day in 1929, "Lucky" was forced into a limousine, beaten, stabbed, and then dumped. "Lucky" was tagged with the nickname "Lucky" because he survived the beating, which was meant to kill him. His droopy eye, and the scars on his left cheek, obvious to all, was a result of that beating. He was informed that his partner or former associate, Maranzano, was the person who ordered the hit. "Lucky" was not one who could forgive and forget. He had Maranzano "whacked" by three of his own men and Bugsy Siegel.

"Lucky" was to have had a meeting with Maranzano, in Maranzano's office and was scheduled to be whacked during that visit but instead "Lucky" had learned of the plan that he was the guest of honor and decided that he would instead hit Maranzano with his people dressed as policemen. They succeeded in knocking off Maranzano.

"Bugsy" Siegel was one of the assassins and shortly after that went to Hot Springs, and met with Owney "The Killer" Madden who had been "banished" to Hot Springs. The mob was supposedly considering Hot Springs to be a gambling Mecca under their control. No one knows for sure why Bugsy abandoned Hot Springs for Las Vegas, but we do know that he did leave for some reason. (That order must have come directly from one of the mob families.) Bugsy was Jewish, therefore, had very little, if any, direct power over the rackets. He depended, instead, upon the protection from the various Italian families to whom he and everyone else in the rackets paid a "franchise fee."

Bugsy was much later killed upon orders of Luciano, who had by that time (1946) been deported from the United States and was living in Sicily. Bugsy's crime? The Syndicate thought Bugsy was using the Outfits (read La Cosa Nostra and Teamsters Union) loans for his personal pleasure.

But, back to Thomas Dewey.

Dewey had found difficulty in charging and making it stick that Luciano was involved in the rackets. That was not understandable considering his prey's vast criminal enterprise, his pay-offs, his graft, and his propensity for violence, but Dewey did finally round up enough witnesses to charge Luciano with ninety plus counts of white slavery. With arrest warrants in hand, the New York cops went to Luciano's hotel, but found that he had left rather hurriedly, shortly after receiving a phone call that an arresting party was on its way. "Lucky" paid $200 per week to a bellman to tip him off if someone came looking for him and when he received that call he skipped out as the officers were coming up the stairs.

The next time we officially know of his whereabouts comes from informants of that day. He drove to Cleveland, left his car and jumped on a train to Hot Springs, Arkansas, where he was evidently welcomed with open arms by Owney Madden, the Chief of Police, the Chief of Detectives, the Sheriff's Department, the Mayor's Office, and all of their people. There was just one problem that developed.

EUREKA! NEW YORK'S #1 CRIMINAL, "LUCKY," FOUND IN HOT SPRINGS

One fine day in 1936, a Bronx Detective, John Brennan, happened to be in Hot Springs searching for a murder suspect who was "wanted" in New York. Brennan probably found it unbelievable when he saw a person he recognized as "Lucky" Luciano arm in arm with the Hot Springs Police Department's Chief of Detectives, Herbert "Dutch" Akers, on the East side of Central Avenue about a block from the Arlington Hotel.

Can you imagine this? The New York City Detective, showing extreme courage, walks up to "Lucky," shakes hands, renews old acquaintances, and asks "Lucky" why he doesn't come back to New York City with him and face the charges brought by Tom Dewey. "Lucky," of course, who has been taking hot baths and enjoying his freedom in an open city like Hot Springs doesn't even entertain the offer. He then asks Brennan to forget he ever saw him in Hot Springs or elsewhere. Brennan supposedly explained to him that he could be in a lot of trouble if he did not report seeing "Lucky" and where. We are not sure of "Lucky's" reply to that offer, but we do know that it was negative.

Register of Prisoners Confined in the County Jail of Garland County, Arkansas

Number of Days	Number of Lockups	Amount
4		
16		
2		
11		
3		
10		
6		
8		
1		
2		
3		
18		
3		
2		
7.6	16	
3		
1		
1		
4		
4		
7		
1		
1		
1		

Name	Sex	Color	When Committed Mo.	Day	Yr.	By What Authority Committed	For What Offense and for What Term	Date of Leaving Prison Mo.	Day	Yr.	Escaped or Discharged if Discharged by What Authority	Number of Days	Number of Lockups
Harry Rosenberg	M	W	12	7	35	G J	Embezzlement	Jail				30	
Wm Houston	M	C	1	13	36	G J	Gr. Larceny	Jail				30	
Cecil James	M	C	1	13	36	G J	Gr. Larceny	Jail				30	
A. E. Morgan	M	W	1	24	36	G J	Embezzlement	4	10	36	Tucker Farm 4 yr	[illegible]	
Alton Windham	M	W	1	27	36	G J	Gr. Larceny	4	6	36	Rel Houston [illegible]	6	
Wm Malone	M	C	2	3	36	G J	Asslt to Kill	Jail				30	
C. C. Robbins	M	W	2	3	36	G J	Gr. Larceny	4	16	36	[illegible] Witts	16	
Buster Hanspart	M	W	3	14	36	MC	Robbery	4	30	36	To M.C.	30	
Theo Holt	M	C	3	16	36	MC	Robbery	4	30	36	To M.C.	30	
Melton Atwater	M	C	3	26	36	MC	Murder	4	4	36	Bond	4	
Andrew Hudson	M	C	3	26	36	G J	Robbery	Jail				30	
W. B. Beramus	M	W	3	26	36	Montgomery Co	Murder	4	11	36	Ret to Montgomery Co	11	Pd by Mo[illegible]
Chas Luciano	M	W	4	1	36	New York		4	4	36	Rel to State Rangers	4	
Eugene McKenzie	M	W	4	2	36	MC	D & D	4	3	36	To MC	2	
Chas Welder	M	W	4	4	36	MC	Liquor	4	4	36	Apl Bond	1	
Clarence King	M	[illegible]	4	4	36	MC	Liquor	4	4	36	Apl Bond	1	
Mrs Edna Russell	F	W	4	4	36	MC	Liquor	Jail				27	
Mrs Z. L. Menges	F	W	4	4	36	MC	Liquor	4	7	36	Apl Bond	4	
Angis McKechan	M	W	4	4	36	MC	D & D	4	5	36	Bond	2	
Ross [illegible]	M	C	4	8	36	MC	Refusing [illegible]	4	8	36	Apl Bond	1	
[illegible] Carver	M	W	4	8	36	"	"	4	8	36	"	1	
Frank Andrews	M	W	4	8	36	Holdover	Move La.	4	9	36	Rel to La.	2	
Arthur Burrough	M	W	4	8	36	M.C.	D & D	4	9	36	Rel [illegible]	2	
Jarrett Ingram	M	W	4	11	36	MC	False Pret.	4	11	36	Bond	1	
W. B. Beramus	M	W	4	13	36	Montgomery Co	Murder	4	25	36	Rel to Mong. Co.	13	Pd by Mo[illegible]
[illegible] Meredith	M	W	4	14	36	MC	Larceny	Jail				17	

Check out line 18, Chas. Luciano, male, white, committed 4/1/36, by New York authorities; released 4/4/36 to State Rangers after 4 days of confinement.

The Detective did notify his New York Chief and managed to get "Lucky" arrested by going through the Arkansas Governor's Office. Here is the number one criminal in the country arm in arm with Hot Springs' Chief of Detectives and a New York City Detective has to be the one who "recognizes" Luciano, and the detective has to be the one who has to raise the alarm.

Anyway, Tom Dewey sent a telegram to Hot Springs Chief of Police Wakelin asking him to arrest Luciano. Reluctantly, Wakelin had Luciano arrested and taken before the bar of justice. (Hot Springs' justice, that is.) It took the scoff law minutes to post the $5,000 cash bond and hc walked out free to return to the streets and his friends whom you might assume were just about any authority in Garland County, Arkansas. He was free again to take to the streets and even take a hot bath. Guess who made the bond. You guessed it, Owney Madden, his old friend from New York City.

Thomas E. found out about this dastardly turn of events and he raised Cain from New York City to the foothills of the Ouachita Mountains. Having his number one target, the biggest pimp in the country, in custody, and then to have him released on a $5,000 bond, which had been posted by Hot Springs' "Boss Gambler," Owney Madden, former New York hoodlum, well known to the New York authorities, was just too much. He didn't care if Hot Springs was the Wild West of the country. He just wouldn't put up with it.

Dewey must have been livid when he called the Attorney General of the State of Arkansas and wanted to know, "What in the cotton pickin' hell is going on?" He also telephoned Governor Marion Futrell and threatened him with bad publicity for the State of Arkansas, saying that he would make it known around the country that Arkansas harbored known criminals. That threat might carry some weight with the Governor of the State, but as had been proven, it didn't amount to much of a threat to a cocky Hot Springs' "Little Combination" or their minions, the Police

Department, the Sheriff's Office or the Mayor and his Office. They had state connections and maybe even federal connections.

Carl Bailey, the Attorney General and a gubernatorial hopeful, when contacted by Dewey, probably said something to the effect that, "Ah, that's just Hot Springs."

At least the Governor somehow managed to get "Lucky" re-arrested and held in jail until something could be done. Governor Futrell pulled out his best threats and personally ordered Chief Wakelin to hold "Lucky" until further orders. Of course, that had to be cleared with Owney who was Luciano's host. Finally, they did arrest him and held him in the Garland County Jail for four days.

At the hearing setting bond and so forth, shenanigans were pulled. Two Garland County deputy sheriffs grabbed "Lucky", taking him away from the officers from Little Rock who were to take him to jail in Little Rock for an extradition hearing. Even though it had been agreed that Little Rock authorities would take Luciano when the bond was set, Garland County Deputies stepped in and hustled Luciano out of the courtroom. It was practically pandemonium in the courtroom but the judge, as one would expect, did nothing to enforce the agreement, instead letting Garland County hold him.

"Lucky" lived in "luxury" in the Garland County Jail, buying meals for everyone including his jailers and his girlfriend who was living with him in his cell.

The Governor believing, evidently, what Dewey had told him, called the director of the Arkansas Rangers who rounded up a party of twenty state Rangers (as they were called then), and four days after Luciano was arrested they went in the dead of night to Hot Springs armed to the teeth to retrieve Luciano for his extradition to New York City.

As an example as to who was in control, the jailer, when he heard footsteps coming down the hall of the jail, and the beating on the door, called the Chief Deputy Sheriff John Ermey wanting to know what to do. Evidently, twenty Rangers armed with submachine guns and shotguns presented a formidable force. He wasn't about to let "Lucky" go without a fight, if necessary. The Rangers, after beating on the jailhouse door, and threatening to break it in, were allowed to enter the jail and took their prey into custody and returned "Lucky" to Little Rock. (The Chief Deputy was the same John Ermey, Chief of Police, who later in 1967, gave our confiscated slot machines back to the mobsters).

Charles "Lucky" had a lot of ideas of grandiosity, even in the big middle of the depression where people were eating from breadlines. One of his ideas which had come true was being in control of the rackets: bootlegging, gambling, loan sharking, numbers, protection policies, prostitution and assorted gangster related passions, rackets held together by murder and mayhem, so powerful that he could name and hold together five Italian families who would "own" all the rackets in particular cities, towns and areas of the country.

No one knows, I suppose, exactly the reasons to assign the different territories to five Italian families: Genovese, Gambino, Colombo, Lucchese, and the Bonnano families other than their power in those areas. They gained their power by having connections with authorities such as Tammany Hall, a group of thugs who engaged in New York politics and in other major cities. They evidently had the muscle to enforce the territories that Luciano had assigned.

It is unreasonable to think that simply because of its size, Hot Springs was not of significance in the world of gambling and prostitution. At least the federal government did not discount its importance in the scheme of things, but was either unable or unwilling to stop the illegal activities. You can bet, too, that the Syndicate was ever mindful of "Bubbles" and did not let that franchise go unheeded. You can bet the farm that the Syndicate got tribute from the English Godfather, "The Killer" Owney Madden and his associates.

It is nearly always a surprise to the uninitiated that even though La Cosa Nostra is for Italians only, they have always had alliances with persons of Jewish, Greek, Irish and other heritage. Gambling and prostitution had to be the crimes of choice in the "Valley of the Vapors." The city didn't have that many businesses to be "shook down" like New York City, Chicago, and other large metro areas. The hot waters of the hot springs brought the visitors, those who came for a good time, as well as the sick and lame. Gambling and prostitution were sold as a necessity to provide nighttime amusement after visitors had bathed during the day.

About the only other businesses in that part of the country, the foothills of the Ouachita Mountains, could be classified as a service industry for the gambling element. Where else were the conditions so ripe for an opportunity to satisfy the thirst of a nation, a naturally hot bath and the anxiety of the turn of a card or the whir and click of a slot machine?

In Chicago, they made alcohol in bathtubs while we made ours on the side of a mountain, from sparkling blue water and corn raised right there on the farm. (As a matter of fact, the stock exchange in New Orleans is reported to have quoted the price of corn by the gallon.) Seriously, the bathhouses in the City, just to the East side of Central Avenue were owned by the federal government, America's first national park, so how else was the City to survive? That was the argument, anyway.

During the day visitors could drink or bathe in the waters that fell as rain 4,000 years ago and now bubbles up at 143 degrees Fahrenheit from 47 hot springs within the valley. Then as now they could swim and boat and fish in the five lakes and three rivers, but the question remains, what were they going to do at night?

This was an argument that the "Little Combination" (Hot Springs's La Casa Nostra) made stick. It was generally believed that Hot Springs would dry up without the games. Figuratively, if there was no gambling to keep the visitors busy at night, could the city survive? (Maybe they would just have to see.) One theory was that people who frequented the clubs were adults. They didn't buy snow cones and hot dogs and didn't visit the Alligator Farm or the Petting Zoo or other taxable attractions, therefore the rackets made the City click with only limited taxes gathered from the adult games.

One of the major drawbacks to this kind of "adult" attractions was that the money made by the rackets was not shared, except indirectly, with the city or the county. That meant that there was a price to be paid by the "other" citizens of the "Valley of Vapors." They either went along with the dictates of the gangsters or else. Just one black ball dropped by the mob against a person could mean banishment from the community. If you didn't work for the "Little Combination" or one of the houses of prostitution or one of the pieces of the service industry, or at least survive on what was left, you might as well move elsewhere.

I have been asked many times if the Mafia or La Cosa Nostra was involved in operations in Hot Springs. My answer is, "Why do you think Frank Costello, the "Boss of the Underworld" who supposedly was the master of the gambling world liked to come to the Valley and relax? Was it business or pleasure? The Valley was far from neutral territory as the story was told and sold in Arkansas and mid-America. This myth somehow made the rackets and racketeers in Hot Springs more palatable to the general public.

"Well, it's alright just so long as the Mafia doesn't control it." And who could prove that "they" didn't control it when it is almost impossible to prove a negative. That was a simple explanation, that the mafia didn't control it and one of those urban legends which took root here in the Wonder State. Possibly no one dared ask if others controlled it for them, enforcing their monopoly and getting their share of the gains.

The Irish, Greek, Jewish, Cherokee Combination proved it. The Mafia must not be connected because all these generalized true blooded good ole' boys operated the rackets, called during that day by the people who owned it, the "Little Combination." It included Madden, Harris, Phillips, Pakis, Columbus, and others. Can you imagine why some Mafia people, who would kill at the drop of a hat for a mere insult in other cities, would let the "Little

Combination" and these people operate with impunity, in control of a cash cow like Hot Springs, a whole town which could be so easily kept under the thumb of a handful of people protected by the city, the county, and the state and maybe even federal and not intercede?

In 1964, about three years before our raids, the federal government records show that the gross annual profit from the Las Vegas casinos, supposedly a state controlled operation, was $240 million dollars while Hot Springs grossed $200 million dollars in a completely uncontrolled operation; no oversight committees, no state restrictions on "pay-outs" or odds, no standardized bookkeeping records, and no onsite supervision. The odds could be from zero to whatever, but imagine having an industry that could completely disregard any state laws, including the nonpayment of state and federal taxes and even have denial of existence.

(Who is stupid enough to keep "books" on an illegal racket? The "Little Combination" wasn't!) Al Capone was charged with income tax evasion, so how could Owney Madden and other members of the "Little Combination" get away with it? There was a whole litany of federal crimes with which they could have been charged. Could it be that they had national influence as well? Who could prove their income?

Controlling the rackets was not easy and without exposure to danger. Any threat to their way of living had and has its potential pitfalls and many have paid for their questioning that control, but we must, as corny as it seems, remember that freedom is not free.

Vapors Club officials, by and through the police under pressure, permitted photographers to take pictures of the bathroom area of the Vapors Club where a bomb had exploded. Newspaper photographers were allowed to take pictures of the bathroom area where the bomb exploded but not pictures of the gambling area. The guard steered them away when they pointed their cameras toward the gambling room (remember there is not supposed to be any gambling), but one brave soul, an enterprising photographer snapped a picture of the tables and the machines and all the action.

—Staff Photo by Larry Obsitnik.

The Picture They Didn't Want Taken

This shot of the gambling equipment in the Vapors casino was taken on the sly. Police and Vapors officials permitted photographers to take pictures of the damaged area but steered them away when they pointed their cameras toward the gambling room. "We've had enough bad publicity," one policeman said. Notice the holes in the ceiling. The blurred objects at right are part of what was left of a wall.

—Staff Photos by Larry Obsitnik

Where One Escaped Possible Death

\n unidentified man stepped into this telephone booth in the obby of the Vapors moments before the explosion occurred. le suffered only a cut above his eye, although the force of he blast hurled bricks and other debris against the wall, knocking holes in it and in some cases embedding the objects n the wall.

rew broken bricks across the ıby, slamming them against the posite wall around the booth. me of the bricks were embedd in the wall.

The glass door of the phone oth was shattered but its occunt escaped with only a cut ove his eye.

The Vapors opens its restaurant d bar at 10 a. m., but the sino does not open until noon, employe said.

Officials said that if the explon had occurred a few hours er many more persons might ve been injured and some might ve been killed.

The club is one of Hot Springs' ıshest and nationally known entainers appear there nightly. Ginny Tiu, child television and night club star, was appearing this week. Harris said the club would have to settle with her and other scheduled entertainers.

"We'll make repairs as soon as possible," he said. He said he had no idea how long it would take before the damage is repaired, but that he didn't expect it would take too long. Workmen had boarded up the front of the club within an hour after the blast.

In the meantime, he said, the club is still undecided about what to do with its more than 200 employes. The payroll of the club is about $12,000 a week, he said.

Harris estimated the damage at $125,000. He said part of the loss would be covered by insurance.

They were ushered out when the guard said, “We’ve had enough bad publicity.”

This bomb had been planted and had exploded in the bathroom of the Vapors Club, one of Hot Springs plushest clubs, obviously not meant to hurt anyone especially, but to carry a message: maybe just a signal to not get too greedy or “why can’t we have a share?

There should be no surprise that a police officer was the person who was acting as the spokesman for the club, limiting access to the gambling area of the Vapors. Police and deputy sheriffs, guarded the clubs. Police types only went to the clubs as protectors using the law to aid in that protection of the clubs and the patrons on the assumption that the clubs were good for the city. (One might assume, too, that they were there to aid the Club in enforcing the limits placed on the reporters and the State Police).

One would have to be blind not to see that this was the program; the “Boss Gambler” saw to it that his people were taken care of. Loyalty to the combination was the price the citizens of Hot Springs paid for what little money came their way. God help anyone who tried to change that system! That included any unmade wiseass who thought he might use the “law” to change the system.

A bomb was planted, too, at the same time in Raymond Clinton’s son’s car. Raymond, Bill Clinton’s uncle, said he could not explain why anyone would do that. No one was ever officially identified as the bomber, but again, I would bet the farm that the “Bomber” paid for his mistake.

LONG TERM MEMORIES

Just kidding?

"Shoot the s.o.b. while you've got him there!" was the telephone response from one lady about eighty-three years old who was "well connected" to one of those movers and shakers (during the day) when she learned that I was in the city (and this in 2007). I was sure she said it in jest, but my reporting friend assured me that she was dead serious. (Oh well, everything is fair in love and war?)

The "Little Combination" tried everything it could possibly think of to maintain control of the city of Hot Springs and Garland County. They evidently thought of it as a civic duty or, at least tried to convince everyone that "They," the mob, were the ones who kept "Bubbles" running, and without that income and support the city and county would fold. When you looked at the tax rolls and saw that the major part of the income from the slot machines, prostitution, prostitutes, and the other rackets was either voluntary or so low that it did not amount to a major portion of the budget you might wonder what would keep "Bubbles" afloat.

A FAMILY TOWN? — IMAGINE THIS SCENARIO

The city had only one main street. There are houses of prostitution on the second floors of most of the business houses, in that day, if they are not occupied by a gambling operation: The Ohio Club, The Bridge Street Club, The Southern Club, the Vapors Club, and others.

Even the staid old Arlington Hotel in that day had an entrance from the Fourth Floor to a house of prostitution next door, The Hatterie. It was, according to some, one of the best houses in town. It set where the exit ramp is now from the Arlington Hotel to Central Avenue. It was torn down some years ago to make room for an exit from the parking garage of the Arlington.

Secondly, how about your family walking downtown on the only main street in town, Central Avenue, with the knowledge there could be another gunfight like happened between the Deputy Sheriff of Garland County and the some of the officers of the Hot Springs Police Department?

What if you now know that several bombs have been exploded in some of the gambling dens, as well as fights at the whore houses, drunks on the street and hucksters on practically every corner.

What if the longtime Mayor of your city, when asked about his salary, said, "Don't worry, Leo will get his." There was no question that he wasn't talking about retribution but reward and who would doubt that the reward would come from the Boss Gambler and his minions?

What if the Chief of Detectives for your Police Department not only was openly walking down your main street with a companion on the walk who was the most wanted man in America, a gangster who was wanted in New York City on 90 counts of promoting prostitution, a person not only known to be a pimp, but a pimp who found homeless, wayward girls to service any man with the price charged by the pimp.

What about a Sheriff who not only allowed that pimp to have his girlfriend stay with him in his cell in the County Jail but allow him to send out for food, not only for himself but all the other inmates in the jail and the Deputies assigned to "guard" him?

And this, while the other "common criminals" would have and did languish in jail because they either did not have the money to pay their fine or did not know someone in the rackets who could use their influence to secure their release. They might have been in jail on legitimate charges or possibly because one of the powers that be wanted them in jail. The Mayor, the Chief of Police and the Sheriff, his deputies and the judges probably had that power, don't you think?

What about a candidate for the Sheriff's position losing an election and then being killed in an alley right there in the city only two weeks later? (*Memoirs of Sid McMath*)

How about the man, who worked at what then passed for a fast food restaurant, who was shot for beating his wife? It was a well intentioned act, but the problem was that the two men who came into town from New Orleans to do the job shot the wrong man. He did survive and the Boss Gambler paid his expenses plus a sum for the rest of the man's life to try to make up for the mistake. The intended victim had never had a trial, but that did not matter in some cases, especially when you are protecting the girl friend of a city father. (*Mark Palmer, interview, 2008)*

What about making the decision as to which school your kids would attend when one school required a trip down the main street, Central Avenue, where gunfights were not all that unusual, and homeless drunks were encountered not all that infrequently.

SID McMATH AND THE GI REVOLT

Sid McMath, while Garland County's prosecuting attorney in 1946, probably said it best when he said that Mayor Leo McLaughlin's administration had been in power at Hot Springs for some twenty-five years and they had built their organization's strength on illegal gambling. He could have tagged them with prostitution, too. (Oh yeah, don't forget the Chief of Detective's scam, stealing cars, then finding them for a reward plus selling illicit guns to anyone who had the money. Or was that the Chief of Detectives Aker's racket?)

McMath said in a later interview,

> "Gambling itself was not so objectionable, but in order to have illegal gambling all the law enforcement officers had to be controlled by the political boss, the judges, the clerks, the prosecuting attorneys, the sheriffs, the chief of police, the mayor and so forth, and they also have to have control of the election commissions, with selected judges and clerks on election day. In other words, they control the community, and they have sufficient power that if you oppose them, you could be in real trouble."
>
> (You can say that again!)

Later, Governor McMath recounted that a friend of his ran for sheriff (after the Second World War) and lost a hotly contested race to a McLaughlin man. Just weeks after the election, his friend was lured into an alley and killed. He also told about a candidate for Mayor running against Leo McLaughlin. After this person, McMath's friend, lost the race, his mortgage came due; it was bought up and he and his family were evicted when they couldn't immediately pay off the mortgage.

McMath said that he, as prosecuting attorney for that district, was prosecuting two jewelry thieves when he received a mysterious telephone call late one night. It was Owney Madden. He agreed to meet Owney on the mountain where he, McMath, lived. It was late night, but Madden insisted that he needed to talk with McMath that night.

A long black limousine was waiting for him on the top of the mountain. Seated in the limo, according to McMath, were Madden and supposedly his bodyguards, one driving and the other two flanking Owney sitting in the back seat. McMath had no idea why there was such urgency. He soon found Madden's mission. He asked McMath to not prosecute two jewelry thieves, giving no reason why he was making the request. After telling Madden that he could not do that, Madden said, "Okay."

McMath says he walked back down the road toward his house on that dark night and he quickened his pace and the hairs stood up on his neck when he was about half way down the road to his house.

Later, after conviction of the thieves and they had served their sentence, Sid saw Madden who told him that he, Madden, had, in effect, told the two thieves that they needed to go back to the cotton fields and not try to stay in Hot Springs. *(Memoirs, Sid McMath)*

If Sid McMath, a decorated Second World War Marine combat veteran and later a two star Marine Corp General, had his hair to stand up on the way to his house after meeting with Owney Madden, you can imagine how the average person must have felt when Owney asked for a favor or gave some "friendly" advice.

Governor McMath recounts the time that he was running in 1946, for prosecuting attorney for the district, which included Montgomery County and Garland County. It was his contention based on his experience in Hot Springs that when the votes were counted in Montgomery County, a sister county, a telephone call was made to determine the vote count there. A quick tally of those votes would tell the “machine” in Garland County how many votes they needed to steal in Garland County to make a winner of whoever they chose —the machine candidates.

Unfortunately for the McLaughlin Administration, the telephone lines between Montgomery County and Garland County were mysteriously cut during the counting of votes in the 1946 election so they could not get the count as to what votes they needed to make a winner out of Sid’s opposition. When asked who cut the lines, McMath simply smiled. (*Memoirs, Sid McMath*)

During the campaign two McMath supporters, former military men, were getting signatures on affidavits from a great number of people swearing that they had not voted even though the records showed that they had. This list included lots of people whose only note of their present existence was a tombstone. The two veterans were held up at gunpoint by two men who took the affidavits. McMath knew the identity of the two people who held up the two veterans.

In other words, the administration used every trick in the book to get reelected, including buying poll tax in names of the dead, and using that poll tax to have someone vote it. These veterans were hijacked of the affidavits by armed men, an incident later corrected through extensive negotiation—turn them back or else. They later recovered all the affidavits gathered by the veterans and the two robbers were convicted of robbery in Garland County, prosecuted by Sid McMath, the Governor elect.

SENATOR ESTES KEFAUVER'S SUBCOMMITTEE ON CRIME

In 1950, "trains and planes carrying the most powerful men in America began to converge on the mountain spa (Hot Springs, Arkansas) for a meeting to analyze the significance of Washington's all out investigation into organized crime." That was the word from the Kefauver Subcommittee people. Television of that day gave its viewers a black and white front row seat to Senator Estes Kefauver's Subcommittee, naturally referred to as the Kefauver Subcommittee. To that date, these hearings were the most famous inquiry into organized crime in the history of the United States. The Committee was well publicized and made Kefauver a household name, but there was very little to show for its effort.

A little known chapter in the Senator's book, if he had written one, might be the fact that he taught school one year in 1931, and coached football in the Hot Springs School System. Another page of that book might be his supposed bitterness when his girlfriend married another suitor, Hubert Coates, who was much later tried for his shooting of the Hot Springs Chief of Police, Oscar Sullivan over a woman, and surprise of surprises, was found not guilty by a Garland County jury.

Coates had an argument with the Chief of Police Sullivan over Coates' attention to a girlfriend of Sullivans, and essentially Coates beat Sullivan to the draw in a Hot Springs drugstore. (Coates was tried and acquitted, not an unusual verdict during that day in Garland County and later.)

SENATOR JOHN McCLELLAN'S SUBCOMMITTEE ON CRIME

Following in the footsteps of some national "crime fighters," Senator John L. McClellan had a Subcommittee hearing where over 600 witnesses were to appear. A great number of these witnesses were subpoenaed and appeared in Washington, D. C. but in my opinion, and others, very little resulted from these appearances. (At least nothing changed in the Arkansas nomenclature. It was business as usual as far as the rackets were concerned.) Once the mob learned they could take the Fifth Amendment, the hearings seemed to be a worthless effort on the part of the Senate.

Among other meager subcommittee results, Joe Adonis, a hearing witness who was Agnes Madden's (Owney's wife) old golf partner at the Hot Springs Country Club, was deported. Willie Moretti, a frequent visitor to Hot Springs hosted by the Madden's, another nervous witness, was assassinated by the mob. They thought he might have "loose lips", which brought on a guaranteed "hit" since the mob thought loose lips sink ships. They couldn't afford to have anyone who might weaken and be tempted to testify about their connections to Hot Springs or any other place. And, in those days, it didn't take a lot to get an order for a "hit."

This was as close as they got to "The" Senator, John L. McClellan's territory. There was much discussion during "the day" as to why nobody (notably McClellan) ever did a "job" on the gambling and prostitution action in Hot Springs since he was from Camden, Arkansas, less than 80 miles away. Quite a few people wondered why McClellan would have a crime fighting reputation, but would not or could not recognize crimes in his backyard. He ran for office on his reputation, managing to contact enough people to get funds to run for reelection, and that included Hot Springs and Garland County.

If not for gambling, then for the interstate transportation of females for immoral purposes also referred to as the White Slave Traffic Act, a federal violation, patently illegal (unless all the girls in the numerous houses of prostitution were home grown!).

Gambling and prostitution were openly illegal and, therefore, the resulting income was illegal and all subject to the same charges which have sent so many thugs to prison; income tax evasion and worse, but a check of the roster of the purported members of the "Little Combination" in Arkansas doesn't indicate any convictions on these federal crimes.

Appearing before a Senate Subcommittee brought on a lot of memory loss. Some who "testified" even forgot the names of their close associates and/or their own names, and even though they had been coached by their attorneys on the Fifth Amendment, the witnesses sometimes forgot the exact words. Reportedly, some seemed to not know or forgot what the words were to the Fifth Amendment. "Incriminate" in one case became "criminate." (Of course, I have known lawyers who have made the same mistakes, me included.)

Remember my admonition about setting your mind to it? Then why could the Senate not bring a few of their subcommittee members to town, subpoena about ten prostitutes or casino workers, who even if "lawyered up," would likely produce at least one who would start the chain upwards. First, to a pimp or a madam or the pit boss, second, to a thug who takes payoff money for protection, and finally to the "Boss Gambler" who runs the rackets. You could even grant immunity to the first informant! Remember prostitutes peddle their trade from house to house, state to state and racketeers too often operate on the proceeds from racketeering which includes prostitution. How simple!

Hot Springs even has plaques on the sides of buildings commemorating the location of particular houses of prostitution. One plaque on the building next to the *Gangsters Museum of America* on Central Avenue indicates that a house of prostitution was on the second floor "in the day," as well as, a "Drive Through Mortuary" on the ground floor. (They made sure you "looked natural.")

(HOKE V U.S., 227 U.S. 308, decided in 1913, upheld the constitutionality of the original language of the Mann Act expanding federal regulatory power over interstate prostitution which

would have given the Federal Government jurisdiction over some of the Hot Springs' rackets, principally, prostitution.)

VINCENT "MAD DOG" COLL, NEW YORK ASSASSIN

Being an Irish enforcer for the Italian Mafia in New York City during the early Prohibition years and being a friend of Dutch Schultz, a bootlegger, a thug, and a mean man meant Vincent Coll ran all the risks, but he also added complications to those risks: Challenging Schultz, by kidnapping other gangsters and assorted faux pas sure to and did shorten his career and certainly shortened his life. Coll was born in Ireland, but immigrated to the United States only a year after his birth.

Dutch Schultz, beer baron and thug in general, employed Coll as an assassin to kill Schultz's enemies. Coll's freelance modus operandi was quite lucrative, but almost guaranteed his need for a great amount of life insurance for his going away which was going to happen sooner or later (probably sooner as we learn).

In addition to just being an assassin in general, Coll went into the sideline business of kidnapping other gangsters, then demanding a goodly sum to ransom them. Obviously, those gangsters who had enough money to warrant kidnapping could be credited with a lot of friends and associates who would probably pay the ransom but take the kidnapping seriously. It took no application of rocket science to figure that this kind of program would be short lived. It is reported that Coll thought the victims would not report the kidnapping to the police, especially, since being criminals, they would have a hard time explaining to the Internal Revenue Service how they happened to have such huge supplies of cash to pay for their release. That, however, did not mean they could do, almost at will, what they always did when they wanted, "whack" the one who crossed them.

"Mad Dog" Coll would have been better off if he had turned himself in to the IRS and/or the FBI or any other authority that wasn't on the take. They could have charged him with stupidity at least. Anyone in their right mind would know this attitude would bring a whacking of all whackings. (As my Aunt Winnie would say, "The boy just ain't bright.")

Coll even had the chutzpa to kidnap "Frenchy" DeMange, Owney Madden's partner in the prohibition business and an associate in his New York's Cotton Club. (This was before Madden settled in Hot Springs.) Coll even telephoned Madden personally telling him the ransom for Frenchy would be $50,000; cash, of course. Madden told him to come on down, and he would pay him. Coll, always cocky as well as "*mad*", walked into Madden's office at the Cotton Club. Owney, obviously wasting no time with a nut case, threw a bundle of cash to Coll while, at the same time, telling him that it amounted to only $35,000. He explained to Coll that he was a little short of cash but would catch him when he saw him again. "Mad Dog" lived up to his name. He chewed on that offer for a few minutes and then accepted, knowing that Madden had always treated him right. He failed to remember, if he ever knew, there is no honor among thieves, and he was about to get a first-hand lesson. He was about to get "whacked" and whacked big time.

Different reasons, different folks. Dutch Schultz, before he died, had tried to corner Coll and was furious that he hadn't already gotten him. The reason Dutch was so mad was that he had gone on Coll's criminal bond guaranteeing that Coll would show up for court, but Coll failed to attend this outing, so Dutch lost his bail money, then couldn't find Coll to collect the money he had lost. (And besides that ole Dutch was embarrassed that he knew a criminal who wasn't good for his word!!)

Coll was christened "Mad Dog" Coll by Jimmy Walker, Mayor of New York City, about two days after Mad Dog's 28th birthday and evidently Coll tried to live up to that reputation.

Dutch had come close to getting Coll earlier but Coll escaped from Dutch's first wave of hitmen. Coll stayed close to his neighborhood but the gunners finally found him. (Some gunners!) The hale of bullets missed Coll, but the shoot-out left a five year old boy named Michael Vengali dead and several other children wounded. From then on Coll was known as the "baby killer", an unflattering name for an unflattering person. (A gangster custom was to spread pocket change around on the sidewalk, hopefully keeping the neighborhood kids between them and the shooters.)

Tiring of the chase trying to collect the money, Schultz finally decided he would keep trying, taking blood rather than money. He worried that he would become the laughing stock of the West Side if he was found to be so easy. (Dutch was not one to take a joke). As a result, Dutch sent one of his people, Bo Weinberg, who knew Coll by sight, with two other thugs, Scarnici and Fabrizzo, to a drug store where Coll was supposed to be on the telephone.

Coll was obviously a slow learner, but he lived long enough to accept a contract paid for by Salvatore Maranzano to have another nice guy, "Lucky" Luciano, rubbed out.

Coll wanted and got an advance of $25,000 with the same amount to be paid on completion of the job, killing Luciano. Just a few months later, on September 10, 1931, not suspecting that he was less than welcome, Luciano was going to visit with Maranzano at Maranzano's office. The plan was for "Lucky" to show up at the office where Coll would also turn up at about the same time and carry out the contract, killing Luciano. Luciano, however, had more lives than a cat if you count each of his close calls as one of his nine lives. He got a tip-off about this plan laid out by Salvatore, so he instead sent over a squad of his own hit men who stabbed and shot Maranzano to death. Coll truly did show up outside Maranzano's office but his appearance didn't set off any alarms. His appearance was fortuitous, turning up immediately after the stabbing and shooting murder of Maranzano, but Luciano evidently had not realized that Coll had been hired by Maranzano to kill him. Although he was the intended killer of Luciano, Coll was left alone by the fleeing squad of hit men because they didn't know that Coll intended to whack Luciano, their employer, on orders of Maranzano. The hit men consisted of two of Dutch Schultz's mob plus Bugsy Siegel, dressed like policemen. They reportedly told Coll when he arrived that there had been a murder and he better clear out.

Can you believe that "Mad Dog" got to keep his front-end money of $25,000 and still didn't have to face the fact that he was the one who had rubbed out "Lucky" Luciano and bear that cross until he, himself, was whacked? He could keep his advance of $25,000 without having to do the job, and no one was left to tell. There was no one to return the money to, don't you see? In this case the proposed hittee, Luciano, became the hitter. Coll should have been called "Lucky" himself, except that he had a date with destiny, and destiny was not going to be kind. Neither would she wait.

Vincent retained the famous (or infamous) defense lawyer Samuel Leibowitz to defend him in the Vengali kid's case (possibly with the $25,000 obtained from the Maranzano job). Leibowitz won an acquittal for Coll that December by destroying the credibility of the prosecution's main witness, George Brett, a man who made a living as a witness at trials. Coll walked free except for that date with destiny.

Vincent had no idea that his days were numbered, even though he had beat the Vengali rap. For some seventy odd days, Vincent was a walking dead man. Someone talked him into telephoning them from a drug store telephone booth on West 23rd Street, early morning, 12:30 a.m. on February 8, 1932. This was in his neighborhood so he felt safe, but little did he know. (Remember Schultz is still looking for him even if he had beaten the Vengali rap.)

Vincent was in the drug store telephone booth talking business with someone, not known to this day, when a black limo eased up to the curb at the edge of the drug store. Vincent was too engrossed with the telephone conversation to notice the limo.

The driver, Bo Weinberg, stayed behind the wheel with the motor running. The second thug stood guard on the sidewalk, while a third went inside the drugstore. The third man's submachine gun was too well concealed under his heavy black overcoat to be seen, even if Coll had looked.

Motioning the innocents aside, the third thug, the shooter, swinging his Chicago typewriter from under his coat, racked the bolt back, leaned forward into a shooting position, squeezed the trigger, and the gun, which was loaded with .45 caliber mankillers, made a deafening roar. The shooter stretched out, pushing the gun ahead and with steady feet, fired a deafening two bursts, one up the left glass window and the other down the right side glass window while the third and final volley buzzed like bees through the booth's door. It didn't take much, only a total of fifteen bullets to finish off Coll. That was the number of bullets dug out of his body at the morgue. (The coroner said, however, that many more shots may have passed cleanly through his body accounting for so many holes in his body.)

The killers ran to the limo, jumped in, taking off at high speed. Whipping out from the curb Bo roared away with a speeding police car right behind them, also dodging other cars. The unsuccessful cops "just happened" to pull up when Bo was speeding away in the obligatory black limousine. Did Bo and his bunch, Scarnici and Fabrizzo, elude the carload of detectives who pulled up just "after" the shooting? (Could the police have been there to insure that the hit men were successful in their whacking and then escaping?) Stranger things have happened, especially when policemen were getting a share of the millions of dollars generated by the mob, including Schulz, Madden, et al. from bootlegging.

People who should know, said that it was Owney Madden, boss of the Hell's Kitchen Mob, New York's biggest bootlegger, (who later became our Owney) who kept Coll talking on the phone long enough for the killers to pinpoint him. The whacking could have very well been for the kidnapping of Owney's partner, "Frenchy" DeMange. (And not the measly $35,000 ransom which had been paid to Coll for "Frenchy".) Destiny sometimes exacts a heavy payback. Owney never denied his part in the execution, simply smiling when asked if he was the person on the other end of the phone.

Dutch Schultz later sent a wreath to Coll's funeral, bearing a banner with the message, "From the boys." The boys, however, naturally did not come to the funeral. Only his widow actually attended the funeral, a sad ending for a "natural born" killer. A final taunt to a "Mad Dog." (I wonder if "the boys" sent a wreath to Schultz's funeral after, he, too, was whacked.)

The services of the two '"hitmen," Scarnici and Fabrizzo went, of course, to anyone who needed their services and had the money to invest. Only a week before, these two "wise guys," both evidently "made men," according to the Mafia Code, burst in on an apartment with pistols and submachine guns blazing, killing three people outright and wounding three others. Their aim was better than their identification skills; they had hit the wrong apartment. None of the three killed or wounded was "Mad Dog."

Fabrizzo, one of Coll's killers, would be murdered just a few weeks later on November 20, the same year, 1932, after a botched attempt on the life of another "hitman," Bugsy Siegel, one of Dutch's most trusted allies and the founder of Las Vegas, aka "Lost Wages." Crime might pay, but usually only for a short time.

Scarnici would make it as far as Sing-Sing where on the 27th Day of June, 1935, he would take a seat in "Old Sparky" and be carried out on a stretcher. Destiny was waiting in a black hearse just outside the walls of Sing Sing.

Now, this leads us to where Owney "The Killer" Madden is connected to Hot Springs. Owney was much smarter and lived a much longer life than Coll and a lot of his friends from his street days in New York City. He died in Hot Springs, Arkansas, living about thirty years longer than Scarnici and, surprisingly, cheating old Sparky and a shot of bad medicine on a prison gurney even though he was once convicted of murder. He died in his sleep in 1965. Owney believed the mob when he supposedly got an alternative from the mob and/or New York City authorities: move to Hot Springs, Arkansas, or you won't move anywhere. That was the talk of the town, that Owney was forced out of New York City and banished to Hot Springs, Arkansas supposedly by the mob, or maybe not.

I choose to believe that the mob wanted Owney to organize and run gambling and prostitution in Hot Springs for his own benefit as well as the mobs. I believe that his "retirement" was a ploy. It doesn't seem reasonable that he left his criminal contacts, a ruthless reputation, a thriving sideline of bootlegging business (the biggest in the United States) and the big city night life to move to Hot Springs. After all, Owney owned controlling interest in one of New York's favorite night clubs, the Cotton Club. (Remember, if it is not reasonable, it's probably not true. That comes from 48 years of experience, either catching the bad guy and prosecuting him or defending him.)

Also, Frank Costello, the Mafia head of the gambling rackets across the United States, was a friend of Owney's and often visited Hot Springs, a town which had more or less developed illegal gambling and prostitution to a science. Owney and the mob found what DeSoto had been looking for about 400 years before, a gold mine. They found a gold mine, but one in another form, illegal gambling and prostitution, backed by the real treasure, "magic" water.

Their Arkansas gold mine was easier to work than the big metropolitan New York City area. There were fewer persons of stature in Arkansas who had to be bought and their price was cheap relative to the possible take and the costs which they incurred as business expenses in New York, Chicago, New Jersey, Philadelphia and other points East and North. Also, Owney had muscle from the Mafia he could call on if needed at Hot Springs but he more or less had his own muscle, the local and county police, and too many times the Governor's Office.

Owney met, courted and married the Hot Springs postmaster's daughter, Agnes. She played golf with Owney's associates from out of state and served as a hostess for most of these gangsters when they came to town, Al Capone, et al.

"CITIZENIZING" OWNEY

In Hot Springs, New York's Owney was a big duck in a smaller pond. You will find he knew the movers and shakers, not only on the local and the state level but even on the federal level or, at least, made direct contributions to federal politicians like Senator John L. McClellan.

This was evident when, in the mid-1950's, Agnes and Owney made a contribution of an unknown amount to the Senator, bypassing the local Democratic fund-raising group, and a short time later gaining citizenship for Owney in the Western District of Arkansas federal court, correcting an oversight of about sixty or so years.

Owney had never received citizenship and he was worried that he would be charged with violation of the Immigration and Naturalization Statutes and deported if he tried to get citizenship at this point in his life. His attorney, Q. Byrum Hurst, evidently talked Owney into going before a former United States Senator who was now a Federal Judge in the Western District of Arkansas, Judge John Miller, who granted citizenship to Owney.

Judge Miller was asked, by the press, how a person with Owney's record, one murder for which he was found guilty and 140 arrests, without conviction, in states other than Arkansas, could be granted citizenship and his reply was that he did not know of that unfavorable record. Owney got his citizenship.

Owney's brother, Martin, aka Marty, was not so well connected (at least not on a first name basis with heavyweights) but obviously depended upon his brother. Owney, and his connections in Arkansas and further Northeast. On September 10, 1953, Immigration Officers took Marty into custody and took him down to the ferry bound for Ellis Island to await deportation. (It would appear they were operating hastily for some other reason, maybe, before opposition could start building? The basis for Marty's problems with his citizenship was his forgetfulness. He had been convicted of burglary charges in 1911, and another felony in 1916, but when he went to Cuba to see the dictator Fulgencio Batista,

Calendar No. 447

84TH CONGRESS } SENATE { REPORT
1st Session } { No. 444

MARTIN ALOYSIUS MADDEN

JUNE 6 (legislative day, MAY 2), 1955.—Ordered to be printed

Mr. KILGORE, from the Committee on the Judiciary, submitted the following

REPORT

[To accompany S. 541]

The Committee on the Judiciary, to which was referred the bill (S. 541) for the relief of Martin Aloysius Madden, having considered the same, reports favorably thereon with an amendment in the nature of a substitute and recommends that the bill, as amended, do pass.

AMENDMENT

Strike all after the enacting clause and insert in lieu thereof the following:

That, the Attorney General is authorized and directed to discontinue any deportation proceedings and to cancel any outstanding order and warrant of deportation, warrant of arrest, and bond, which may have been issued in the case of Martin Aloysius Madden. From and after the date of enactment of this Act, the said Martin Aloysius Madden shall not again be subject to deportation by reason of the same facts upon which such deportation proceedings were commenced or any such warrants and order have issued.

PURPOSE OF THE BILL

The purpose of the bill, as amended, is to cancel the outstanding deportation proceedings in the case of Martin Aloysius Madden and to provide that he shall not again be subject to deportation by reason of the same facts on which the present proceedings are based. The bill has been amended to provide for the cancellation of the outstanding deportation proceedings rather than to grant the beneficiary permanent residence, since he was previously lawfully admitted for permanent residence.

Private Law for Marty

and then tried to get back into the United States, which was then under the dictatorship of Batista, he failed to list these peccadillos and was, therefore, in violation of a United States prohibition against allowing entry of convicted felons unless they were cleared by Immigration Authorities. (He probably just forgot that he had ever been convicted of any criminal activity, even though he never seemed to have an occupation inside the law.) (See the Private Bill passed by the United State Congress. It helps to have a "connected" brother.)

Entreaties on Marty's behalf were made to Catholic Cardinal Spellman as Marty was a devout practicing Catholic. The Cardinal refused to step in. Marty and his friends even went to Tom Dewey, Owney's own nemesis asking for his help. He, obviously, having a long memory, didn't step in.

Evidently, the officers were very serious (for some reason) and were taking him to the docks not only to take him to Ellis Island (the site of departures of undesirables) immediately upon arrest, ready to load him on an outward bound ship that very night. They completed their run to Ellis Island leaving him there, but he stayed for less than an hour when the duty officer was advised by telephone that Marty could be released on $5,000 bond. Just before loading him up, there was a stay of execution and the state execution of the warrant came from an obviously influential person, but whom? There were those who said it was due to effort of U.S. Senator John L. McClellan. Do you really think this could be so?

That done, Owney then got the Private Law passed through the United States Senate and House of Representatives making it possible for Martin "Marty" Madden, to stay in the United States. (It is a good thing that we have corralled political contribution abuse. Haven't we?)

Davis Knows Names In Slot Switch

10-20-67

By BOB SALLEE
Democrat Staff Writer

State Police Director Col. Lynn A. Davis told a panel of Little Rock Jaycees Thursday that he can prove the identity of persons in Hot Springs who permitted 15 seized slot machines to fall back into the hands of gamblers instead of carrying out destruction orders by the Municipal Court.

Davis said he felt the Garland County Grand Jury was the proper one to file charges but he left the impression that if the jury fails to act, he might take some action of his own.

His remarks came during an interview which was being prepared for telecast Sunday on the Jaycees' weekly show, Challenge 67.

Panelist Frank Watson asked the question which brought Davis' reply.

Davis agreed with Watson that the situation amounted to malfeasance in office by those involved, whom he declined to identify by name.

"I know who they are and I can prove who they are," he declared.

The 15 slots were seized by State Troopers Aug. 17 during a raid.

They turned up later during another raid and were identified by Davis as being the same ones ordered destroyed from the earlier raid.

Davis explained how he knew. When Troopers confiscated them the first time, they were marked with the exact time and date they were taken in addition to where they had been seized.

Davis said the 15 carried those markings and there was no question about them being the same ones.

Much criticism has been leveled at the State Police, Davis commented, accusing them of picking on Hot Springs.

He explained that raids were carried out without the knowledge of Hot Springs Police "because just the existence (of slots, etc.) proves that local authorities haven't coped with it."

An editorial in one of the Hot Springs newspapers entitled "Rape of a Resort," brought a stinging reply from Davis because of the implication that State Police had done something illegal.

Davis said the Palmer newspaper chain sought to blame State Police raids on Hot Springs gambling with the upsurge of traffic deaths on the highways.

Detailed statistics on the traffic situation were requested by them, Davis said, but when the figures showed that deaths were actually fewer, "they didn't use them."

Davis emphasized that at no time have troopers been pulled off the highways to raid gambling establishments. Supervisory personnel and off-duty officers were used, he explained.

"We're not picking on Hot Springs. Why, there's no other place in the United States that has a situation like this."

Then he reminded the panel that for years Hot Springs operated wide open gambling, the city collected a tax on illegal slot machines and off-duty policemen worked in the casinos.

"Where else can you go and pick up 111 slot machines in a little red barn?" he asked.

Davis said he is not carrying out a personal vendetta against gambling but simply enforcing the law.

Panelist John Selig wanted to know about complaints Davis has received about the working relationship between state and local authorities.

Davis said he has received no complaints officially, although unofficially he understood that Pulaski County authorities, and those from Hot Springs, resented raids without first notifying the local officials.

"We have full police powers and again, I would like to say that the existence of it proves that somebody isn't doing their job."

Watson wanted to know Davis' feelings on the question of legalized gambling and mixed drinks in view of proposed constitutonal revision.

He offered a personal opinion that it would be the state's "biggest mistake" to extend wagering legally beyond the parimutuel windows at the dog and horse tracks.

Liquor by the drink was something else, Davis commented. "As for the other matters, I don't know . . ."

Moderator Hugh Pollard wanted to know if Davis was finished with Hot Springs but he replied, "No, I can't safely say that."

On private clubs, Davis said that legitimate private clubs with year-round memberships are within the law but troopers would be obligated to act against those which do not measure up.

The word on the street was that slot machines were hard to destroy—needing to be melted in a furnace.

How else could you explain how difficult it was, plus having to be done out of sight?

THE EYES HAVE IT — ANOTHER EYEWITNESS

But back to 1967 when Smokey flares up!

An informant, Smokey, told me the day after the slot machines which we had seized weeks earlier were supposed to have been destroyed (but weren't), that it was one of the highest ranking city police officers who had ordered the machines taken back to the repair shops, undamaged. These same officers were present when these machines were returned to the repair shops after they were "saved" from what was reported to be a roaring fire. My informant had been present when some of the machines we had gotten in our *first* raid on the four clubs were taken by the police to the gravel pit to supposedly be destroyed, then those few brought there were returned to join the other machines for repair and redistribution.

Smokey seemed an appropriate name. He was at the gravel pit when a few of our machines were delivered on instructions by some of the Officers of the Hot Springs Police Department. The driver who was bringing the slots to the gravel pit was motioned as to where he should park. He jumped out, dropped the tailgate of his truck and slid two or three slots out the back of the truck.

Subsequently, one of the ranking police officers opened his car trunk and took a "sludge hammer" to one of the machines. Smokey described the "technique" of the officer as a great show of "forbearance." In other words, the officer obviously was attempting to make it look like he was banging the machine around, while really he was simply making a few dents in one of them. Smokey advised me that he all but wrestled the hammer from the officer while telling him, "You don't know how to wield a sledge hammer." Smokey really started hammering away. Little did he know that there was no intention of doing any harm to the machines, only a few brought out for show, and just enough to say that they had done what they swore to—destroyed the machines and equipment.

Who was going to prove differently? Frankly, we knew from experience that we could be in court for the next few years doing our best to prove that the machines had not been destroyed. How are you going to prove a negative? Do you think they could have found fifty people who would swear that they saw the destruction of the machines? (How about 500?) Evidently, they had little trouble finding the eight who swore by way of a sworn affidavit that the machines had been destroyed. They were policemen.

Smokey was giving the selected machine holy hell when one of the higher ranking officers told an officer of lesser rank, "Get the damn sledge hammer away from the crazy fool who is swinging it." The officer asked how he could take the hammer away from the informant. The officer said that had been tried several times with no success. The ranking officer advised the other, "Tell him that the hammer is yours and that you have just gotten an emergency call and have to go." (Sure, he had to leave immediately.) Grabbing the sledge hammer he threw it in the back of his police car and left post-haste in a cloud of dust.

The pickup truck driver was then told to load the two or three machines up. He did so, leaving the gravel pit with the two or three he had come with, plus dents in one of the machines. (The Chief later said that the machines were on fire when he left and surmised that someone could have gotten some pieces from the pile. He said slot machines were hard to destroy, the same story told by the Little Rock Police many times before. They had proclaimed in the past that it took a blast furnace to destroy the little devils. Imagine the savings we made by proving that a dose of diesel fuel and a match would work.) The Chief swore that the machines and gambling equipment were on fire when he left, and someone must have come along and salvaged some of the parts. Obviously, he had never been around a fire fueled by 20 gallons of diesel fuel, stoked by plywood crap tables and 25 slot machines encased in wood! Also, miracles of all miracles, these slots they "burned" had the date of seizure and the initials of the ASP officers that seized and inventoried them on the inside of their case but that information was the same on the machines that we later seized at the shops. (I ask you, how could that be?) Well, that is the same story later told by the Chief of Police to the Hot Springs Civil Service Commission who was obviously trying to defend the Chief and the Police Department.

Looking back on it, I am surprised that I thought nothing of developing this case to the court level or never insisted on taking it to court. No one had ever told me to take a case to court or not, but I was smart enough to know that it was useless. This would have been a perfect opportunity to further embarrass the "Little Combination" and the movers and shakers of Hot Springs to keep the matter in the news, but in that day it didn't work that way. I do know that in the beginning, I determined that, in cases like this, I would not tie down Troopers who should be on the road reporting on cases other than corruption. And too, we had the machines and had put the city and county on notice that if they did not enforce the law, the state police would. I decided to do nothing further about these machines, one of the many decisions I made "on the run."

These were machines that had been numbered for city and county tax purposes. Sure enough, on the bottoms of the slot machines were numbers which identified each machine for tax purposes. The county tax collector, in the past, surveyed businesses that had the machines. The collector's man turned the machines up on the countertop, took the number from the machine, a simple number like 25, 37, and so forth, made a note of the business and the number from the machines they had in their place of business and gave it to the tax collector. Taxes were then assessed against the business. It seemed that the usual tax was $10.00 per machine and another amount for the other gambling equipment and larger sums for small casinos and larger casinos and bookmaking businesses.

Forty years has somewhat mellowed my feelings for most "Little Combination" people not only in Garland County but in Pulaski County and Little Rock as well. This does not, however, make me have any warm fuzzy feelings toward the officers of high rank who were then in the Hot Springs Police Department, especially when they were two of the eight people who signed the affidavit swearing that the original twenty-five machines had been destroyed when they knew they were to be turned back to the "Little Combination," taken to the repair shop for storage and returned to the gangsters.

ADEQUATE DESTRUCTION TAKES PLACE — ADDING INSULT TO INJURY

Little did we know, in the beginning, except by deduction, that the machines were not destroyed when turned over to the Police Department but returned to the gangsters. We chose to not have that happen a second time.

The second time around, after our raid on the repair shops, we had possession of the machines and kept it. It never was a case of what to do with the machines. In any event, they were to be destroyed after being used as evidence if a trial had taken place. Of course, no trial ever took place, therefore, the law required that they be summarily destroyed as gambling equipment per se, which we did right then, hauling them to the gravel pit. (Also notice, that in this case, we didn't ask the Attorney General, or any judges, for their opinion as to the destruction of the machines, an important point to be made.)

Juice Joints are things that should have proved worrisome to anyone who had ever lost money at one of these casinos. We found at the repair shops where there were stored with many slot ma-

ovember 20, 1819
he Oldest Newspaper
he Mississippi
hing Company, Gazette Building, Little Rock
Little Rock, Arkansas. Second Class postage

, October 6, 1967

Enforcement Lesson

State Police Director Lynn A. Davis has now given the state the best lesson yet in what it takes to break the back of the notorious casino gambling operation at Hot Springs.

What it takes is law enforcement of the kind exemplified in a State Police raid Wednesday which climaxed in the destruction of more than 100 slot machines, valued as high as a quarter million dollars.

Not even the affluent commercial gamblers of Garland County can long withstand losses and pressures such as those they have experienced under the relentless enforcement policy of the FBI-trained Lynn Davis. This week's raid was the most successful of a series that began uncertainly in the spring and gathered assurance in the summer after Davis became director. When the state officers started raiding clubs and seizing slot machines and other equipment, casino-type operations were shut down and slot machines were withdrawn into hiding. Now the police are tracking the slots down in their hiding places. Last week a trailer-load of slot machines, evidently owned by Hot Springs gamblers, was seized in Saline County. This week's big haul in Hot Springs came from two places where the machines were in storage and repair.

Davis's work as police director continues to lend luster to his own career and to constitute a solid credit for the Rockefeller administration. Winthrop Rockefeller came into office committed to law enforcement and his commitment is being fulfilled.

Grand Jury, Please Note

This week's major gambling raid at Hot Springs has raised intriguing and important questions for investigation, variously, by local, state and federal authorities.

State Police Director Davis found that 18 among some 100 slot machines seized in two Hot Springs repair shops had been "destroyed" before by Hot Springs police after earlier raids. This time the State Police presided over the destruction themselves. The slots were smashed, burned, and were to be covered over by a bulldozer and it seems improbable that even a Hot Springs slot machine can survive such a Carthaginian fate. The question, however, for the reform-minded Garland County Grand Jury is: Why and how did the slots survive the first time around?

A second question is under examination by the Federal Bureau of Investigation. State Police report that some slot machine parts taken in the raids look new. If these parts were brought across state lines, their use in re-building slots may have constituted a [illegible]

From the People

'Trained' v. Discerning Minds

To the Editor of the Gazette:

Admiral Sharp, urging escalation, tells us that the war may be over in five years. Five years more of this war will leave our cities in chaos, an additional 40 to 50 thousand of our young men dead (at the 1967 rate), even greater numbers of Vietnamese dead, and America morally bankrupt.

What we are doing to our young people is tragic. I talked with a pilot who had flown many missions in Vietnam, and he seemed to have no conviction that he was serving a worthwhile cause. Making a sad jest, he said it was just a "dirty job" he had to perform or face court martial.

To show how conservative the Armed Services are, he told me that a superior officer had questioned him suspiciously on finding him reading Salisbury's book on Vietnam. The young man had bought a New Testament to take with him on his return to Vietnam. It is amazing to learn that the military permits this seditious book to circulate freely among servicemen. However, I suppose that God has been officially declared to be on our side. Recently one general sent new troops into battle with these encouraging words, "Good luck, good hunting, and God bless you."

I can only admire those young men who have the moral courage to refuse to serve in a war they sincerely believe to be un- [illegible]

(Communications on any subject are welcome. Letters should be under 500 words and typewritten if possible. All letters are subject to editing. Each letter must be signed although signatures will be withheld on request. No published letters will be returned. No un-published letters will be returned unless self-addressed envelope is enclosed.—Editor.)

year, from the groves of learning march brigades of mortarboards equipped with the wisdom to take orders and the courage to drop napalm and atom bombs on the just and unjust alike.

John Allen Adams.

Arkadelphia.

The 'Price'

To the Editor of the Gazette:

An Open letter to the President of the United States, Lyndon Johnson.

Dear Sir:

Mr. Johnson you are not paying the price of the war in Vietnam. You have no one personally involved. You are only making additional profits with few taxes.

Can you tell the 16,000 boys who have died in Vietnam that you feel the price is right. Can you tell the thousands in Vietnam, now, laying their lives on the line that the price is right: [illegible]

is not worth the blood of one American boy. If you are reading your mail these days, you will know that everyone who is against our continued involvement in Vietnam, is not a peacenik, beatnik, cussers and doubters, but are down to earth good American citizens, who incidentally, vote.

G. L. Zies.

Fort Smith.

Rich and Poor

To the Editor of the Gazette:

Dividing the wealth by taxing the rich and giving to the poor has been the panacea for restoring the health of every sick nation since the dawn of history.

"The Great Society" poverty programs represent such a move. History is against its success. The longer the program continues the wealthier the politicians wax and the poorer the poor become. I am not so naive as to say it cannot be done but history says it has been tried and failed many times before. Also, the very fact that nations dished out public funds for such purpose seemed to hasten the country's downfall.

Prof. Alexander Tyler wrote nearly 200 years ago: "The average age of the world's greatest civilizations has been 200 years. These nations have progressed through this sequence: From bondage to spiritual faith, from spiritual [illegible] chines and slot machine parts which the "Little Combination" had hoarded all those years. Some of these were even made (supposedly) by the Spa Amusement Company in Hot Springs, Arkansas, owned by Dane Harris, a player in the rackets. This would prove that they weren't shipped interstate, a violation of federal law, wouldn't it? (He says, tongue in cheek!)

Chances are you have never seen a "juice joint" as most of them never see the light of day or at least not after they are installed.

GAZETTE

Troopers Seize Slots Believed Already Burned

From Gazette Press Services 10-5-67

HOT SPRINGS — Three persons were arrested and charged with possession of gambling equipment here Tuesday after State Police seized more than 100 slot machines in raids on two buildings identified by State Police Director Lynn A. Davis as slot machine repair shops.

Davis estimated the value of the machines at between $150,000 and $250,000 and said 18 of them were among those "supposedly destroyed" after State Police raids August 17 at the Bridge Street, Ohio, Citizens and White Front Clubs.

All except the 18, which Davis said were damaged and bore markings made by officers during the previous raids, were burned under Davis' supervision Wednesday afternoon.

Davis said he had obtained "a verbal order" from Municipal Judge Earl Mazander to destroy the machines. Mazander also issued the search and seizure warrants Davis used in the raids.

Among the three, two-ton truckloads of equipment hauled to the bonfire were a shipping crate that Davis said was specifically built for slot machines and a "juice joint" that he said was used to control play on a dice table.

The 18 slot machines supposedly destroyed under the supervision of Police Chief John Ermey were taken to Little Rock for storage. Davis said Mazander had requested that they be held as "evidence," but he was unable to say what the evidence was to be used for.

The three men arrested were identified as Tony A. Frazier, E. P. (Lefty) Wallman and John Sampson, all of Hot Springs.

the night and the fire kept burning.

If anything larger than a silver dollar remains this morning, it will be beaten with a sledge hammer, and finally, the remains will be covered by a bulldozer, the State Police said.

Davis Tells Club He's Disappointed

In a civic club speech shortly after the bonfire, Davis said it hurt him to say that the 18 machines were supposed to be destroyed under a court order.

"Eight witnesses said they witnessed the destruction and yet we find 18 machines obviously barely damaged and some not damaged at all," he said.

The State Police aren't picking on Hot Springs, he said, and raids have been made in other towns. However, he said, Hot Springs happened to be the only place in the state where a large number of slot machines were known to be located.

The machines were being held for the time "when the pressure is off to open back up," he said.

—Associated Press photo.

State Police check repaired slots seized in Wednesday raid.

Raids Are Proof He Keeps Pledges, Rockefeller Says

GAZETTE 10-7-67

Governor Rockefeller said Friday that the latest State Police raids on Hot Springs gambling carried out "what I had promised I would do."

Spa Judge Charges 3 After Raids

Civil Service Probe Held on Spa Police Role in Seizures

HOT SPRINGS — Warrants were issued Friday by Munici-

25
5¢
$7.50
JACKPOT
7 7 7 $60
25¢

Troopers Put Torch To 18 Slot Machines

HOT SPRINGS (AP) — State Police Director Lynn Davis set out Monday to prove that you can too destroy a slot machine without melting it in a blast furnace.

He turned his State Troopers loose on 18 of the devices, which they battered into pieces with sledge hammers. They burned the remains in fuel oil then and buried them.

That's what was supposed to have happened to the machines once before, after they were seized in a State Police raid here, but they turned up again Oct. 4 in a raid on the Spa Amusement Co., an alleged slot machine repair shop. Davis said he identified them by their serial numbers.

The Hot Springs police were in charge of the first demolition assignment, and Davis insinuated later that Police Chief John Ermey and another officer were present when someone made off with them.

That's why Municipal Judge Earl Mazander ordered the machines held, but he declared them contraband and ordered them destroyed Friday after an investigation failed to incriminate Ermey or his officers.

A Spa Amusement Co. employe testified that he had found the machines battered and burned and that no policemen were present when he retrieved them.

He said he repaired the machines, and he advised investigators that the only way to put them completely out of commission was with a blast furnace.

Monday's sledge-hammer destruction took place in a gravel pit north of here.

"We want to show how thoroughly a slot can be destroyed with a sledge hemmer," Davis said.

Run of the News

The Political Strategy Of Focusing Public Attention

By KARR SHANNON

In just about every governmental administration, state and national, the dominant political strategy is to give some move or accomplishment dignity by identifying it with whatever contemporaneous desire of the general public that happens to be the most powerful.

That move or accomplishment must be strikingly emphasized over and over, especially if there has been some administration blunder, weakness or frailty that the administration wants twilighted. When something goes wrong, or there's a multiplicity of failures in various categories, it is the policy of the chief executive — governor or president — to play down or ignore such shortcomings while directing the attention to some creditable accomplishment.

That was the policy of FDR. When things were going wrong in general, he would distract public attention by pointing to, or bringing up, some fascinating something in his favor. Press conferences offered great opportunity for such maneuvers.

LBJ resorts to such strategy, but he can't match the genius of FDR.

Orval Faubus is a past master at such tactics.

WR's Horn-Tootin'

And Gov. Winthrop Rockefeller is not doing so badly for a novice. Right now he has at least two things going in his favor — the courage and accomplishments of his State Police director, Lynn Davis, and the skill and tenacity of his insurance commissioner, John Norman Harkey. The governor never tires of bugling the merits of these two men. He brings it in during press conferences, and on teevee and in public speeches throughout the state.

And the people apparently are gobbling it up. The State Police raids on gambling, directed by Mr. Davis, are unprecedented in scope and persistence. Lavish praise is coming from both press and pulpit. If the election were held today it's a pretty safe bet that this one thing would re-elect Mr. Rockefeller.

A Hint to the Wise

It has been hinted — not officially — that something of the same strategy will be used by the Constitutional Revision Study Commission in drafting a proposed new state constitution. There may be one or two features of the proposed charter designed to be so attractive, so fascinating . . . that the people will forget that the proposal takes away their right to elect their Supreme Court and circuit court judges and their right to elect their secretary of state, auditor, treasurer and land commissioner; that they may forget that they will be burdened with an annual legislative session that runs 90 days instead of the present biennial 60 days, and that they will be charged with higher taxes and unlimited salaries . . . The favorable factors may be made so glittering as to place in the shadows the provisions that give the legislature unprecedented power and that make the governor a virtual dictator.

Poets Like Autumn, Too

Much has been said about how poets capitalize on the spring season for their rhymes. Also it is during this season that the amateurs are "inspired." Any newspaper publisher will vouch for that. It is during spring that the slush of rhyming rubbish hits the editor's desk.

But auaumn, too, has always been a season beloved by poets. Some of it, like spring poetry, is sheer doggerel. But much of it—by the renowned poets—is logical, inspiring. Listen to this:

John Greenleaf Whittier: "Heap high the farmer's wintry hoard. Heap high the golden corn. No richer gift has autumn poured from her lavish horn."

Thomas Hood: "I saw old autumn in misty morn, stand shadowless like silence — listening."

Bliss Carman: "There is something in October that sets the gypsy blood astir; We must rise and follow her, When from every hill of flame . . . She calls and calls each vagabond by name."

William Carruth: "A haze on the far horizon, the infinite tender sky. The rich ripe tint of the cornfields — and the wild geese flying high."

Robert Browning: "Autumn wins you best by this, its mute appeal to sympathy for its decay."

William Cullen Bryant: "The melancholy days are come, the saddest of the year; Of wailing winds and naked woods and meadows brown and sere."

Senator Wiley Helped to End Foreign Policy P...

LAY ON YOUR BACK TO SEE IF YOU ARE BEING CHEATED

During play on a dice table, commonly known as a crap table, a player, of course, wants a particular number to come up on the dice. At the appropriate time, when the house especially wants the house number to come up causing the dice shooter to lose, the house can insure the shooter loses. No, it isn't a miracle. The house can absolutely guarantee that they can make a certain number on the dice come up whenever they want.

To do that they employ a "juice joint." A tad of lead is inserted under certain "house" numbers which will stop the roll of the dice at these "house numbers" when they come in contact with the force of a magnet. Now where in the world would a magnet be? Why, of course, *under* the crap table. At the appropriate time, a houseman leans on a compression switch which causes an electrical charge to run through the copper wire under the table which causes the dice to stop on the spot which has been "leaded." Needless to say, the dice most likely wind up causing a "snake eyes" or a "crap out" at a propitious time insuring that the player loses. It is comforting to the house to know they have an experienced person handling the switch to the juice joint. He must be observant enough to hit the switch at the very moment the dice are about to roll to a stop naturally. It would be somewhat embarrassing to have the dice, in the middle of a roll, slam down on the felt, locked in position. (In a less cultured environment the dealer, in that situation, as well as the house, might become an exhibition of complete destruction plus a certain amount of mayhem.) In other words, some might get fighting mad when they find that they have been cheated when it appeared all along that this was a "square house."

Oh well, that's why they call it gambling. You are gambling that the house is on the up and up. The next time you go to a bust-out joint be sure to get on the floor and look under the table and see if the bottom is wired. (He says with a grin on his face!)

GATOR AND THE LITTLE RED BARN

Little did I know that this was the day. Amazingly, after the initial load of slot machines had been burned, a person from Hot Springs called me giving me the address of a house where, according to him (or her), a little red barn held many slot machines.

This was a call out of the blue. The informant, who I named Gator did not say to "leave my name out of it," but I respected his privacy and to this day have never advised anyone of his identity. I only talked to him once. He *or she* said she had been convinced of our being serious, and that she had finally found someone who would take care of the casino problem. This was the day or so after we burned the original haul of slots. She said that the kids in the neighborhood pulled back boards on the side of a little red barn at a Hot Springs residence, put their hands in between the planks and moved their hands around until they found where they could put their money.

Obviously, it was very difficult for the kids to hit a jackpot as there was none other than the nickels "dropped" by the kids. (They still had about the same luck as those who played the slots at the ending of the racing season.) I was told by old timers that the machines at that time were screwed down so tight that they "squealed." (Take the suckers for all you could, while you could.)

This person to whom I assigned the name, Gator, described the little red barn, giving me the address and all the identifying information. Information from informants can be a trap of some sort so you must be wary. I was. This was just too good to be true. What she described seemed like the mother lode—at least 25 or 30 machines. Little did we know! He explained that she had never reported this matter to law enforcement in Hot Springs as they and the person who had the machines were in the same boat and she, the informant, would be the one punished rather than the barn owner. I didn't ask why she was reporting these machines to me.

111 Slots Seized In Raid

State Troopers on a raid in Hot Springs Saturday found 111 slot machines neatly stored in this "little red barn," as oficers called it, including 19 which bore stickers proclaimng that that they had been made by the Spa Amusement Co., which is a violation of federal law.

Scene is at the rear of the Harry Columbus estate at 222 Bell Aire, an exclusive section near the Hot Springs Country Club.

UNLIKELY SPOT — Columbus' residence, above, nestled among trees looked like anything but a place where police would be likely to find a cache of illegal one-arm bandits. Below is a close-up of Columbus' mailbox. He is a brother-in-law to Jack Pakis, a well-known Hot Springs figure.

DAVIS CHECKS SLOTS — Davis, right, displays one of the locally manufactured slots, of a variety previously unknown to lawmen. It features five different ways to "hit the jackpot." At far right, Davis inspects the sticker, which identifies it as being made by Spa Amusement Co., and assigned to the Vapors nightclub.

Davis Says 'Gambling Era at End'

Another Resort Raid Nets State Police 111 'Slots'

By EDNA LEE HOWE
and
JOHN LONGINOTTI

Arkansas State Police raided red storage barn at the me of Harry Columbus, 222 ellaire Drive, fashionable subvision across Malvern Road om the Hot Springs Country at 8 a. m. Saturday, seiz-111 slot machines.

olumbus is identified as manager of the Southern Club, long since closed, and as a brother-in-law of Jack Pakis, an owner of the club.

No charge has been filed but Col. Lynn Davis, state police director who led the raid, said he anticipated an arrest.

Davis valued the machines, all in working order and partially stored in wine-cellar fashion, at $150,000 "at the old price but worthless" in view of present conditions. "They'd be a poor investment, right now!"

"This is the end of an era in Arkansas," Davis stated flatly during a press conference at the firing range off the Hot Springs-Benton highway as the huge pile of slots was ground to bits by a bulldozer and then doused with 30 gallons of diesel fuel and set afire before being dumped into a trench ar buried.

"Gambling days in Arkans are at an end," Davis declare

Davis, accompanied by a co tingent of state troopers an members of the department Criminal Investigation Divisi (CID) had raided two repa shops in widely separated are of the city at 615 second ar 29 Westbrook on Wednesday last week, confiscating over 1 slot machines and numero parts, later destroying them the site of yesterday's destru tion.

The ones taken from the bar at the Columbus home, how ever, were all in working co dition, and, according to Davi 19 of them were manufacture by the Spa Amusement Con pany, identified as owner of th repair shop on Second street.

Davis would not identify th company as owner of the 1 slots taken yesterday, but a other source close to the situ tion and considered unimpeac able, said they did belong t that firm. They comprised th largest group of workable m chines taken in a state polic raid here.

During recent such raids her Davis said approximately 3 slot machines and parts suff cient to bring that number t 400 had been confiscated. The worth was estimated at half million dollars by Davis.

Davis said he was confide there were still approximate 230 machines in Hot Spring but that some of these cou have been moved elsewhere.

"I have a fairly good ide where they are," he said, ind cating that other raids might b in the offing.

The State Police are holdin 18 slot machines, among thos seized in raids last Wednesda and determined, from markin to have been a part of th gambling loot seized in simil raids on four downtown clu Aug. 17 and supposedly d stroyed Sept. 22 at the sam firing range, as "evidence" instructions of Municipal Judg

It is a mistake to, at first, question an informant about his motive. He could begin to become sentimental and hang up.

(These machines proved to not be the namby pamby light-weight electronic stuff they have today in poker rooms, but heavy cast metal, weighing about 80 pounds. Several troopers have jokingly told me that they were sore for weeks after carrying the slots down to the first floor of most of the clubs that were raided on our first "official" visit to Hot Springs.)

We did a rolling reconnaissance around the barn and the neighborhood and decided to get a search warrant for the barn. In justifying the search warrant we recounted that a confidential informant had told us that the little red barn contained slot machines. I expected to get the third degree about the barn, but didn't. We kept the location under surveillance until we got the warrant and moved in. Using several vehicles, including commercial delivery surveillance vans, we made sure nothing came out while we were getting the warrant.

The lady who answered the door at the house was served the search warrant. Even though we had legal right to search the red barn, I felt it would be more courteous if I gave her a chance to voluntarily give me permission to look in the barn by furnishing us a key. She refused. When we pried the lock off the barn door and swung the doors open, light fell on the biggest stack of slot machines I had ever seen outside Las Vegas. One hundred eleven machines we counted as we lugged them out to the rented truck to be hauled to the gravel pit and burned.

There was not enough time for the slots and the other equipment to "cut and run." They were ours. We had them under air tight surveillance. People said and believed, "It couldn't be done," but we just did it. I had said that same thing, gambling couldn't be stopped in Arkansas, since the time I had been in grade school, but then was then and now is now. *We had earned them and we were going to take them to the gravel pit to be burned.*

DEMOCRAT Today's News Today

Y EVENING, OCTOBER 7, 1967 12 PAGES ★ PRICE 5c

111 Slots Confiscated; Some 'Made in Spa'

By BOB SALLEE
Democrat Staff Writer

HOT SPRINGS — State Police today seized 111 slot machines from a storage building on the fashionable estate of Harry Columbus, 222 Bellaire, in an exclusive residential area of Hot Springs near the Hot Springs Country Club.

State Police Director Lynn A. Davis said this was the largest collection of working slot machines that troopers have seized to date, and he disclosed that at least 13 were of a new variety which had been manufactured by the Spa Amusement Co. at Hot Springs.

Spa Amusement Co. was the scene of a raid Wednesday in which almost 100 slots were taken from the company's repair shop.

A plate inside the new machines carried an inscription: "This machine made by Spa Amusement Co."

Davis said the machines were of a kind he had never seen before.

He indicated this would be the clincher to federal charges against the firm for manufacturing slot machines illegally.

Davis identified Columbus as the brother-in-law of Jack Pakis, a well known Hot Springs figure and operator of the Southern Club.

Columbus is listed in the Hot Springs city directory as manager of the Southern Club.

H. Dane Harris, resident agent of Spa Amusement Co and operator of the now-clo Vapors night club, and P are generally thought to competitors in gambling cles.

When asked about this t Davis smiled, raised his brows, and said, "So did

Davis and seven tr came to Hot Springs F r night and moved in on the lumbus estate at 7:30 a.m. day after obtaining search seize warrants from Hot Sp Municipal Judge Earl M der.

The Columbus home is ...hood of homes i...

Hot Springs earlier this year totaled 11 in less than two months by April 18 in which more than 55 slot machines had been seized in various private clubs.

On Aug. 17 state troopers, led by Davis, seized 25 slot machines and hundreds of pieces of equipment from four clubs in Hot Springs.

On Sept. 9 Davis led State Police on raids against alleged "bookie" operations in North Little Rock and areas in Pulas...

...ward to it.

The source said the doors of the truck flew open on the busy downtown street before the police had acted.

Davis said today that the load of machines taken from the Columbus property would be taken to the spot where the other machines had been destroyed and burned.

The site is near Interstate 30 at the edge of town.

Total slots taken in the raids at Hot Springs this week by state police are now more than 200. Eighteen of those seized Wednesday were "supposed to have been destroyed" from raids made on four Hot Springs clubs on Aug. 17, according to Davis.

Davis said that the machines taken today included two of the "old silver-dollar type" and that several had masking tape iden...

(By the way, I never got a note acknowledging that we had done what they had failed to do over the years. Oh well, they were busy.)

The thought occurred to me, why didn't they, the gangsters, get rid of the machines when they saw that we were serious and the answer was, obviously, we got credit for being everywhere and all the people around town would be looking for machines being moved. As a matter of fact, the police did later arrest one of the employees of the repair shops driving a truck containing slots and found a truck load of machines at another gravel pit in Malvern about thirty miles away.

One of the best suggestions sent to the newspaper, at that time, was to take the machines to a "legal" state (only Nevada at that time) and sell them. That was a unique idea. (Oh, to have those 1,000 or so old time slot machines back and to have them to auction off on e-Bay.) They were made of what I believe is described as pot metal and some had the head of an Indian with feathers and all. Some of them were named "Jennings." (To this day I still get asked if I kept at least one of those machines and the disappointing answer is that I didn't. Of course, if I had kept one, it would have been illegal and I would have had to lock myself up!)

Needless to say, this time we didn't ask for any anyone's permission to destroy the machines, taking them directly to the gravel pit. When the truck pulled away it was "loaded to the gills". It creaked and moaned and the worst part was that it was a borrowed truck. I knew it would be a miracle if it made it, but it did after much encouragement.

Davis Says the Gambling Era Is Over

(Continued From Page 1.)

gambling here or anywhere else in the state," said Richard Wootton, a young lawyer who led the effort to pass Amendment 55.

"I'm sure there are people who would like to try to bring back gambling," he said, "but I think they're wasting their time —certainly in the foreseeable future."

Says Emphasis Has Shifted

Like others, Wootton sees a turnabout in thinking toward gambling by the city's business community. In the first place, he said, the major tourist outlook now is toward the convention trade rather than the individual tourist, which means a change in the type of person who comes to Hot Springs.

"These people [convention delegates], while they enjoy nightlife and entertainment, are not here primarily to go to casinos," Wootton said.

This is ironic because it was largely with an "amusement tax" on the city's busy gambling devices that the $1.26 million modern new Convention Center was built.

In the second place, Wootton said, industry (nine major plants in recent years) has come to Hot Springs, creating a broader based economy. This is evidenced, the young lawyer noted, by bulging bank deposits and increased sales tax receipts.

"I think people have realized gambling is not the only thing that can keep you going," he said. "In the past the man on the streets had to turn to a gambling or tourist related source for income. Now we even have a shortage of skilled labor for our plants. People are no longer as dependent on an open-one-day, shut-the-next, boom or bust economy."

Amendment Defeat Was End, He Says

This change of thought — and thus the end of the era — came about in November 1965, Wootton feels, when the voters of Arkansas soundly defeated Amendment 55 and Hot Springs businessmen and civic leaders, faced with the feeling of the state on gambling, began their turn to industry and conventions.

The pressures from the gambling interests are still here and there are several cases in court or pending over the situation, so many businessmen and public officials declined to talk on the record or be quoted by name.

One former official felt that the adverse publicity that has come to Hot Springs in recent years through the mass media was a major factor in the finale.

"People are no longer naive," he said. "They turn on their television sets and listen to newscasts and read the papers. And the papers and news media are not going to sit by and watch this thing continue. There'll be little clubs and honky tonks that will try to open up, but they're absolutely no good for any community and the people here will put an end to that. And anything that is bigger is going to attract the attention of the newspapers."

No governor can stand the heat of adverse public comment, he said ("Faubus was the [illegible] agitation against it brings about some kind of action.

"I found a sentiment out in the state that the people didn't particularly care about what is going on in Hot Springs so long as it didn't get out of hand and become an eyesore to the state."

—Photos by Larry Obsitnik and JAY of Hot Springs.

Hot Springs Slots—Then and Now

The top picture shows a row of slot machines in the Vapors club in 1963 at the peak of illegal gambling in Hot Springs. The bottom photograph was taken Thursday, at the height of State Police destruction of gaming equipment seized in raids at Hot Springs.

Other Events Created Stir

Other events in 1963 and early 1964 led to the public's attention: Mainly a mysterious bombing of the plush Vapors, thought by many lawmen to be part of a gangland attempt to move in, and a surprise news conference held at Hot Springs on March 18, 1964 by William Hundley, the chief of the Justice Department's Organized Crime and Racketeering Section. It was not known by the press that he was even here, but in his statement, he said that he and his agents had toured the town's glittering gambling spots, and "from what I saw down here [illegible] operated then as a private club, put in some gambling to help pay its way. Smaller gamblers wanted part of the action and got it.

At one point, a public official remembers, "There was a great deal of trouble of small joints wanting to operate and that's where it got a little out of hand."

Finally, in 1959, Dane Harris, a Hot Springs native, opened his plush Vapors in the north end of town. Using gambling revenue from his casino, one of the swankest in the South, he brought in big name entertainment. The era had reached the bigtime.

Then came the Faubus shutdown. There was a brief flurry to reopen as private clubs, but gambling mostly in the form of slot machines came back, the press noted it and the clubs were closed again. The gambling was reduced to smaller operations, "bustout joints" and shoving by the smaller gam- [illegible] through the liquor outlets and the clubs. Parents were visibly disturbed.

The Grand Jury's interim report in September reflected this feeling in the community.

It not only ordered a crackdown on the liquor stores and clubs, but on any activity that it felt was unlawful or unethical. Among these were the alleged use of public officials to check the clubs for gambling equipment in order to assess the "amusement tax." The Jury also told all public officials to do their duties.

The feeling that gambling was not what it used to be in Garland County was evident by this sattement from the Jury:

"We are in a very promising period. ••• This [economic] growth has been prevalent even though illegal operations such as gambling have been curtailed in recent years."

This sort of attitude, Father Smith feels, indicates that the era is ended.

[illegible] come to naught had not Davis taken over the leadership of the State Police.

"With the advent of Colonel Davis," he said, "my promises began to materialize into reality."

Part of his campaign was to clean up Hot Springs. When he took office in January, he gave Col. Herman Lindsay, the 20-year veteran director of the State Police, the go-ahead to raid the clubs. After a stuttering start, Lindsay's troopers pulled out a number of slot machines from the clubs. But it wasn't until 13 days after Davis took over in August that the big raids began. On the first one, led personally by Davis and without the knowledge of local lawmen, the State Police seized $70,000 worth of the equipment (Davis' estimate) from five of the small clubs.

Where before, lawmen had trouble obtaining search and seize warrants, newly elected Municipal Judge Earl Mazander was quick to go along. The equipment was burned (although some of the supposedly destroyed slots eventually found their way back to the gamblers). The local authorities began to make a few raids.

Then early this month, Davis hit the repair shops, seizing hundreds of thousands of dollars worth of hard-to-replace gambling equipment and parts. The supply of slot machines at Hot Springs was being depleted. Altogether Davis estimates that his troopers destroyed between $500,000 and $1 million worth of gaming devices.

His prize seizure though, is a "juice joint," a device that can control the throw of dice. He said this one instrument "is indicative of the whole mess. It points up the fact that when you're in an illegal activity, you can go a step further. Inasmuch as it's illegal anyway, why not go ahead and use a juice joint."

Davis Urges Continued Vigilance

Davis thinks his ending of the Era only means more vigilance by lawmen.

"I think that the only way to stop gambling in Arkansas," he said, "is through hard and constant honest law enforcement and this is what we plan to continue. We are keeping an eye out all over the state for any evidence of organized gambling."

This is a statement many Hot Springs people want to hear.

"I find a great deal of public sentiment for Davis' action: the former public official sa "If he just treats Little Ro and Pine Bluff and other tow the same way. It's all okay if just won't discriminate agai Hot Springs."

Hurst Declares Era Not Over

One of the few voices speaking up for gambling at Springs is that of state Sena Q. Byrum Hurst. And he doe see an end of the Era.

"I've been here all my li he said, "and I've seen this happen before. I've seen ga bling machines hauled out burned at the fairgrounds I've seen them come back.

"This may be new to Rockefeller. This may be new Mr. Davis. But not to us have lived here always. D will find that he can't carnality out of human bein

Era Is Over

come to naught had not Davis taken over the leadership of the State Police.

"With the advent of Colonel Davis," he said, "my promises began to materialize into reality."

Part of his campaign was to clean up Hot Springs. When he took office in January, he gave Col. Herman Lindsay, the 20-year veteran director of the State Police, the go-ahead to raid the clubs. After a stuttering start, Lindsay's troopers pulled out a number of slot machines from the clubs. But it wasn't until 13 days after Davis took over in August that the big raids began. On the first one, led personally by Davis and without the knowledge of local lawmen, the State Police seized $70,000 worth of the equipment (Davis' estimate) from five of the small clubs.

Where before, lawmen had trouble obtaining search and seize warrants, newly elected Municipal Judge Earl Mazander was quick to go along. The equipment was burned (although some of the supposedly destroyed slots eventually found their way back to the gamblers). The local authorities began to make a few raids.

Then early this month, Davis hit the repair shops, seizing hundreds of thousands of dollars worth of hard-to-replace gambling equipment and parts. The supply of slot machines at Hot Springs was being depleted. Altogether Davis estimates that his troopers destroyed between $500,000 and $1 million worth of gaming devices.

His prize seizure though, is a "juice joint," a device that can control the throw of dice. He said this one instrument "is indicative of the whole mess. It points up the fact that when you're in an illegal activity, you can go a step further. Inasmuch as it's illegal anyway, why not go ahead and use a juice joint."

Davis Urges Continued Vigilance

Davis thinks his ending of the Era only means more vigilance by lawmen.

"I think that the only way to stop gambling in Arkansas," he said, "is through hard and constant honest law enforcement and this is what we plan to continue. We are keeping an eye out all over the state for any evidence of organized gambling."

This is a statement many Hot Springs people want to hear.

"I find a great deal of public sentiment for Davis' actions," the former public official said. "If he just treats Little Rock and Pine Bluff and other towns the same way. It's all okay if he just won't discriminate against Hot Springs."

Hurst Declares Era Not Over

One of the few voices now speaking up for gambling at Hot Springs is that of state Senator Q. Byrum Hurst. And he doesn't see an end of the Era.

"I've been here all my life," he said, "and I've seen this all happen before. I've seen gambling machines hauled out and burned at the fairgrounds and I've seen them come back.

"This may be new to Mr. Rockefeller. This may be new to Mr. Davis. But not to us who have lived here always. Davis will find that he can't take carnality out of human beings."

—Photo by JAY of Hot Springs

Col. Lynn Davis: Did he really end an era?

Hot Springs Gambling: An Era Ends

PAGE 1

'Whole Damn Thing' Over, Former Official Declares

By LEROY DONALD
Of the Gazette Staff

HOT SPRINGS — On the morning of October 7, Col. Lynn A. Davis, the slim director of State Police, set fire to 111 slot machines seized a few hours earlier behind the plush home of a night club manager here. As the flames rushed down the trial of diesel fuel to engulf the battered gambling devices, he proclaimed: "This is the end of an era!"

Is it?

After a century of winking at Arkansas's laws, has Hot Springs gambling—which prompted a Justice Department official to label it the largest illegal gambling operation in the nation—reached its end?

A survey last week of those who are supposed to know indicates that it has.

"It's the end of the whole damn thing," said a former public official, who as a lifelong resident of the area has seen the gambling ups and downs.

The opinions of when the end of the era came vary considerably.

Certainly, all agree, Davis' raids on Hot Springs clubs and slot machine repair shops and storage places and the resulting destruction of from 400 to 500 slot machines and other gambling paraphanalia was a devastating blow.

But the beginning of the end, many feel, can be traced to the passage in 1961 of Robert Kennedy's anticrime bill; former Governor Orval E. Faubus' shutdown of the casinos, in 1964; the defeat of Amendment 55, the legalized casino gambling bill, later in 1964; election of a new slate of county and district officers last year; the positive action of the Garland County Grand Jury now in session, and chiding from state newspapers.

In the 100 years that Hot Springs has been known as the place to find action outside the law, similar occurrences have happened. And the gambling has shut down, then opened up, then shut down and reopened again and again. Only this time, things seem to have all fallen into place to truly put an end to Hot Springs' wide open era.

There still is a hard core of those who think gambling is essential to Hot Springs' tourist business and want it back, but their outlook generally is regarded as foolish.

"I would certainly feel that as long as he [Lynn Davis] is in charge of the State Police, you're not going to have

(See GAMBLING on Page 13A)

DEMOCRAT ••• Sunday, December 10, 1967

nition Chafes as He Awaits Court Ruling

LYNN A. DAVIS
. . . State Police head

sees where it could rule in his favor.

Asked what he would do if the court rules against him, Davis said Saturday:

"I actually don't know. My wife and I were just sitting here (at home) talking about that. We haven't made any plans for such eventuality. Of course, if it rules in my favor, we will just go on without any interruption."

Who takes over in his place if he is ruled ineligible? Davis said he had not discussed this with the governor, so he wouldn't know.

Has the governor been helping him out financially? Davis said, "I heard or read somewhere that I was drawing $40,000 a year. That would really be some kind of a salary."

Then, he admitted that, if he had to leave without any salary, "The governor might feel sorry for me and give me some kind of gratuity."

If Davis is ruled eligible by the Supreme Court, he would be in line to draw all of his salary from Aug 1

to remove the words "10 yea next preceding his appointment." It could leave in the requirement that he be a resident of Arkansas.

Would the legislature do this? Most observers at the Capitol believe they would although

WR Is Called For Hearing In Hot Springs

HOT SPRINGS (AP) — Governor Rockefeller is among 28 persons who have been subpoenaed to appear Monday as defense witnesses in a hearing on two motions. One seeks to disqualify Circuit Court Judge Henry M. Britt of Hot Springs as the presiding judge in the trial of nine gambling case defendants.

The other asks for an immediate jury trial for the defendants, all accused of keeping a gambling house.

The hearing is scheduled for 9 a.m. Monday in Garland County Circuit Court here.

The motion says Judge Britt will be called as a witness to prove that the "constitutional rights" of the defendants have been violated.

The motion also alleges that Judge Britt "has shown bias and prejudice to each defendant."

The motion asking for an immediate trial notes that the defendants were indicted seven months ago.

Sam Robinson filed the motion for his clients, eight of whom were arrested in State Police raids at the Ohio Club last April 5 .

The eight indicted by the Garland County Grand Jury are John E. Atwood, Willie Jack Digby, Dana Ray Milner, Raymond McCarthy, George Collins, Harold J. Milner, Howard Johnson, all of Hot Springs, and Coolidge Conlee of Forrest City.

Another defendant, Sam LaVelle Jr., was indicted by the Grand Jury on a charge of keeping a gambling house at the Ohio Club, but he was not arrested in the raid. All nine pleaded innocent to the charges at their arraingment.

WR, judge called in gambling hearing

HOT SPRINGS (AP)—Twenty-eight persons, including Governor Rockefeller, have been subpoenaed to appear next week as defense witnesses at a hearing on two motions, one of which seeks to disqualify Circuit Julge Henry M. Britt as the presiding judge in the trial of nine gambling case defendants.

The second motion notes that the defendants were indicted seven months ago and asks for an immediate jury trial.

A hearing on the motions is scheduled for Monday morning in Garland Circuit Court at Hot Springs.

The motion asked that Britt be called as a witness to prove that the "constitutional rights" of the defendants had been violated. It alleged that Britt "has shown bias and prejudice to each defendant."

Eight of the nine persons were arrested last April 5 in State Police raids at the Ohio Club in Hot Springs.

The eight indicted by the Garland County Grand Jury were John E. Atwood, Willie Jack Digby, Dana Ray Milner, Raymond McCarty, George Collins, Harold J. Milner, Howard Johnson, all of Hot Springs, and Coolidge Conlee of Forrest City.

Sam LaVelle Jr., the other defendant, was not arrested in the raid but was indicted by the grand jury on a charge of keeping a gambling house at the Ohio Club. All nine pleaded innocent to the charges at their arraignment.

Among the other witnesses subpoenaed were Britt, Prosecuting Attorney Walter Wright, State Police Director Col. Ralph D. Scott, City Clerk J. Harold Smith, Municipal Judge Earl Mazander, Police Chief Joe Grain, former Police Chief John Ermey and several members of the State Police.

State Police arrested 33 persons in Garland County during gambling raids last March and April.

On May 1, the day before Mazander was to hand down his decision on the cases, the Garland County Grand Jury indicted 26 of the defendants.

The following day Mazander found 25 of the defendants innocent and dismissed the charges against the other eight.

This was pure intimidation. They had no intention of bringing anyone to a real trial.

WR AND JUDGE SUBPOENAED TO APPEAR

Historically, the best way to defend a case such as these is to keep having the case set off. You simply have the Judge set the case for a hearing, then the night before "something happens" to necessitate having the case set off for another date; lack of a particular witness, illness of the defense attorney or the prosecutor or some such excuse. The only problem with that, as far as the State Police were concerned, was that the prosecution or the judge or someone else would find it impossible to find the complaining witness, many times the state police, to advise them of the postponement so they would make a trip to Hot Springs only to be told the case had been set off. It did not take many such "wild goose" trips to wear the ASP witness down. That would be just the time the case would be called and the ASP witness would not be present to testify. (I have always heard, "It's not what you know but who you know.")

It was because of this that I decided to simply go after equipment and not people. We would spend our effort in getting illegal equipment and destroying it. However, some of my associates either did not get the word or were so mad at the system that they wouldn't let pass an opportunity to even the score with the bad guys, so they arrested some of them. Sure enough the delay began.

The machines could have been used as evidence if a trial had taken place but we never considered a trial as being worth the effort since we had been successful in the raids, but the same people were fairly safe in public office, the prosecuting attorney, the judge, seemingly, the entire legal system.

Some statistics as to how rampant the violations of the state law were:

Belvedere Country Club began the 1959-60 fiscal year with 12 machines and later installed 74 more. The Southern Club, Southern Bar and Southern Grill started that fiscal year with 21 machines and completed it with 44. By the end of the fiscal year, 1959-60, there were 846 coin-operated gambling devices located in Arkansas which could be found in 450 places of business, which shelled out $189,139.75 for federal tax stamps. Embarrassingly inexpensive when you consider what it cost to try to control it!

The *Arkansas Gazette* reported that federal tax in the amount of $150,500 had been paid during the fiscal year of 1960-61 on 602 machines. Those figures seemed to justify the United States Department of Justice's tag of Hot Springs being the biggest illegal casino operation in America and was certainly appropriate when you considered Hot Springs, Little Rock and Pulaski County. Hot Springs was the focal point because of its gangster's visits and their meetings there, but I wonder who furnished the machines distributed throughout the state and how they could justify a federal tax on gambling paraphernalia, in itself a violation of the law?

The law required that the slots be summarily destroyed as gambling equipment per se. They were of no use other than in gambling and were subject to being destroyed forthwith (without waiting for some expert or an attorney General's opinion) to say they were designed for use as gambling paraphernalia. We knew that trials would only lead to obfuscation or "wooling around" of the officers and would lead, as usual, to a $50 to $100 fine.

To bring the charges of possession of gambling paraphernalia made it too easy for the scofflaws, the legals and the illegals, the judges and the operators of the gambling establishments and their attorneys, to tie up police officers for days and days. The case would be set for trial, then postponed for some reason, then reset and again postponed. Eventually, even the most hardened veteran of police work loses faith in the system.

FORREST CITY, FAYETTEVILLE AND EVERYWHERE ELSE

I had given the "go ahead" to finding and shutting down all gambling operations wherever they might take place, but depended upon the officers in the field and in the command positions to know where, when and what to do, and they did.

We didn't have the advantage of having a list from the *Arkansas Gazette,* dated August 14, 1960, which listed not only the individual who had purchased a federal stamp on those gambling machines, but also the names of the businesses and where they were located. I knew about the casinos but not all that much about the machines being located in stores, restaurants, and thc club houses, even at the Fayetteville Country Club.

Years later, after leaving office, I checked the newspaper files and found even more information. Not only were Little Rock, North Little Rock, Fort Smith, Hot Springs, Springdale and other major cities represented in that number, there were also machines at Strong, Lake Village, Royal, Bearden, Hampton, and dozens of other "hot beds" of gambling activity. (Said tongue in cheek!) Some of these machines were reportedly pinball machines, but I know for a fact that one of my great disappointments was leading a raid south, almost to the Louisiana/Mississippi line and finding that it was closed because they had been tipped off.

That same article dated about 1961 indicated that fifty people in the state paid a $50.00 federal tax for gambling operations, an occupational tax, which was required of bookies.

The article also stated that Hot Springs businesses placed additional machines in operation during racing season at Oaklawn Park.

It takes a lot of help to make this many raids; and that help has to be good! For example, the Arkansas State Police.

OWNEY, BOBBY KENNEDY AND SENATOR McCLELLAN AND THE WIRE SERVICE RESCUE

"This resort town has been having some interesting visitors lately," Senator Estes Kefauver said. "One is a suave, portly, well dressed New Yorker named Frank Costello." Costello's presence alone would have justified the interest of the Kefauver Committee. The Senator himself referred to Florida as the number one gathering spot for the underworld figures like Costello, Accordo, Giancanna, and others but ranked Hot Springs as the nation's number two gathering spot for men with Costello's general reputation, gambling, loan sharking, and assorted crimes in which the La Casa Nostra or the mob engaged.

At one point a group of young thugs was trying to take control of Owney's wire service which transmitted race results from the race track to various betting parlors around the country. These guys were too young to know that upstarts like them usually met the same fate as a northbound bug traveling ninety miles an hour into a southbound windshield. Fortunately for them, Carlos Marcello, mafia capo, had his hands full with his other problems (like deportation). Owney was older now, but he still knew how much the cash cow, gambling, meant to the "Little Combination" and the mafia.

About that time Owney disappeared from the Hot Springs scene for a short period of time, and it later developed that Tony

Accordo, absolute capo or boss of bosses in Chicago had been visited by Owney, also known in earlier years as the "Duke of the Westside." Tony assured Owney that he had some muscle which could be utilized if he needed it.

A few months later, Accordo personally visited Hot Springs. In addition to other subjects, Tony's pending six year sentence for income tax evasion was discussed. The Bureau (FBI) tried, unsuccessfully, to monitor the conversations, but only succeeded in physical surveillance.

At least three of Accordo's associates consulted Madden. The mafia, La Cosa Nostra or the Syndicate as it is sometimes known is a business that rivals some of the biggest corporations in America and they can't leave very much to chance. Who is going to control prostitution, gambling and shylocking (lending money at exorbitant interest rates), and other rackets in Accordo's Chicago, the "Windy City," if Accordo goes down river? Also, who will provide protection of the Hot Springs rackets when needed? Good question and one that needed to be decided. Another indication of Madden's influence.

On June 7, 1961, the *Associated Press* ran a story that Bobby Kennedy was pushing for a new federal law regarding the Hot Springs racing wire service coming from New Orleans through Hot Springs to the Little Rock bookies, under sublease by Madden to Barney Levine and other bookies in Little Rock. Kennedy said the New Orleans thugs were trying to move in on the wire service. (Which thugs? The thugs had already moved in, lock, stock and barrel.) The newspapers of that day reported that Madden, nearly seventy years of age, was still actively a part of and participant in the crime syndicate and believe it or not he had certainly not severed ties with Carlos Marcello, New Orleans Capo.

History doesn't readily record what happens to top waters who don't know just how deep the water runs! Believe it or not, some of the top waters might think a few bombs placed here and there would make an impression, but not with these types—Madden's, Accordo's, Costello's, Luciano's and other Mafia types. The Dixie Mafia, a bunch of southern fried gangsters who some thought might be trying to muscle in couldn't even come close. (They were not Italian and just couldn't seem to build such a reputation.)

Unlike New York and Chicago and other large cities under the control of the Syndicate, Hot Springs had very few businesses that could be "shook down." All other businesses were considered to be a service industry for gambling and related businesses—ice, booze, snacks, hotels, motels, taxicabs, auction houses, and other businesses essential to the gambling industry, if not to the non-essential businesses, those not part of the rackets.

It was common knowledge by those "in the know", that Hot Springs was an ideal place to take refuge if you were wanted. If you had the money, you had the protection. As a matter of fact, the local constabulary, city, and county claimed that this was so, if you were not violent. If you were just the run of the mill gangster, non-violent, just trying to stay out of the clutches of the law, you had a place in Hot Springs. This story was about as believable as the, "They Said, It Couldn't Be Done" story which was closing down the biggest illegal casino operation in America.

You could be as violent and as hot as a firecracker and still find friends in the Valley.

If the non-violent protection myth held water, then why did the Hot Springs and Garland County law enforcement officers take under their wing Frank "Jelly" Nash, a Leavenworth Federal Penitentiary escapee; "Pretty Boy" Floyd, a hold up man and a killer; "Lucky" Luciano, the biggest pimp in the country; Alvin "Creepy" Karpis, an admitted killer who in 1946 sent the Hot Springs Police Chief and the Chief of Detectives, and a Madam, Maxine Jones, all some of Hot Springs's finest, to the penitentiary for harboring a fugitive and assorted other crimes in Hot Springs, in direct opposition to the propaganda that the Hot Springs movers and shakers only protected non-violent criminals.

THE McCLELLAN SUBCOMMITTEE ON CRIME

In August 1961, a team from Washington, Senate "racket probers," descended on "Bubbles," part of a Subcommittee chaired by Senator John L. McClellan. The racket probers made no secret of the fact that their main target was Owney Madden's wire service which came into Hot Springs courtesy of Carlos Marcello, capo of the New Orleans branch of the La Cosa Nostra.

Bobby Kennedy, who was United States Attorney General felt that a prosecution in Hot Springs would be a distinct service to the nation, and he made no secret of the fact that he wanted Madden to have a front seat at the trial. Q. Byrum Hurst, Owney Madden's personal attorney, said that when the subject of Bobby Kennedy came up, Owney asked a rhetorical question, "How can he do that to me when his father and I were partners during prohibition."

(Good question! How did one bootlegger, or several, wind up being known thugs, and one other wind up being the father of the President of the United States of America?)

Bobby, President Kennedy's brother, was the chief counsel for the Committee, while John McClellan was the Chairman. Kennedy had drawn up a list of forty individuals as targets for the hearings. It could have been, too, a try to get Carlos Marcello, the originator of the wire service and a Kennedy hater. (It had been reported that Marcello had given a bag containing $500,000 to a Richard Nixon supporter for Nixon's campaign against Jack Kennedy.) This seems a lot of money but not an unreasonable amount when you consider what Marcello, Madden and the others took in. (I have not absolutely verified this but it seems reasonable and comes from several good sources.)

Bobby, not too long after Jack Kennedy's election, while rummaging around in his files of warrants, had found an extradition notice for Marcello who had been granted citizenship to Guatemala as a favor (for money) to the dictator at that time. Bobby had Immigration and Naturalization grab up Marcello and hustle him to a waiting plane taking him to Guatemala, where they dropped him like a hot rock. Those authorities didn't know what to do with Marcello, so they first put him in jail, then, took him by jeep about thirty miles into the jungle, dropped him without survival gear and left him. It was said that he still had on his stylish loafers and his high dollar suit when they dropped him. They were sure, according to unimpeachable sources, that he would never make it back to civilization, but he did.

Marcello made it back to the United States by hook or crook and, literally, by the seat of his pants, and swore to even the score with Kennedy. He is said to have told three associates, "Don't worry about that little Bobby son-of-a-bitch. He's going to be taken care of." *(The English Godfather*, page 191).

(Who knows but that he might have! Possibly even both, Jack as well as Bobby.)

Senate investigators had not overlooked the fact that one of Madden's wires from Hot Springs' Ritter Hotel crossed over US government property, on the East side of Central Avenue, the National Park side, which was illegal. Owney could be prosecuted, fined, and even jailed if the situation was not quickly rectified. Transmitting gambling information from one state to another across federal government land might be exactly the lever Bobby Kennedy was looking for to get both the Hot Springs operation, run by Owney Madden and the New Orleans operation run by Carlos Marcello.

Owney called a meeting of all his bookmakers when he learned of the interest in the racing wire by Bobby Kennedy and suggested that they close down from August 5th as he believed a new law was about to be passed making race-wire services illegal. Faced with the prospect of a jail sentence in the winter of his years, Madden also made arrangements for his casino interests to be bought out.

The McClellan Subcommittee made it known (finally) that they were going to call Owney to testify before the Committee.

The *Arkansas Democrat* printed:

"Owen Madden, formerly of New York City, told our reporter he would tell the committee nothing. Hot Springs witness James Vitro, reportedly an employee of Madden's, also said he would not answer questions. The third witness was Julian Lytel of North Little Rock who, according to his attorney, would answer only to his name and address." — *Arkansas Democrat,* September 1, 1961.

And this is what they did (or did not do)! From the questions reportedly asked by McClellan, it would appear that neither he nor the Committee knew anything about the Hot Springs illegal operations other than the wire. Nothing about the gambling, prostitution and assorted other nefarious activities. Complete ignorance of the gambling, prostitution, and other nefarious activities even though the Senator was from a town about 84 plus miles from Hot Springs and had campaigned and gotten contributions from all over the State including Owney and Agnes Madden, Garland County and Hot Springs and logically from the racket fraternity.

The record would appear that the witnesses were asked *generic questions rather than specific questions* showing more illegal activity than the Madden wire across government property. The Committee seemed, by the questions asked, that they were on a fishing expedition and not much of one at that. Senator McClellan, for example, asked Mr. Madden about his citizenship. He surely knew whether Madden had been granted citizenship or not. If citizenship had been previously granted then the question was useless and begged to bring out an objection based on the Fifth Amendment against self incrimination. If he had not been granted citizenship they could have filed suit on that basis attempting to deport Madden immediately.

At the hearing in Washington, Senator McClellan began by asking Vitro and Madden to identify themselves. Each gave him their names and addresses. When asked several times about his occupation, Madden stated that he was retired for several years. McClellan asked him, "retired from what?" Madden pleaded the Fifth, stating:

"I refuse to answer on the grounds of ..."

Gaz. Sept. 1-61 Gambling

—AP Wirephoto

Arkansas Witnesses Remain Silent

James Vitro (left) and Owen (Owney) Madden (right), both of Hot Springs, sit before the Senate Investigations Subcommittee at Washington with their attorney, Charles Lincoln of Little Rock. Vitro and Madden declined to answer the Subcommittee's questions yesterday on the ground of possible self-incrimination.

Madden, Pal Plead Fifth As Probers Apply Heat To Hot Springs Gambling

From Gazette Press Services

Washington, Aug. 31.—Owen (Owney) Madden, an old New York mobster now in Arkansas, and James Vitro, his associate, invoked the Fifth Amendment today in a Senate investigation of gambling.

Madden, now 70 years old and hard of hearing, told the Senate Investigations Subcommittee he was retired. But he refused to say what he had retired from or whether he ran a horse race wire service at Hot Springs.

Lytle Silent On Race Wire At Little Rock

By JAY LEWIS

Gazette Washington Bureau
1203 National Press Building

Washington, Aug. 31.—C. Julian (June) Lytle of 5127 Broadway, North Little Rock, was called before the Senate Investigations Subcommittee which is investigating gambling but refused to answer any questions today. On the advice of his attorney, J. B. Dodds of Little Rock, he invoked the Fifth Amendment to avoid giving answers which he said might incriminate him.

The questions dealt with a racing news wire service, which Julian B. Adlerman, Subcommittee counsel, said was operated in Little Rock by Lytle and others. Such a wire service provides the information that a bookie must have to carry on his wagering business.

Lytle was asked if he operated the service at Little Rock in conjunction with Cecil B. Hill, Harold F. Dunaway and F. C. Barnett.

He was asked if he supplied racing news to the following persons: Junior Finley, Joe Wilson, Harry Vandergriff and Sloan Bennett.

Asked About 'Chase'

He was asked if he had been "chased around by the police in Little Rock" from one address to another. He was asked if he had had his place of business at one time or another at the following addresses: 1020 Main Street, 908 Main Street and 910½ Main Street, all in Little Rock, and 611½ East Washington Avenue, North Little Rock.

Lytle refused to say whether his principal business operation was a racing news service, or

(See LYTLE on Page 2A.)

Joseph Marcello and Joseph Poretto, Madden's reputed associate, refused to tell whether the Nola News in New Orleans was a cover for a race wire operation and supplied race results to Madden among others.

Leo C. Nulty, a Subcommittee investigator, testified that he had found records at Nola showing its gross income from 1954 through 1960, "ostensibly" from printing work, was $1,952,338.24. Yet, he

(Related Article on Page 12A.)

said, its expenditures for paper and printers ink in this period amounted to only $4,057.10, while its telephone bills totaled $30,933.36.

Stopped a Squeeze?

There were intimations in the hearing that Madden had gotten help from Chicago tough characters to prevent Poretto from taking over his operation.

Chairman John L. McClellan (Dem., Ark.) asked Poretto whether he knew Chicago mobster Murray (The Camel) Humphreys, and whether Humphreys had "told you to get out of Hot Springs and stay out."

Poretto said an answer to that might tend to incriminate him.

"Have you been back to Hot Springs since?" McClellan demanded.

An answer to this, Poretto said, might incriminate him, too.

Vitro refused to tell his occupation when called to the witness chair, but Madden, asked the same question, said "I'm retired. For quite a few years."

Retired 'From What?'

"From what?" McClellan asked.

"I refuse to answer," Madden said, then changed it to "respectfully decline to answer on ground it may tend to incriminate me."

He and Vitro both said they were hard of hearing.

Madden refused to say whether he once was "a resident of New

(See PROBE on Page 2A)

Madden and Pal plead the fifth, saying they would maintain silence ... and they did.

To which McClellan said, "I suggest you say 'decline to answer.'"

A freshman interrogator would recognize this as a softball question, designed to go nowhere and if answered would go nowhere. They could prove his bootlegging activities, his racket connections and enough other charges to spend days gathering testimony for his prosecution. But this was not to happen and you can draw your own conclusions as to why the appearance led nowhere.

Jerome Alderman then took over the questioning. He went through a series of questions asking Owney if he was a naturalized citizen, to which Owney objected as to relevancy. The questioning of Madden seemed and proved to go nowhere.

For the Internal Revenue Service, Michael Connaughton, testified as to how he had traced the wires from Hot Springs' Ritter Hotel with a telephone company lineman. It proved to be a long and often hazardous job, according to him, taking them over rooftops, through a forest and halfway up a mountain. The total amount of wire strung was at least a mile in length; and it was of the commercial type and not too suitable for outdoor wiring.

This hearing would have been a perfect time and place for the IRS to have presented tax records and related documents concerning the rackets and the racketeers. A number of other gangsters had been prosecuted on tax evasion charges; Al Capone and Tony Accordo, for example, and I feel sure they could have come up with sufficient evidence to at least raise a question about the Hot Springs rackets.

When Owney's testimony was over he caught a plane straight back to Arkansas. A reporter for the *Arkansas Democrat*, who had been covering the hearings, was also on the flight. When Owney climbed aboard and walked down the aisle, he passed Senator McClellan, who was already in his seat, buckling his safety belt. The two men smiled, shook hands and exchanged a few words together.

As Q. Byrum Hurst Sr., Owney's lawyer, put it, when asked about any blame put on McClellan by Owney, reported there were no hard feelings, "It wasn't McClellan's fault. It was young Bobby Kennedy that had done it." (Ibid, Page 193-194)

(That's what they call throwing good money after bad. Owney's trip to Washington and getting no more than his name and address for the expense and trouble, yet, no one seemed troubled by these developments. One good development was, though, that there were no hard feelings between Hot Springs "Boss Gambler" Madden and the well-known fearless crime fighter McClellan who got political campaign contributions sent to him from Agnes and Owney personally, bypassing the Democrat Party Committee of Garland County.)

Attorney General Kennedy said he could not believe that there was no connection between organized crime and Hot Springs gambling, but a review of the event seems to prove that the McLellan Committee was bound and determined to prove Bobby wrong. They had the FBI, IRS, INS and the entire weight of the United States government behind the efforts to prove him right, that there was a connection, but they failed miserably in proving anything.

Did anybody notice this lack of effort?

Lee Mortimer, in his *New York Confidential* column, wrote, "*I'm just wondering* (or am I being naïve?) why Senator McClellan of Arkansas never mentions Hot Springs, with its open gambling, slot machines and easy gals to entertain visiting Mafia and labor-union big shots from all over the country? They come to take the baths and reminisce with Owney 'The Killer' Madden. Hot Springs makes Saratoga in the old days look like piker money. The Springs is where the Boys cut up the rackets and assign the boodle that McClellan is investigating." (Ibid, page 190-196).

WERE THE "GOOD OLE' DAYS" GOOD OR BAD ... AND FOR WHOM?

Well, who did it hurt? It helped people keep their jobs while providing entertainment to the masses. How comfortable would those who say they would like it back like it was in the "old days" when they consider that their Chief of Detectives for their Hot Springs Police Department, Herbert "Dutch" Akers, said in a confirmed statement:

> *"When I decided to steal with the rest of them, I wasn't able to align myself for a 'cut-in' on the large money from the gamblers. So, I made mine from various other sources." — ("Hell in Hot Springs," Liberty Magazine, Part I, July, 1939)*

This statement by Akers was confirmed by one of the FBI Agents testifying in the Alvin Karpis harboring trial of Akers, and the Chief of Police and others later that year. The federal agent said Akers told him,

> *"I was totally honest when I went to work for the Hot Springs police force. I'm not the only officer in the United States to have gone crooked." — (New Era,* 26 October 1938, Testimony of FBI Special Agent E. J. Connelly.)

That's good, Dutch, and original. (Ed.)

Dutch Akers was right. He had lots of crooked company, and much of it right there in Hot Springs As a matter of fact, you could safely say, he was right again, It seemed all were crooked or worked alongside other crooked cops. Nine other officers, through a series of charges of protection, bribery, hindering apprehension of felons, and related crimes were dismissed from the force or went to the penitentiary. Dutch was bringing discredit even on this bunch.

Crabgrass, Again

The rackets enjoyed support and "some" from the state level.
Is that Governor Faubus behind that mask?

WHY PICK ON HOT SPRINGS?

Everyone seems to have overlooked Pulaski County.

Just as a matter of interest can someone explain this scenario as anything other than a "fix" from top to bottom:

1. Arkansas law forbids gambling of any kind;
2. Casinos are running in all parts of the state, Hot Springs, Little Rock, North Little Rock and elsewhere before 1967;
3. 800 plus slot machines are on locations in Arkansas for which the federal government collects taxes on an illegal activity;
4. More than 50 Arkansas bookies buy federal tax stamps;
5. Racing results from around the U.S. are collected in New Orleans by Mafia Capo Carlos Marcello, then sent to Hot Springs, Arkansas via telephone racing wire to Owney Madden, Boss Gambler, relayed to Hot Springs bookies and then sent by Madden via illegal telephone wire to Barney Levine, Boss Gambler of Pulaski County, Arkansas then sent to bookies in Pulaski County and elsewhere in Arkansas;
6. Arrest records indicate nothing more serious than sparse misdemeanor arrests and usual fines of less than $100 and these arrests occurring infrequently, maybe once every two or three years and then for only selected people;

As far as McClellan is concerned, it had been previously reported that he had received substantial campaign contributions from Owney and Agnes Madden. Could it be that he really wasn't a crusading crime fighter like so many believed? It especially raises a question when he didn't do more about illegal activities in Arkansas, almost in his back yard. Even in Pulaski County, the seat of state government, for some reason or another, he failed to root out crime, although it, too, was almost in his back yard.

New York newspapers, the *Times* and the *Daily News,* "descended" on Hot Springs and the *News* concluded that "Bubbles" was the biggest non-floating dice game in the land. They simply restated what the United States Department of Justice, J. Edgar Hoover, Bobby Kennedy and other lawmen had said on more than one occasion, "Hot Springs is the biggest illegal casino operation in America." Bobby Kennedy put the pressure on Governor Orval Faubus who ordered a close down of the games. (For a little while, until it cooled off!)

One response was from John Ermey, the Chief of Police and Owney's next door neighbor, who oversaw the return of the slot machines in 1967, who said, "The citizens of Hot Springs want an open town. We've had people run who want to close up, and they got beat."

The chief should know how the elections were won and he proved that he would go to any lengths (legal or not) to protect the rackets, like returning slot machines to the racketeers after, not only swearing that they had been destroyed, but getting other police officers to swear to the same thing. (But this was par for the course.) (Ibid, Page 196)

ARKANSAS DEMOCRAT

NINETY-EIGHTH YEAR

An Independent Daily and Sunday Newspaper

K. A. ENGEL, *Publisher (1926-1968)*

C. STANLEY BERRY, *Publisher* — MARCUS B. GEORGE, *Editor*

ROBERT S. McCORD, *Editorial Page Editor* — GENE HERRINGTON, *Managing Editor*

Page 6A — Wednesday, October 30, 1968

Mr. Good Guy

Maurice "Footsie" Britt is the Mr. Good Guy of the Republican party. Whether he s auctioning off strawberries in Bald Knob, advocating old-time patriotism in Hot Springs, or touring the tornado-damaged city eenwood, Britt presents a warm and ..n quality that people are attracted to.

For example, in the college straw-vote Britt has gotten more votes than even Gov. Rockefeller at five schools. Even the Democrats like him, as evidenced by the praising nd hand-shaking that he has received from le 35 Democratic senators, who are open- and fiercely hostile to the Republican par- and Gov. Rockefeller. People like Britt ecause he doesn't take himself too seriously - a characteristic that sets him apart from ost of the tight-lipped regulars around ov. Rockefeller.

While the job of lieutenant governor is rgely a ceremonial one, this doesn't mean at it can't be performed with decency and ith courage. Britt has demonstrated these ualities. He has apologized publicly when has been wrong — an almost unheardof ing for a politician to do. But at the same ne, he has refused to be backed-down either partisanship or crudity. Anyway, s pretty hard to intimidate a guy who has pro tball for the Detroit Lions and

And what a Lt. Governor! — The former all-American football player for the Arkansas Razorbacks, lineman for the Detroit Lions and the most decorated soldier in history who lost an arm in the second world war, has never lost his courage.

MOCRAT Price 15c

0, 1967 ★ ★ ★ ★

State Police Surprise Pulaski Gamblers; 12 Nabbed In Raids

Felony counts of "keeping a gambling house" were filed against 12 suspected Pulaski County bookies Saturday after State Police Director Lynn A. Davis directed raids on 11 places.

All were private homes except the Westwood Club, which has been padlocked several times in the past for the same reason. Owner K. Barney Levine, who once made a big show of turning his gaming room into a part of the nightclub, was among those arrested.

Police seized a quantity of gambling paraphernalia, including crap tables, boxes of dice and other items used in the conduct of a gambling business.

All of those arrested were freed after putting up $100 cash bonds.

Those arrested, their home addresses and the place where they were nabbed were booked as:

1. Sloan F. Bennett, 23 Brooklawn, Rte. 5, which is the Henson Loop Road.

2. Robert Raymond Bennett, 38, 2915 Dalewood, Rte. 5, Henson Loop Road.

3. Kenneth W. Matthews, 23, 6717 Ponderosa, 904 W. 25th, Apt. E, North Little Rock.

4. Kenneth Shelby Brown, 53,

(Related pictures on Page 2A)

211 W. 6th, North Little Rock; picked up at the same address.

5. Ralph H. Lafferty, Rte. 6, North Little Rock; picked up at the same address.

6. Ovid G. (Preacher) Mathis, 59, 11 Abby Lane, 12221 Col. Glenn Road.

7. Roger O. Treadwell, 29, 8 Delrose Drive, 9617 Base Line Road.

8. Raymond H. Kyzer, 61, 2719 High, 7201 Mabelvale Cutoff.

9. Granville D. (Sonny) White, 38, 4900 Westwood, 9617 Base Line Road.

10. Ed Herndon, 49, 6500 Highway 161, North Little Rock, picked up at the same address.

11. Joe T. Wilson, 54, 5108 H, Little Rock, 4712 Alpha, North Little Rock.

12. Levine, picked up at the Westwood Club.

Davis made a point of emphasizing that none of the addresses were in the Little Rock city limits, but five were in North Little Rock. The rest were outside both cities in the county rural area.

The raids were carried out by CID agents and other officers selected from various departments in the State Police, Davis said.

He added that the Pulaski County Sheriff's Office and the North Little Rock police were not consulted, nor did they participate in the raids, which began at 12:15 p.m.

In an unusual maneuver, Davis had all of the arrested sus-

Democrat O. D. Gunter

THEY RAN 'OUT OF THE MONEY'
. . . Levine (left); Treadwell (glasses), White (right)

Can you pick out the ASP CID Agent apart from the bookies? (Hint: It is the intelligent-looking man second from left, right behind Barney Levine.)

1967 — A MATTER OF SECURITY

It was pitch black outside my office at ASP Headquarters with no outside security light. Alone, except for radio operators in the rear of the building, I heard a knock on the office side door, one seldom if ever used. It was the weakest point of our security system, a simple single panel wooden door.

Making sure that my sidearm was handy (on my hip) I answered the knock and in walks one Gene Young, Governor Rockefeller's personal security chief, loyal to the bone.

Gene asked for a minute of my time, then walks over to the single wooden panel door, opens it and in walks a Texas lawman. I could tell he was a Texas lawman because he was about medium height, wearing cowboy boots, a ten gallon hat and one of the biggest sidearms I have ever seen. He was, I learned, the Chief of Police for San Angelo, Texas.

Following the lawman was obviously the honoree, Zakar Garoogian, in handcuffs and even more obviously nervous.

Zakar had been arrested in San Angelo planning or participating in a burglary. He claimed to be a member of the Dixie Mafia, a loose knit group of good old boys, and supposedly Southern bred, whose *modus operandi* consisted of pulling multiple burglaries in a single night in a small town, overwhelming the police department of that particular city.

Garoogian had convinced the Chief of Police that he had information that was worth a better deal on the charges which had been

WR Prefers That 'Unhealthy' Rumors Not Be Published

By GEORGE DOUTHIT
Democrat Staff Writer

Gov. Rockefeller said Saturday that all the rumors about threats on his life and sabotage "are not healthy" and he would rather see them terminated than published.

The governor, who returned at 2:30 a.m. Saturday from Palm Beach, Fla., and the Republican governors conference, also said he was still hopeful that the State Supreme Court will rule State Police Director Lynn Davis eligible but if it doesn't he will move in the special session to remedy the law blocking him.

Rockefeller called a press conference early in the afternoon at the mansion to talk specifically about events at the Republican governors conference and also to answer any questions on reporters minds about other subjects.

He said the Republican governors are convinced that sentiment in their states has not yet crystallized on the Republican presidential nomination and they didn't take a stand on it. They did emphasize that the Republican governors, with 26 in number, are now in the majority and that they should be allowed to play the leading role in developing the Republican platform next summer.

One item they discussed was the domestic policy as it relates to some 500 federal agencies doing business in the states, the governor said.

Asked about the extraordinary security measures around him at Palm Beach, the governor said:

"I evaluate it this way. If we have a visiting governor or senator in Arkansas, we always provide a state police escort. This is customary in other states. On the trip to Florida, because of the discussion about this, not only the state police but the sheriff's office and the city police were alerted.

"I don't know what all they did provide but I did not make any special request. Our state police suggested that Lt. Jim Ross go with us and until this situation is clarified, the state police will be anxious and cautious."

When can the press expect some kind of clarification of this whole business," one reporter asked. Rockefeller said:

"I have no way of knowing, but I can say this. The way Col. Davis is handling the situation at the present moment is the way it should be handled, on a professional basis. He is not giving me daily reports on what's happening and I am not asking for them."

See WR on Page 2

HOPEFUL ON DAVIS
. . . WR eyes remedy

Labor Fears Johnson Could Lose

AFL-CIO Plans Effort to Oust Conservatives

made against him. The information he had, supposedly concerned plans for the assassination of Governor Winthrop Rockefeller.

Garoogian, the Chief, and several others had come in a plane from San Angelo, Texas to Little Rock. I didn't know which plane or what plane, or any of the other particulars and didn't want to know. His mode of travel didn't matter; it was that he had come from Texas to Arkansas, supposedly voluntarily. I could imagine what his story would be, though, if he came to trial. Naturally he would plead that he was forced to come and he could hardly voluntarily agree to extradition from one state to another without more formality. Whether he agreed to come to Arkansas or not, it was a dangerous proposition. What if he came to trial in Arkansas? He would claim that he was unwillingly forced to come here and therefore he could possibly escape prosecution if he was charged here.

Was the story he told believable? Maybe, but most likely not and I was betting that it was not. He knew of no particulars, no names of participants, no times, and no circumstances which would lead me to believe that no real planning had been done to execute the Governor. I would stake everything on this being jailhouse talk, but each threat had to be fully investigated to determine if true or not. I have known of some of the most outlandish stories, completely unbelievable and not logical, turn out to be true.

But to publicize threats or rumors of threats was, in my opinion, a mistake. That kind of information simply caused more people to consider the deed.

For example, an engineer at one of the most sensitive United States Arsenals located in a northern state was convinced that J. Edgar Hoover had been kidnapped and was being held for ransom. He was so convinced of the truth of that scam that he contributed money to the ransom and even after we arrested the perps and he said he understood the scam, left a note on his refrigerator addressed, "Mr. Hoover, Help yourself to the cold cuts in the frig and I'll be home shortly." His "contact" convinced him that she was in touch with a special agent of the FBI and she communicated with him through a microphone concealed under the dashboard of her car.

We tapped his phone and electronically tied her phone to his, taking her telephone calls to him posing as a Chicago FBI agent, proving conclusively that it was a scam.

Now, here I am facing "The Killer" Garoogian. I asked Garoogian for names of people, times and places, none about which he could be specific, or even close to specific; more likely idle jailhouse talk.

Time, I suppose proved me right, because Win died quietly in his bed in 1973. A great man and a good friend to me and to Arkansas.

A VISITOR FROM THE EAST ... CHICAGO, THAT IS

The most serious threat I ever received was from Carlos, a Chicagoan with a record as long as my arm including an alphabet of assorted crimes up to and including contract murder.

Without revealing my sources I can tell you that our two crews met Carlos at the airplane terminal. He came off the plane and confidently went to the baggage check, but before he got even close, he passed the exit door which just happened to open as he was passing by. He was urged through the door and into a nondescript taxicab. One of his two new companions, as they pushed him into the back seat of the cab, stated something to the effect, "Let's take this one", loud enough that any bystander could hear, allaying any suspicion of foul play.

Carlos had little option. As a matter of fact he had none. He knew he was going for a ride and chances were good that he wouldn't be riding back on his way to safe haven.

Pulling out from the curb the cab went several hundred feet, stopped momentarily and picked up one other passenger, a young skinny guy, pleasant-looking, who looked a lot like me. When we didn't take the obvious road, right, to lighted downtown Little Rock but instead turned toward Scott, Arkansas, a dark swampy countryside, Carlos became quite concerned and began making threats when he realized who we were. (As well he should.)

When he asked if he was under arrest we told him we didn't think so. He asked a lot of questions concerning his future. He was assured that he would not have an opportunity to carry out any threats and that his future looked short. He believed a promise. He assured us that he would be able to identify us since we made no secret of our identity. We told him to take a good look at all of us and put in a good word for us. He didn't ask, with whom, but he got the gist of the conversation and became much more amenable within a few minutes—about the first time the cypress trees started appearing on the dirt farm road.

In Carlos' world it was not good news when your captors made no attempt to hide their identity. Obviously the captors normally would have no fear of identification as there would be no one to identify anyone. (Doesn't that make sense?) It did to Carlos.

The closer we came to Scott, the more swamps lit up by the moonlight began to flash by the car, and the more questions were asked between the occupants such as, "Is this the one?"

Carlos' bags were taken by a person who could have been Carlos if the question had ever arisen. The second car advised us by a "back channel" on the radio that we had not been followed from the airport and no one had raised a question. (Disinformation is sometimes preferable to leaving a hanging question, like, "What happened to that guy, my seat mate from Chicago who had so many interesting stories."

Among ourselves we agree that this particular swamp was where 'she' was at. Naturally Carlos wanted to know who "she" was, and when he realized where he was he knew he was no longer in Chicago, in the bosom of his friends.

When we casually mentioned that "she" was Beaulah Hogg, he seemed unable to resist asking who Beaulah Hogg was. We tried to explain to him that "she" was an alligator, probably our biggest, but not the only one. He seemed to question our veracity until finally, following the directions of one of my companions, we "found" the right swamp. Dark, crawly, murky water seeming to flow over your ankles, along with snakes, two pound frogs, lition ARKANSAS

ENTH YEAR—No. 66 Second-Class postage paid at Little Rock, Arkansas LITTLE ROCK, WEDNES

a

Jets
ed
s

U.S. Air
dumped
mbs today
nist build-
Cambodian
e North

ig strikes,
fortresses
of explo-
Communist
nd troop
ind three
of the Bu-
Camp 86

Commu-
illery at-
ie Ameri-
last week
h is only
Combo-
ong and
ops have
up in the
in Cam-

B52s un-
of bombs
nist an-
positions,
as along
rth Viet-
theast of
t at Con
tnamese
e from
long the

y again
after a
nmunist
acks. A
1st In-
in last
special
vo Com-
70 men
positions
the Bu

patrols
ing for
h Viet-
them
photo-
wound-

st Ger-
it oper-
years
in 1965
y. He
y frag-

Democrat

ACTION ANGERS GOV. ROCKEFELLER
. . . At jail press session with Davis

Murton Foe Won't Relent

A member of the State Prison board said today "under no consideration" will he approve Tom Murton as state prison superintendent, despite the urgings of Gov. Rockefeller.

The governor, who has said that Murton, superintendent at Tucker Prison Farm, is his choice for the top job, was scheduled to meet with the prison board later in the day.

Grady Woolley, El Dorado, the board member and strongest opponent of Murton, said when he arrived at the State Capitol today that the reasons he gave last week for not wanting Murton as prison superintendent still apply today.

Woolley today, however, went a little further and hinted that if Murton became prison superintendent that the board would not have much control over his actions. Woolley virtually said

Officers in Texas Probe Alleged Plot To Assassinate WR

By THE ASSOCIATED PRESS

An unidentified drifter being held in connection with a series of post office burglaries is being questioned in San Angelo, Tex., about an alleged plot to assassinate Gov. Rockefeller, The Associated Press learned Tuesday night.

Maj. Kenneth McKee, director of the Highway Patrol Division of the State Police Department, said he had learned of the purported plot about 6 p.m. Monday and that two State Police officers had been sent to Texas.

The AP learned that the two men were Maj. Bill Streubing and Capt. Buck Halsell, both of the State Police Department's Criminal Investigation Division.

State Police Director Lynn A. Davis, contacted at the Pulaski County Jail where he was imprisoned Tuesday after being held in contempt of court for

"That's the only thing I can think of that's important enough for anyone to want to kill me," Davis said.

Reports from San Angelo indicated that the recent gambling raids in Arkansas also may have been involved in the alleged plot against the governor.

The San Angelo Standard-Times, quoting "well-informed sources," reported today that high ranking Texas intelligence officers had spent most of Tuesday afternoon and night talking to the man in custody.

The man was quoted as telling police only that he had information about such a plot, the newspaper said.

Taking part in the investigation along with Streubing and Halsell, who arrived in San Angelo about noon Tuesday, are Dub Capran and Forest Burleson, two intelligence agents of mosquitos and every kind of creature one could imagine when they are going to take part in a "whacking."

When Carlos, walking about a foot off the mushy tarp of the musty swamp was returned to the car he understood the message he was to carry back "home" and he expressed his thankfulness many times over for his chance to return home.

The message was this: "If any thing happened to me, my family or Win Rockefeller and/or his family, retribution had already been assured, bought and paid for with bonus money in the bank for the successful mob whacker. We made sure he understood the message applied to any and everybody who had a connection and after we quoted a few names, I believe he was assured that we knew who and where.

(Anyone who might feel empathy for Carlos might consider the disregard he had for at least eighteen people, some good, some not so good, who had no chance for a full life. His contracts had no escape clause.)

Carlos never mentioned his guns, which we had intercepted, and he was obviously overwhelmed that he had a chance to see Chicago again and by the time he got there his pants were probably almost dry.

A DIME SAVES THE GOVERNOR ... AND OTHERS

Barely reported, if at all, was what I refer to as the Memphis Incident.

The Governor and a plane load of staff and others were descending to land his Falcon jet at the Memphis airport. More than a little concern was expressed when the landing gear failed to deploy. The wheels just refused to drop down regardless of the number of attempts.

Conferring with a number of people, the crew was still circling to use as much petrol as possible in case the solution couldn't be found. Even though there appeared to be no alternative but to do a belly landing, flat on top of the Memphis Airport runway, it came to someone that maybe the manufacturer might have some ideas.

Sure enough the crew was advised that under the carpet running down the center of the plane, there was, about halfway down the aisle a steel plate which when removed gave access to the landing gear and down there was a handle which could be used to crank down the landing gear.

Hallelujah, a great solution, just rip the carpet up and start screwdrivering before the petrol runs dry. Where is the screwdriver? Who has a screwdriver? The silence was deafening. This, not being a mile high garage, housing a handy screwdriver, brought on the attitude of close yet so far. Despair had not set in but it could be seen from there when the Governor, a World War II combat veteran, remembered that a dime sometimes fits a screw head.

It worked. The landing gear came down for a three point landing proving once again that you might not know where help is coming from, but ask for it anyway.

LYNN DAVIS

NOT SO GRAND JURY

Days before my appearance before the Pulaski County Grand Jury, the Prosecuting Attorney claimed to need the name of the informant who gave me the information which led to the arrest of the twelve Pulaski County bookies.

The Grand Jury could have only pleaded ignorance of the law, and, in this event, it would appear that neither the judge who had called the grand jury nor the Prosecutor had "read the law" and were, therefore, just as ignorant or they just didn't care. (And this is a compliment when you consider the usual treatment given to persons facing gambling charges in Pulaski County. Felonies were always reduced to misdemeanors and usually resulted in fines of $50.00 or less.

It was clear and had been for years that the bookies lead charmed lives. Their criminal records indicated that they had been arrested a total of 118 times for felonies, 112 of which were for bookmaking and related crimes, and all of the them had lead to no more than $100.00 fines. One of these was Barney Levine who not only was a leading bookie but owned the Westwood Club, one of the biggest casinos in Arkansas.

Due to the heat that we had applied the Westwood was closed and the gambling equipment had been stored. On our raid we found 30,000 pairs of dice emblazoned with the name "Barney." These were the same type in existence today but just happened to be found in conjunction with other paraphernalia. (I never did figure out why he would have that many dice. He must have found a real deal buying them in the bulk.) Barney and the boys got their horse racing results over the sports wire owned by Carlos Marcello, New Orleans' Mafia Capo which came to Owney Madden who subleased it by way of Hot Springs.

As I told my latest informant who cautioned me about the dangers involved in what they had planned for me brought me no more alert than I was already. In my opinion what he told me he knew first hand, that they were going to put me in jail if I refused to name my original Pulaski County informant, was crazy. Little did I know?

About two weeks later I received a subpoena to appear before the grand jury and breaking with my usual procedure, I told my wife at breakfast that morning that I might be in jail by that afternoon. She passed that "earth shaking news" off saying something like, "the judge would be crazy to do something like that." She took the news with about as much aplomb as she took some other stories I might tell, that is, not seriously. Very seldom did I confide in her, believing that the less she knew, the less she would worry, but in this case she knew this couldn't happen. (What a case of misjudgment!)

Here I am before the 16 people on the "grand" jury, tried and true citizens, who are, as reported by my "court informant," supposed to either get the name of my "bookie informant" or put me in jail. Seconds after being asked for the name of my "bookie informant" again and again and getting a refusal, the foreman of the grand jury couldn't wait to spring the trap. He said to the prosecuting attorney in a much practiced second grade sing song verse:

"If he will not tell us the name of his informant let's take him before the judge. The judge will make him tell."

Taking me before the circuit judge I again refused to reveal the name and he, in a "show of force," told his Bailiff to take me to the county jail and hold me until I purged myself and revealed the name. Before leaving with the Bailiff I would swear I told him that I wouldn't tell until hell froze over.

Gazette.

Little Rock Forecast
Cloudy and mild with a chance of rain. A high of 66 is forecast today and a low of 42 tonight. Yesterday's high was 56, the low 35.
(Weather Map on Page

DNESDAY, DECEMBER 6, 1967. 30 Pages ★ ★ ★ ★ 10 Cents

Davis Won't Name Gambling Informer, Is Jailed by Kirby

Staff Photo by Gene Prescott

Colonel Davis (right) was in a jovial mood just before entering the jail.

Judge Holds ASP Chief In Contempt

By GEORGE BENTLEY
Of the Gazette Staff

Circuit Judge William J. Kirby held Col. Lynn A. Davis, director of the State Police, in contempt of court Tuesday for refusing to answer "certain questions" asked firs[illegible] the Pulaski County Gra[illegible]y, then by Judge Kirby.

Judge Kirby ordered Davis held in the County Jail until he decides to purge himself of contempt by answering the questions.

Judge Kirby declined to reveal what the questions were. "That's the Grand Jury's business," he said.

The contempt citation was for refusing to name a confidential informant who gave information to the State Police that led to raids on alleged bookmaking activities in Pulaski County on September 9, Davis disclosed later Tuesday at a news conference that Governor Rockefeller called at the jail.

Eisele Pledges 'Sound' Action

G. Thomas Eisele, the governor's legal adviser, said action would be taken "on a sound and legal basis" in an effort to get Davis out of jail. This is expected to be in the form of a petition to the state Supreme Court to review the matter.

Davis was asked at the news conference if he planned to spend the night in jail. "I'm prepared to stay here, frankly, until hell freezes over," he replied.

Davis was taken to the jail at 1:30 p.m., four hours after the Grand Jury went into closed session in a conference room near Judge Kirby's chambers.

Davis, one of five witnesses subpoenaed to testify before the Jury, was the last to [illegible]led into the Jury room. [illegible]ry questioned him from [illegible] to 11:25 a.m., then instructed him to wait in the adjoining witness room.

The Jury remained in session during the noon hour, without calling any witnesses, but apparently sent word to Judge Kirby that his assistance would be needed, because Judge Kirby remained available in his chambers during this time. Prosecut-

Only 'Gamblers, Criminals' Can Be Pleased, WR Says

By ERNEST DUMAS
Of the Gazette Staff

"No one can be pleased but the gamblers and the hardened criminals," Governor Rockefeller said Tuesday of the arrest of his State Police director.

The governor was plainly enraged when he walked into the Pulaski County jail just before dark to visit with Col. Lynn A. Davis. He was stern and unsmiling when he and Davis met with newsmen 20 minutes later in a conference room at the jail.

Mr. Rockefeller interrupted a speaking trip in Northwest Arkansas to fly back for the meeting. He said he returned "to express my moral support to Colonel Davis and to express the full support of my administration."

He said he considered the jailing of Davis to be political harassment, directed at both him and Davis.

"I find it hard to believe otherwise," he said.

Mr. Rockefeller previously has praised Davis for directing raids on gambling spots in Garland and Pulaski Counties.

He said he was shocked and saddened by the jailing and that he was worried about the impact on the state, especially on impressionable young people.

Governor Rockefeller and Davis said at the news conference that the ground for Davis being jailed was his refusal to tell the Grand Jury the names of the person who gave the information to Davis that led to State Police raids on 11 alleged bookmaking operations in Pulaski County on September 9.

The governor defended Davis' refusal to identify his confidential informant.

"We know that the prerogatives of law enforcement people have been drastically reduced in recent years," Mr. Rockefeller remarked. If they are required now to identify the confidential sources of their information, their jobs will be made even harder, he said.

"Releasing the names of informants will absolutely demoralize law enforcement officers in the United States" and lead to anarchy, the governor said. Davis added that it would "put every law enforcement officer in the nation out of business."

'War on Crime' Nets Davis and 2 Others

Mr. Rockefeller said, "Colonel Davis and two reporters are the

Davis Sleeps on Pink Sheets But Lacks Other Comforts

Col. Lynn A. Davis was given a more private cell than

Not Without Backing

AT THE JAIL HOUSE DOORS OPEN WIDE

The Judge's bailiff, who was months later attacked and knifed while taking a prisoner to the Pulaski County Jail, said to me on the way through the tunnel leading to the jail, that he wanted me to know that he had nothing to do with this thing. This statement made me walk at least a foot taller.

When we got to the jail very few reporters were present but once we got inside being booked in, every camera and reporter within a hundred miles (*or so it seemed*) wanted something to film, my leaving the courthouse going to jail. They had not anticipated the judge would direct us to leave by the way of the back door, and to go through the tunnel, which led from the courthouse to the jail. Anything to thwart their getting pictures of my being jailed. That way, the press wouldn't get moving pictures of my being held by the "profiteers" or so they hoped.

The Pulaski County Sheriff, while I was being booked in, called me aside and told me that the press wanted him to bring me outside and then he would lead me up the steps to the jail so they could get some film of the event.

I told the Sheriff that I had no objection if that was what he wanted to do, but, if I were him, I would check with some of my political advisers to find out if they wanted him to be filmed jailing the Director of the Arkansas State Police. Turning around he took about one step and turned back saying as if in shock, "Why, of course, I don't want to do that."

All I did, in effect, was to remind him that they may lose, and he would be the one who would be remembered as "the officer who turned the key" to lock the cell door and that his criminal friends would throw him to the wolves if it came to that.

My cell was standard garden-variety jail cell space—surely nothing you would want your mother to see you in for real. I sent word to the Major, who was my assistant, that I needed him to send someone to my house to get some sheets.

Shortly after reaching my humble abode, my own personal jail cell, I called Sue, my wife, telling her that I was in jail and needed some sheets and covers for my bed. Sure enough she said, "Where are you, really?"

That's my wife. Frugal as she is, she sends some pink sheets that her mother had given us for our wedding back in 1952, about fifteen years before.

A JAIL, A BUNK AND PINK SHEETS

My jailing had a certain touch of "Ned and the Primer," (a grade school "reference book" for the first grade.)

What I had been told would happen, did.

The message I got from the informant who met almost daily with the Circuit Judge, was that the Judge was going to have the Pulaski County Prosecuting Attorney call me before the Grand Jury, and if I refused to name the informant who had furnished evidence which had led to the arrest of the 12 bookies in Pulaski County he would hold me in contempt of Court and incarcerate me in the Pulaski County Jail. I was supposed to stay there until I "purged" myself by naming the informant. This same treatment had been given to two newspaper reporters who refused to name their contacts for a story on corruption in Pulaski County.

Sure enough, I expressed to my source that the Circuit Judge would be crazy to jail the Director of the Arkansas State Police, the highest-ranking police officer in the state. I expressed to him that I believed that would be the straw that broke the camel's back, so to speak. Bookmaking and casino gambling had been a staple of the state and the state government as long as I could remember. It was true what the United State Department of Justice said about Hot Springs. It was the biggest illegal casino operation in America. What they either didn't know or didn't say out loud was that Hot Springs was not alone in promoting gambling operations.

J. Edgar Hoover, it is said, railed against the absence of sensitive information on Owney Madden, sure that he was involved in racketeering, but he wasn't able to prove it conclusively. The emphasis was obviously on Owney and Hot Springs, not Pulaski County.

Knowing Mr. Hoover, having worked for him for 6½ years, and his insistence that it be done his way and *now*, I can imagine the heat he must have brought on the agents assigned to Madden's case. If I were to guess, I would guess that he suspected the political power that the gangsters had, but would not have known for sure just how high that political influence went or if he did, he was, even with his power, unable to remedy it.

I might be mistaken but I can't believe that Mr. Hoover didn't try to root out the mob and the "mob" included our homegrown mob, the "Little Combination," and their influence in Little Rock as well as Hot Springs. At one time he sent 52 agents to Garland County to work on Owney and his crew.

About two weeks later, after being told of the plans for my jailing I got a call from the Pulaski County Prosecuting Attorney saying that a subpoena for my appearance before the Grand Jury would be served on me the next day. I told the Prosecutor that the subpoena would be unnecessary, and that I would appear at any time and any place he wanted. But he said he would send one anyway. (They couldn't afford to have it appear that I was cooperating!)

Well, that was one of the many times I have been proven to be wrong—the judge being crazy. The next day I received a subpoena just like the Prosecutor had said. He must be crazy, too, I thought. How wrong can one be in matters of life? I have always approached life in a not too serious manner. Normally my wife never had any idea of some of the things I did on the job while I was a Special Agent with the FBI and this attitude did not change when I came to the State Police.

I later found that a subpoena was always issued in cases like this. In this way the person coming before the grand jury can be made to look like he is only coming because he was made to come by order of the Circuit Judge.

After my appearance before the Grand Jury, I was taken before Judge Kirby in his chambers, and told I would be in contempt of court until I "purged" myself by giving him the name of my informant and when I refused he ordered me taken to the Pulaski County Jail. But not before I told the Judge that I wouldn't tell until hell froze over. (Said with a smile on my face after being sentenced to jail.)

However, believe it or not, I didn't believe the extent of the corruption until I saw it myself. I did believe, however, that retribution would not take long, which I later found to be true. The question was, retribution for whom, me or them,

CELL MATES, BISCUITS AND GRAVY AND MAYBE JIMMY CAGNEY?

Cellmates? Maybe, sure, that's it—Jimmy Cagney. Can't you just hear Jimmy cocking his ear when he hears scratching near the slammer's kitchen directly across from my cell giving myself and Jimmy a perfect view of the flour barrel. The inmate cooks, of course, didn't go to the trouble of putting the lid on the 25 pound flour barrel. They were only interested in cooking blackeyed peas and biscuits, dishing out meals, morning, noon and night and counting the days they had to spend in that hell hole before they could get their adult beverage of choice.

When Jimmy looks out from between the bars, the scratching stops, leaving only a cloud of flour floating in the walkway between the cells and the kitchen. Jimmy eases over to the side of his six by eight hole again and again hears scratching and at the same time sees a dead giveaway, clouds of white flour drifting down the hall. Not wanting to miss a good jailbreak through the hole somebody might be making, he looks out over the hallway and sees the cloud of flour coming from the flour barrel and at the beginning of the cloud of flour he sees a mouse no bigger than a minute. At the same time he hears and sees a portly guard ambling or slowly shuffling down the hallway.

Jimmy, also known as "Widowmaker Willy," shouts out (as it goes in good stories), "You dirty rat."

This outburst is meant only to scare Biscuits, a name I had selected for my mouse because of his propensity for flour. Willy's shout is meant only to alert Biscuits to the danger of the screw's appearance giving Biscuits time to hide. The alert comes just in time giving Biscuits a reprieve from discovery. He simply hunkers down covered with flour blending in to tomorrow's biscuits and gravy. The "screw" (commonly known to be a guard, except by us in the Fictional Crime Writers Club) whistles at one of the cooks, and pointing to the platter on top of the stove takes a sausage biscuit from the best cook they have had in thirty days.

The screw had gone no more than half past the kitchen when he finished the sausage and biscuit and signaled his wanting a second one. My imagination has faded away as "Widowmaker Willy" did, in due time, but, in reality, I now have two mice. (Promise, stir crazy? Maybe.) The names, Biscuits and Gravy, seemed appropriate. There was only one mouse, then when I looked again there were two. I can assure you Biscuits and Gravy were real, but "Willy" was evidently a figment of my imagination, and at least didn't leave jail with me the next morning. (At least I think he was not on the booking sheet.)

I took comfort in the thought that Biscuits and Gravy, my pet mice, could, I am sure, have left at any time they wanted. It's just that they didn't want to leave. Where else could they find warm shelter, having almost anything they wanted to eat anywhere at any time? Where else would they find a barrel of white flour with the top off? Not in the mid 1960's.

I had no idea that there would be so much support, but no matter what, I believed what I told the Judge, "I won't tell you the name of my informant until hell freezes over." I had it straight from experience that it didn't matter whether the grand jury knew who my informant was or not. They weren't going to show any appreciable difference in their MO (*modus operandi* - method of operation) anyway. The grand jury was going to act as they always had for at least fifty years. This might have been somewhat over the top, but I believed it then, and I believe it now.

I shall never forget the Arkansas Baptist Association, and congratulations and offers of support from many churches of all denominations, preachers, police officers and individuals who wrote letters of support, to me and to the newspapers. Being a police officer and being known for going to jail to protect an informant, yielded an avalanche of information from other folks, information on which I depended and used in some of our raids.

Reaction Against Jailing Davis Mounts

Reaction to the jailing of Col. Lynn A. Davis mounted Wednesday — all of it condemning the move and commending the State Police director for his "courageous effort" at enforcing the law.

Forty-eight persons by mid-afternoon had signed their names to a statement that was to be sent by telegram to Governor Rockefeller following Colonel Davis' release by the Supreme Court.

Most of the signatures were collected after a meeting of a West Little Rock civic club. The club's rules forbid political activity and the members and others signed as individuals.

"We commend Colonel Lynn Davis for his courageous effort in law enforcement in Arkansas," the telegram said, "and we deplore the jailing of the head of the State Police for his refusal to divulge the identity of informants in the pursuit of his duties.

"It seems disrespectful for a man of his position and integrity to suffer the embarrassment of confinement and we ask those reponsible for reconsideration and his release."

The group's statement said the incident focused additional national attention on the city and state and that the resulting "poor publicity ... continues to lend credence to those who would belittle us in the eyes of the world."

LR Photographer Circulates Statement

The statement was circulated by Greer Lile, a photographer, who said it was "time for us to stand up and be counted." Lile originally said the plan was to print the statement and signatures in newspaper advertisements but the telegram to Governor Rockefeller was substituted after Davis' release.

Lile said the statement was not intended to imply any disrespect for the Pulaski County Grand Jury, which had Davis jailed for refusing to disclose the name of an informant whose information had led to State Police gambling raids in Pulaski County. "The point of law is something we didn't want to get into," Lile said. "The actual jailing is what was critical to us who signed the petition."

Seven Ministers Issue Statement

A similar statement was issued by seven Baptist ministers, also acting individually. They commended Davis for his "courageous effort in law enforcement in Arkansas and particularly in the cleaning up of illegal gambling" and deplored jailing him for refusal to divulge the identity of informants "in the pursuit of his duties as a law enforcement officer." The signers were Rev. S. A. Whitlaw, Rev. W. Harold Hicks, Rev. W. O. Vaught Jr., Rev. Lawson Hatfield, Rev. Jerre Hassell, Rev. R. H. Dorris and Rev. Erwin L. McDonald.

Mr. McDonald, editor of the Arkansas Baptist Newsmagazine, earlier Wednesday had gone to the County Jail with Representative Paul Meers and Dr. Tom Logue, both of Little Rock, and visited briefly with Davis to tell him of their support in person and to express their appreciation for his service to the state.

Mr. McDonald said Davis was brought from his cell to a conference room for the visit. The visitors left him magazines and a box of candy.

A spokesman at Immanuel Baptist Church, of which Mr. Vaught is pastor, said that about 400 people who attended the church's Wednesday night prayer meeting unanimously adopted a resolution commending Davis and deploring "the type of interpretation of the law that places the state's highest law enforcement officer in jail while at the same time known gamblers and racketeers are allowed to violate the law and to go unpunished." It said that if such practices continue, "our whole democratic form of government will be in jeopardy." Mr. Vaught said that he and a group of his Church members prepared the resolution.

CUAG Chairman Deplores Situation

James B. Gannaway, a Little Rock lawyer, who is chairman of Churches United Against Gambling (CUAG), issued a statement on CUAG's behalf which said that "citizens of Pulaski County are justifiably amazed that newspaper reporters and the director of the State Police are jailed while year after year well-known gamblers and bookies of this county whose names appear periodically in the newspapers as having been arrested again and again for gambling activities go free and hurry back to their trade."

Gannaway called the situation "extremely deplorable" and urged "immediate remedial action."

"Since Sheriff [B. Frank] Mackey, Prosecuting Attorney [Richard B.] Adkisson and Judge [William J.] Kirby are the three officials most intimately connected with law enforcement in Pulaski County, surely one or more of them must be in a position to suggest corrective measures. It would be most appropriate for these officials to make any such suggestions to the public without delay."

The Young Republican Club of State College of Arkansas at Conway issued a statement Wednesday supporting Davis and saying that Judge Kirby's action "serves only the welfare of those criminals already in prison and those under search by state law officials."

Television Poll Supports Davis

KARK-TV Channel 4 asked its viewers Tuesday night whether they thought the police should be required to identify their informants. More than 5,000 had responded by 10 p.m. but a tabulation of the votes at 9:30 p.m. showed 3,583 responding negatively and 1,188 saying yes — a negative response of 76 per cent.

Radio Station KLRA broadcast an editorial reflecting the station management's official position on the jailing of Davis, which it said had resulted in "the entire nation again laughing at Arkansas."

It also noted that Davis and two newsmen were the only ones who had yet spent a night in jail in the gambling crackdown of recent months.

"The point is well-taken," the editorial said. "These three individuals are the only ones who have been jailed for any length of time. Their jailing came on contempt of court charges, something for which bond is not available.

"Those who have been arrested in the gambling crackdown have remained in jail only long enough for their lawyers and bondsmen to quickly get them out, if they were ever, actually, inside a jail cell at all."

The station subscribed to Governor Rockefeller's statement that the question of law was one that could be resolved in some less dramatic way.

Calls Inundate The Courthouse

Courthouse officials were inundated with telephone calls Wednesday.

Judge Kirby's office received numerous anonymous calls, apparently all condemning Davis' jailing.

Sheriff Mackey said the numerous calls he had received were critical of Kirby. One caller identified himself as Clarence Smith and offered to take Davis' place in the cell, at a fee of $1 a year, which he said he would waive. The sheriff explained that this could not be done without a court order.

The prosecuting attorney's office also was flooded with calls, critical of Adkisson.

Colonel Davis himself was the recipient of many expressions of support. He showed newsmen at the Supreme Court hearing a sheaf of telegrams and special delivery letters from local and national areas, including many from directors of state police departments of other states and from his former associates in the FBI, all supporting him.

One woman delivered a fruitcake to him at the jail and someone else brought him flowers.

—Staff Photo by Larry Obsitnik

Colonel Davis shows stack of messages.

Davis

(Continued from Page 1.)

point. Adkisson said that he found two court decisions in other states dealing with the issue and he said that both were in favor of disclosure.

Eisele handed the Court what he said was a list of 15 to 20 court decisions in other states that he said upheld Davis' stand. Eisle said that one of the cases referred to by Adkisson involved a private investigator and was not in point.

Davis later came to the Capitol and met newsmen in Governor Rockefeller's reception room. Davis exhibited a stack of telegrams he said came from well wishers in Arkansas and across the nation. He said that

From the People

Reaction to Col. Davis's Jailing

To the Editor of the Gazette:

One always places himself in the position of an egotistic neophyte when he attempts to express himself on the actions of another, particularly when he is not completely informed as to the merits or demerits of the action taken. However, I feel compelled to place myself in this position as a result of the recent decision by Circuit Judge William J. Kirby to incarcerate our State Police Director, Col. Lynn A. Davis. I hasten to admit again that I am uninformed as to both sides of the issue; but according to the information available through the various news media, it appears that Judge Kirby's action was taken as a result of Mr. Davis's refusal to answer a certain question asked him by the Pulaski County Grand Jury.

Although Judge Kirby's decision might have been in accordance with "due process," as an ordinary and uninformed member of the electorate it seems to me there must have been an alternative that would have prevented the casting of the issue into the crucible of public debate.

For the past several years Arkansas and its citizens have worked diligenty to improve our image throughout the country, and then Judge Kirby and other representatives (Prosecuting Attorney Richard B. Adkisson and the Pulaski County Grand Jury) of the Judiciary Branch, with decisions such as this one, do more to destroy and tear down our image in one decision than all of us, in years of work, have done to build it up.

It is indeed a dark day in our history when actions and decisions are based more on political affiliations and political obligations rther than what is right and just for our state or country as a whole. When our Grand Juries persecute those responsible for enforcing the law, certainly the demise of our "system" is in sight.

My sincere hope is that something can be done to rectify this ridiculous situation, and perhaps erase part of the smear that has been cast on our great state and its citizens.

Rick Campbell.

Little Rock.

* * *

To the Editor of the Gazette:

In regard to Colonel Davis's arrest I wish to say it is a

(Communications on any subject are welcome. Letters should be under 500 words and typewritten if possible. All letters are subject to editing. Each letter must be signed although signatures will be withheld on request. No published letters will be returned. No un-published letters will be returned unless self-addressed envelope is enclosed.—Editor.)

shame for our officials to have our law enforcement officers jailed for enforcing the law. About the only way to clear the mess up is to defeat Judge Kirby and his backers at the election box. Truly it hurts some of the die-hards so bad to see a Republican in office that they would go to any means for their own political power.

Joe J. Hobbs.

Poughkeepsie.

* * *

To the Editor of the Gazette:

Circuit Judge Kirby and Prosecuting Attorney Adkisson should be tarred and feathered for their action against Col. Lynn A. Davis.

This writer, about to leave the state for several months, is removing from his auto every idenification that might show he came from it, including the securing of new license plates from another state before leaving.

A. S. Bernard.

Malvern.

* * *

To the Editor of the Gazette:

It is a matter of intense shame to this citizen that State Police Director Lynn Davis has been treated so contemptibly. Though the term contempt has been used to describe his actions on withholding certain information, I submit that it is much more appropriate for the petty persons who were responsible for placing him in jail. I am filled with frustration and dismay that such things can still occur in Arkansas.

J. C. A.

Little Rock.

* * *

To the Editor of the Gazette:

Arkansas need not hang its head in shame, it should now raise the head in a spirit of resurgent pride!

In which of the 50 states do we find a state Police director who is fully dedicated to true law enforcement, and the destruction of organized crime? ARKANSAS! In which of the states are wealthy, organized, politically entrenched criminals being hit broadside? ARKANSAS! In which state can a citizen give information to the highest police officer in the state, against organized crime, with full assurance that he will be insulated against criminal reprisal? ARKANSAS! In which state can a father smile with approval upon hearing his son say, "When I grow up I want to be like our police director"? ARKANSAS!

Arkansas has stepped into the forefront of the fight against organized crime; it has started hitting the places that has bred total disrespect for law among the poor for years. Arkansas has, by its actions, said that it preferred the world to know that it was purging organized crime ..., rather than giving silent approval to it! Arkansas has said to the world that it believes that it is more honorable to admit a bad past and correct it than to have a bad past and perpetuate it under wraps! Arkansas has a right to be proud!

James E. Shock.

Enola.

* * *

To the Editor of the Gazette:

Surely there are legal procedures that Judge Kirby could have utilized to test the right of Colonel Davis to withhold confidential information, without having him placed in jail. The issue at stake is one that deserved a more dignified approach. A move for his impeachment would not be out of order.

I am not in position to pass judgment upon all of Governor Rockefeller's actions as governor, but if he continues to appoint men to head the departments of government who are as efficient and courageous as Colonel Davis has thus far proven to be, I shall be in favor of keeping him in the governor's office.

S. A. Wiles.

Malvern.

* * *

To the Editor of the Gazette:

My husband and I tour quite a bit and when I am out of state I am always proud to say "I am from Arkansas." After reading the morning paper (December 6) when they put the director of the State Police in jail, now I will say, "I'm from Texas."

Busch Baker.

North Little Rock.

From the People

The Arrest of the Top Policeman

To th Editor of the Gazette:

The jailing of the director of the Arkansas State Police on Tuesday, December 5, on charges of contempt of court, will surely be recorded in legal history as the greatest travesty of justice in our time. It is obviously nothing more than another attempt to ridicule the governor and, on that basis alone, must be condemned by all who regard the courts as the seat of justice and mercy.

The event of Tuesday caps a long series in recent Arkansas political history designed to harass the Republican governor but with the undesirable side effect of embarrassing the state in every quarter. The leading officials of the Democratic Party, with notable exceptions, seem obsessed with their task of total harassment of the governor both personally and as governor, completely disregarding the fact that the man was elected to the office by a majority of the people of Arkansas.

In the early summer elections of 1967, the Gazette lamented the fact of the office of governor of Georgia being filled by Lester Maddox and, commented to the effect that "surely, the state of Georgia had now become the laughing stock of the nation". May I now submit that, the state of Arkansas, at the hand of a few Democratic office holders possessed with petty jealousies, has replaced the state of Georgia, if in fact that sovereign state ever had the dishonor, as the laughing stock of the nation.

Charles R. Alford.

LittleRock.

* * *

(Communications on any subject are welcome. Letters should be under 500 words and typewritten if possible. All letters are subject to editing. Each letter must be signed although signatures will be withheld on request. No published letters will be returned. No un-published letters will be returned unless self-addressed envelope is enclosed.—Editor.)

To the Editor of the Gazettt:

Re: Statement page 2A, Dec. 6, 1967, Arkansas Gazette, by State Representative Paul Meers.

How faith-building to find a politician with the courage of his convictions.

Independent Voter.

Marshall.

* * *

.To the Editor of the Gazette:

It is my opinion that the arrest of Mr. Lynn Davis, head of the Arkansas State Police, is but proof of the lack of cooperation from various agencies of state government toward Mr. Rockefeller's appointment by this act. Unless Colonel Davis is given a certain amount of cooperation by other departments of state government, the public will naturally get a faulty impression of his success in cleaning up corruption in the state. I raise my voice, therefore, in praising the work this man has done in the short time he has held his position as head of our State Police.

Governor Rockefeller voiced his concern in an interview shortly after Davis's arrest that the young people of the state might change in their respectful attitude toward him. I hold that this incident will not deflate our interest and support of him, but will only serve to strengthen it, giving basis to the poppular idea of the unfairness shown him by other "men in Arkansas law."

Arkansans might remember that it was their vote that counteracted legalized gambling in this state. Therefore, it is the responsibility of our enforcement agency to prevent its occurrence in our state. This must be done by means our police deem best. It can not be rational of us, therefore, to lose faith in Colonel Davis and his diligent men. Mr. Davis is not a fugitive, so why should we question his professional ethics? If anything has resulted from his arrest it is that he is now a martyr to the young people of Arkansas. And this is how I, as a young person, can show him and all other Arkansans that he has our support

Dan B. Farley.

Hendrix College.

* * *

To the Editor of the Gazette:

I just wanted to say congratulations to Colonel Davis on his stand.

Colonel Davis appears to be doing a good job and a long needed one.

Mrs. R. C. Hannay.

Little Rock.

Left A Deep Impression—

COLONEL LYN DAVIS, sagacious new director of the Arkansas State Police, is an impressive, convincing speaker who doesn't need or use notes to say what is on his mind.

He talks like a man who knows his business, law enforcement — who knows what the Arkansas State Police needs in order to become one of the best police forces in the nation. And he apparently has the determination to work toward that goal.

He makes it plain, however, that the State Police Department cannot be enlarged and improved without better support from the public — unless law-abiding residents demand that the Legislature provide better financial support for this law enforcement agency.

After hearing Colonel Davis, forthright speech, members of the Management Club of the Batesville Manufacturing Club obviously were impressed by this man who seemingly is of the highest caliber in his field.

Even though Colonel Davis was born, reared and educated in Arkansas, Gov. Rockefeller was criticized for appointing him to the position because he was living in California (as an FBI agent). Nonetheless, a great many Arkansans (excluding Hot Springs gambling interests) are beginning to realize that Rockefeller made a wise choice, notwithstanding that Davis' residency requirements are being challenged.

And That's The Way It Is—

ONE OF our rural correspondents sent in this clipping:

Every town has a liar, a bluffer, a sponger, a smart aleck, a richman, some pretty girls, a girl that giggles, a weather prophet, a neighborhood feud, two or three lunatics, a woman that tattles; a man who knows it all; more loafers than it needs; men who see every dog fight.

A boy who cuts up in church; some man who makes remarks about women; a grown man who laughs at everything he says; and only one man who doesn't know how to run a newspaper — he's the editor.

A Few Footnotes—

COLONEL DAVIS' sense of humor crops up frequently in the course of his public speaking. While talking about Arkansas State Police budget problems, he commented: "We can't predict how many inmates escape from Cummins and goings."

Incidentally, the Management Club of the Batesville Manufacturing Club is composed of 83 men and one woman.

BATESVILLE
sip mills oftentin
such as the one
School the other
between two boy
schools all over t
I mention the
twisted and false
rounds.

Time to Trav
ACROSS

Enforcing Laws

On the recent wave of law enforcement in the state.

Arkansas Union Labor Bulletin: The new state police director, Lynn Davis, has shown us that, after all, the law can be enforced.

His method is candid; his approach, direct.

It is a new experience to most of us. The state police had in recent history been only a company of traffic cops. They are now concerned about other law violations. * * *

Rev. Erwin L. McDonald in the **Arkansas Baptist Newsmagazine:** * * * The burning of the three truckloads of gambling equipment seized sometime ago by Col. Lynn Davis and his State Police, and this at the order of Hot Springs city officials, is enough to make everybody, including the gamblers, prick up their ears. At least here are considerable gambling devices, variously estimated to be worth between $15,000 and $70,000, that will not be back in operation again, now or ever.

The real cause for rejoicing is not that certain business places have been raided and certain illegal equipment has been destroyed, but, rather, that the substantial citizenry is finally asserting a leadership to make Hot Springs and Arkansas the great city and the great state that they have every right to become. * * *

The Denver Post Dec. 6, 1967

Police Head Jailed Over Name Silence

By ROBERT L. SHAW
LITTLE ROCK, Ark. — (AP)

HARASSMENT
Rockefeller said he believed the jailing of the 32-year-old

INTERNATIONAL ASSOCIATION OF CHIEFS OF POLICE, INC.

1319 EIGHTEENTH STREET, N.W. • WASHINGTON, D. C. 20036 • AREA CODE 202—TELEPHONE 265-7227

QUINN TAMM
Executive Director

December 8, 1967.

Director Lynn A. Davis
Arkansas State Police
P.O. Box 1751
Little Rock, Arkansas 72201

Dear Director Davis:

The Division of State and Provincial Police would like to express our congratulations and support for your position in refusing to disclose the name of an informant.

We commend you for your stand and offer the assistance of the Division of State and Provincial Police in whatever manner you deem necessary.

Sincerely,

Will Bachofner

Will Bachofner,
Chairman, Division of
State and Provincial
Police

To the Editor of the Gazette:

The Democratic Party appears to have found the sure way to lose friends and need acquaintances.

Our Governor Rockefeller is being exposed to a lot of dirty politics, but, other than running a little fever once in a while, he shows the possibility of becoming the best governor Arkansas has had in 12 years.

Ex Democrat.

Little Rock.

★ ★ ★

To the Editor of the Gazette:

The jailing of Colonel Davis of the Arkansas State Police was nothing more than a cheap political gesture.

Judge Kirby should be impeached, if that is possible under an outmoded set of laws in this state. On the other hand the decent people of the state resent his action as it has highlighted throughout the nation why Arkansas is thought of as a backward state — to be avoided by big business.

Governor Rockefeller has done more to give the state dignity, integrity and honesty in government than any governor it has ever had and if this writer were he, I would say to hell with it and hand it back to the spoilers.

Name Withheld.

Hot Springs.

★ ★ ★

To the Editor of the Gazette:

Mr. James E. Shock listed four good reasons why Arkansas can be proud of Col. Davis's intrepid and correct action in protecting his source of information. A fifth question he might have asked is: In what state do law enforcement officers have to contend with unfriendly and obstructive tactics

(Communications on any subject are welcome. Letters should be under 500 words and typewritten if possible. All letters are subject to editing. Each letter must be signed although signatures will be withheld on request. No published letters will be returned. No un-published letters will be returned unless self-addressed envelope is enclosed.—Editor.)

of certain court judges and Grand Jury members?

We who try to go about our business of providing for our families and earning money to pay taxes look on such shackling tactics as the ones exercised last week by the Grand Jury and judge with fearful apprehension.

Name Withheld.

Fayetteville.

★ ★ ★

To the Editor of the Gazette:

Every gangster in the country must have been able to sleep a little better while Arkansas State Police Director Lynn Davis was incarcerated in jail.

My sympathy is extended to Mr. Davis and all the ideals for which he stands. It is apparent to every honest citizen in the United States that Governor Rockefeller's efforts to bear down on organized crime are being circumvented.

It is impossible to comprehend how any jurist could completely forsake the administration of justice and invoke his personal wrath upon a highly qualified, competent police executive like Director Davis. It appears to the country that the judge in this case has taken his vengence out on all the honest, Godfearing citizens of Arkansas. After all, the actions of the State Police are just an expression of the responsible segment of Arkansas's people.

This letter is submitted in the interest of justice and with the hope that no honest society will stand idly by and permit a policeman to be indiscriminately jailed for executing his duties.

Duane H. Lowe.

Sacramento, Cal.

★ ★ ★

To the Editor of the Gazette:

The letters column has recently been filled with angry missals aimed at Judge Kirby and the Grand Jury for the incarceration of Col. Lynn Davis.

It's time something nice was said about the judge. It's through the efforts of such men as Judge Kirby and the three Faubuses on the Penitentiary Board that we can realize what we got rid of last November after 12 years.

Now that there is a new administration with bright, new, and competent faces, such antics stick out like a sore thumb. The die-hard hold-overs attempt to hang on to an era fast on its way to a well-deserved oblivion. The people, who have now had a taste of how it could have been all along, are reacting appropriately.

By the way, Representative Paul Meers is to be commended for his statement concerning the arrest of Davis. He showed the spirit of the new class of younger Democrats by coming out for principle instead of party.

Reggie Populus.

Hamburg.

DEMOCRAT

Today's News Today

SDAY EVENING, DECEMBER 6, 1967 48 PAGES * PRICE 5c

Legal Action Begun To Free Col. Davis

Spent Night In Jail

By GEORGE DOUTHIT
Democrat Staff Writer

Legal moves were under way today to get State Police Director Lynn Davis out of the Pulaski County Jail where he was put Tuesday by Circuit Judge William J. Kirby for refusing to divulge the name of an informant.

Davis was expected to remain in the jail only as long as it takes his attorneys to appear before the Arkansas Supreme Court on a writ of habeas corpus. The high court is expected to at least grant bail, which was refused to Davis by Kirby.

Sources indicated that it might be after lunch before legal action could be set in motion.

Davis said today he acted "just like any other prisoner" during his night in jail in an unlocked cell but he said he probably only got about two hours sleep.

Davis, looking a little haggard, said he did some paper work and conferred with troopers who came to see him.

This morning, he talked in his cell at length with Maj. Bill Miller, head of the Safety Education Division of the State Police.

The State Police director said it was "just a conference."

He said he had received many telegrams and cards from throughout the nation in support of his position. He said his wife also had received 53 telephone calls in support of him.

"So, I hope not everyone's against me," he said.

Davis' incarceration came about Tuesday afternoon when

Democrat/McCants

DAVIS WHILES AWAY TIME IN JAIL
. . . As legal forces work for his release

Has Few 'Comforts'

Davis Retains Sense Of Humor on Jailing

By THE ASSOCIATED PRESS

State Police Director Lynn A. Davis retained his sense of humor Tuesday, even as he was being jailed for contempt of court.

He suggested at one point that Associated Press Newsman Robert Shaw, who portrayed "Superman" Davis in a recent gridiron show, might and was furnished with an old wooden chair and a cot.

Has Pink Sheets

The jail also provided his pillow and a thin pad for a mattress, but a state trooper brought him the pink sheets that he used to cover the pad.

Davis told newsmen when he was brought upstairs to see Gov. Winthrop Rockefeller that the sheets also brought him an AM-FM transistor radio, a package of cigarettes and an overnight kit.

Mackey said Davis, like other prisoners, would be permitted to see an attorney and members of his family, but that Davis had asked that no other visitors be permitted to see him.

Davis told his wife and son over the phone not to come

THE SUPREME COURT HEARING

As the Supreme Court said after hearing my case:

"The Arkansas Supreme Court just have never had any cases like this where the prosecutor and the police were on opposite sides."

At that time, the Grand Juries of Arkansas counties were selected by a circuit judge who chose three people who, then in turn, chose the remainder of the grand jurymen. As shown by the transcript from the Arkansas Supreme Court proceeding, circuit judge Kirby had said, after I had been called before the Grand Jury,

> "Well now, as I understand it, and all of the grand jury, has all agreed, and the colonel here also agrees, that the question asked him, and that he refused to answer was, what was the name of the informant. And now the court wants to ask you, I have decided that it is material, and I think under Section 43-916 I can propound the same question to you and of course, if you refuse to answer you will be in contempt of this court and be dealt with contempt. Now, what is the name of your informant?"

The record before the Supreme Court the next day, after my one night, two day stay in the Pulaski county Jail, showed that I refused to name my informant on the grounds of my fear for his life and property. I believe the transcript left out my assertion that I would not tell till hell froze over.

Justice Jones of the Arkansas Supreme Court said,

"There is nothing in the record before the Supreme Court that would reveal the nature of the investigation being conducted by the grand jury or what information, if any, the grand jury desired, or hoped to obtain, from the individual whose identity Davis refused to reveal. The context in which Mr. Davis is not in the record before us."

Justice Jones wrote,

"The record does not reveal what, if anything, Davis had indicated it would be if he did so indicate...even if the record was complete" ... "the answer should have been given in the secret confines of the grand jury room and not in the judge's chambers or in open court."

(At least ten people had been granted admission to the judge's chambers to see this drama which obviously was supposed to end in the jailing.)

A Supreme Court Justice very aptly noted that there were very few reported cases on the subject of police officers refusing to name informants who led them to be the "bad guy," and prosecuting attorneys and police officers are usually on the same side and were usually on the same team; and that police officers were never asked the name of an informant.

The Supreme Court decision said,

"Surely the statute contemplates more than simply hearing the witness refuse again to answer the same question propounded to him in the grand jury room, without first ascertaining the nature of the information the question is designed to produce."

The prosecuting attorney claimed that the evidence could only be obtained through the testimony of Davis. He said nothing about all the evidence obtained in the raids. He said nothing about all the other witnesses available to testify. The only question was:

"Who is your informant?"

It takes no special intelligence to know that this was exactly what was wanted, the name, so that they could find the "rat." The person they so wanted to identify could have been another bookie, or a disgruntled customer, or one of many different persuasions. The fact that he (or she) identified twelve should have been a valuable clue. He (or she) happened to know everybody, their addresses, their modus operandi (MO) and other good information, all of which turned out to be true.

The *Arkansas Gazette* said in commenting editorially on the contempt case:

> *"In the legislative argument over the Davis' eligibility bills, the contempt citation had been used against him. The Supreme Court decision left the legislature with even less reason not to give Governor Rockefeller legislation enabling him to reappoint the man who, in all probability was the ablest and most qualified Director of Police the state has ever had."*

The jailing proved just how serious they were. It stood to reason we had to find the remaining machines and identify the state's bookies and do so in a short period of time. There were already rumors circulating and bets being taken on how long I would be around, legally or illegally. There was, after all, a legal case that contended that I wasn't qualified as Director because I had not physically lived in the state for ten years next preceding my appointment. The other side was pushing hard.

(I was not fearful for my well being but I still kept a short piece of Scotch tape on my car's hood which, if found loose, would be a pretty good indicator that someone had been under my hood. (And they would not have been checking the coolant level.) Looking back on it that seems to be good sense rather than paranoia.

Little Rock Forecast

Fair and cool. A high of 58 is forecast today and a low of 36 tonight. Yesterday's high was 68, the low 52.

(Weather Map on Page 7B.)

Gazette.

ER 7, 1967. 64 Pages ★ ★ ★ ★ 10 Cents

Davis Is Freed From County Jail By Supreme Court

Chief Justice Harris hands out the Court's order.

Justice Byrd Opposes Move In 6-1 Vote

By ERNEST VALACHOVIC
Of the Gazette Staff

The Arkansas Supreme Court Wednesday freed Col. Lynn A. Davis, the State Police director, from jail where Pulaski Circuit Judge William J. Kirby had sent him Tuesday afternoon for refusing to name an informant in a gambling investigation.

A petition for Davis' release was filed about 1 p.m. and the Supreme Court, after a 10-minute hearing that began at 2, voted 6-1 to grant it. Associate Justice Conley Byrd voted against granting the petition. No reason was given for his decision.

The Supreme Court, which ordered Davis released without bond, didn't rid him of the contempt of court citation by Judge Kirby. The Supreme Court directed Davis' attorney, G. Thomas Eisele, to submit a brief within 10 days on the

Davis case transcript on Page 10A

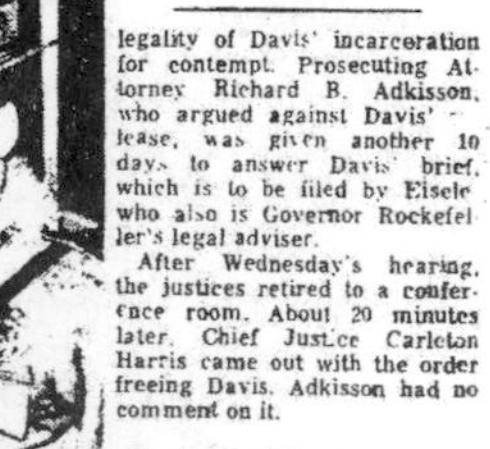

legality of Davis' incarceration for contempt. Prosecuting Attorney Richard B. Adkisson, who argued against Davis' release, was given another 10 days to answer Davis' brief, which is to be filed by Eisele who also is Governor Rockefeller's legal adviser.

After Wednesday's hearing, the justices retired to a conference room. About 20 minutes later, Chief Justice Carleton Harris came out with the order freeing Davis. Adkisson had no comment on it.

Davis Confident Of the Outcome

Davis said later that he thought the state Supreme Court would "find in our favor" after reviewing the complete record. Davis said that despite his experience in the Circuit Court, "I have a high regard for the system nonetheless."

Davis was in his State Police uniform when he arrived in the courtroom in the Justice Building. He was accompanied by

Staff Photos by Larry Obsitnik

Davis reads the order; Sheriff Mackey at the left.

Our Readers' Views

(To our readers: This is your column. You are invited to use it as an open forum for discussing matters of general interest. You may use a pen name or initials if you wish but we must have your name and address as warrant of good faith.—The Editor.)

In Defense of Davis

Dear Editor: It is a matter of intense shame to this citizen that State Police Director Lynn Davis has been treated so contemptuously.

Though the term contempt has been used to describe his actions on withholding certain information, I submit that it is much more appropriate for the petty persons who were responsible for placing him in jail.

I am filled with frustration and dismay that such things can still occur in Arkansas.

J.C.A.
Little Rock

Dear Editor: Arkansas gets another black eye, and the Republican Party gains ground in Arkansas. That's the result of the jailing of State Police Director Lynn Davis for "contempt of court."

Things have come to a pretty pass when people who are trying to stamp out crime are jailed while repeat law violators are never placed inside the bars.

They Say Today

"I am filled with frustration and dismay that such things (jailing of Lynn Davis) can still occur in Arkansas." (J.C.A.)

"How much longer is the present administration going to fight the enemy with one hand and pat it on the back with the other?" (Observer)

This sad event is being publicized across the nation and in other countries. It stands to damage Arkansas more than the episode at Central High School 10 years ago.

Just about time our state begins to shed its Bob Burns and Thomas Jackson image, something like this has to happen, and it has to happen in our largest city, the state's capital—Little Rock.

FED-UP-TO-HERE,
North Little Rock

Dear Editor: My congratulations to Lynn Davis. Through the contempt charge and jail sentence, he has become famous — not notorious, but famous. His stewardship as State Police director has been excellent, but not sufficiently noticed or appreciated by the public.

But the people of Arkansas, and the nation, will now have their eye on Lynn Davis, and his good accomplishments.

More power to him.

D.R.C.,
Little Rock

What Leadership!

Dear Editor: While Americans were dying by the hundreds in Vietnam, slaughtered by Russian MIGs, missiles, mortars and other munitions, our Great Society leaders attended a Russian Embassy banquet celebrating the 50th anniversary of the Communist conspiracy which is set to take our own country; which, for the last 50 years, has been responsible for the worst blood-bath in all history.

For U.S. leaders to toast the Soviet Communists, our arch-enemy, on the 50th anniversary of this Red menace is cause for alarm. It is horrifying!

How much longer is the present administration going to fight the enemy with one hand and pat it on the back with the other? How much longer will patriotism and sanity be dirty words? How much longer are we going to maintain the Red "hot line" and attempt to build "bridges of understanding" to a gangster group that understands nothing that is civil and decent?

What leadership!

OBSERVER,
Malvern

Another Gusher?
PUBLIC INDIGNATION OVER DAVIS' JAILING
POLITICAL OIL FIELD

JUST ONE BLESSING AFTER ANOTHER

Expect it, get ready, then be patient!

Those who long for the "good old days" when the "Valley" was booming with gambling, prostitution and racket money (most of which went to the casino people and the movers and shakers and their people), ask why did "I" choose to close down what was so "good" and so much fun. I would bet 10 to 1 they are younger than 45 years old. (Oh! I forgot, though, there are no bookies around to take the bet???

To these people, I pose this question, "What if you knew what Dutch Akers, Hot Springs Chief of Detectives, knew about shakedowns, illegal gambling, prostitution, the payoffs and the other illegal activities in your city but you were not in a position nor of a disposition to make a living from these activities. Obviously, you would have to tolerate thc corruption but get none of the money from the illegal activities, except maybe your wages which they let you earn.

Some say they miss the fun the City must have had then, even if they had not experienced it, relying instead on fond stories from the selective memories from the "old timers".

Sure, you would be able to gamble and carouse around but not for long unless you had a racket of your own. The odds just aren't in your favor since the "house" always takes a percentage of the take and usually takes much more if the games are unregulated and the less money you have to start with the less time you have to play. I know of no gambler who consistently wins at any gambling game. The odds are just not in the favor of any one player *consistently* beating those odds and especially when the mob can set the odds at any time without any oversight.

Hot Springs was the temporary home for the likes of "Lucky" Luciano, who was sentenced to thirty to fifty years in the penitentiary in New York and subsequently deported to Italy on 90 prostitution charges; Frank "Jelly" Nash, a killer and an escapee from Leavenworth, Kansas Federal Penitentiary who died while trying to be rescued; Alvin "Creepy" Karpis, a bank robber and killer who was not released from the federal penitentiary until 2008, and imprisoned in Alcatraz for longer than anyone else in history; Frank Costello and Al Capone, both Mafia capos and the architects of the Saint Valentines Day Massacre; Earl Young, killer and bank robber; "Curly" Slaughter, cop killer, bank robber; Sonny Lamb and dozens more of the world's worst people by any standard you might want to apply, were "holed up" in your city under the protection of your police and other law enforcement agencies walking the same streets as your children?

Lynn Davis was plucked from FBI ranks for the job of State Police Director by Rockefeller. Notwithstanding the fact that his eligibility was in question due to residency requirements, Col. Davis proceeded to demolish the myth that gambling laws cannot be enforced in Arkansas. In December the Supreme Court

The list could go on and on and include some of the city leaders, the movers and shakers, like Owney Madden, who was reputed to be the "Boss Gambler" in this, his adopted city, who owned two or more casinos in Hot Springs, while stating that he had never worked a day in his life, still found it necessary to watch closely for those who wished him ill or in other words wanted to kill him. Madden, being arrested at least 140 times without any conviction in New York, except for one murder, seemingly speaks more about his power over frightened jurors and witnesses than the quality of his charges.

City Edition **ARKANSAS DEMOCRAT** Today's News Today

NINETY-SEVENTH YEAR—No. 78 | Second-class postage paid at Little Rock, Arkansas | LITTLE ROCK, MONDAY EVENING, DECEMBER 18, 1967 | 28 PAGES | PRICE 5c

In N. Vietnam

3 U.S. Planes Downed

SAIGON (AP) — American planes continued raids on North Vietnam's heartland for the fifth straight day today, and the U.S. Command reported the loss of three jets Sunday—two of them downed by Communist MIG interceptors.

The U.S. Command did not immediately reveal details of the raids today, but Tass, the Soviet news agency, said American planes made a "massive raid" on Hanoi's northeastern district.

American spokesmen reported one MIG probably downed by U.S. fighters in the several swirling air battles over Hanoi Sunday. The American casualties were an Air Force F105 Thunderchief and an F4 Phantom brought down by a MIG21 and a MIG17. The three crew members aboard the two American planes were missing.

The third American plane downed, another Phantom, was hit by ground fire over North Vietnam's southern panhandle. One of its two crewmen was kiled and one was rescued.

Including Sunday's casualties and a Phantom shot down Saturday by a MIG21, U.S. records list 36 American planes and 99 MIGs shot down in aeria combat so far in the war. A total of 765 U.S. warplanes have been reported lost over the North.

A freakish break in the monsoon weather—which began last Thursday—has permitted the heavy raids on key North Vietnamese targets after a one-month lull which permitted the Communists to rebuild shattered facilities.

North Vietnam's carefully hoarded MIGs apparently were out in greater numbers Sunday than in the previous days of the renewed assault, when only four to six of the Red interceptors would dart in and out of American formations.

In the five days of renewed aerial combat, the MIG pilots have downed three U.S. jets, while the Americans claimed only one "probable."

Little ground action was reported.

Vandals Stage Raid

NEW YORK (AP) — Vandals broke into Dyker Heights Junior High School in Brooklyn Sunday night, smashed furniture in five classrooms and set fires that

DAVIS, EISELE AFTER HEARING COURT RULING
. . . Eisele contacts governor's office with the news

Democrat Glen Moon

Making Room for Successor

Davis Says He's Moving Out of His Home, Office

Lynn Davis told a press conference at State Police headquarters shortly before noon that he was moving out immediately from his office and his home at headquarters as a result of an Arkansas Supreme Court decision today.

He said he did not intend to accept nor did he expect to be offered another job in the Rockefeller administration nor a consultant's job at State Police headquarters.

He indicated he has hopes that the special session of the legislature in February will change the law to make him eligible to once again take the position.

Davis told newsmen he has been living off of savings and borrowed money since he took the job Aug. 1, but he assumed from a previous conversation that Gov. Rockefeller will reimburse him for the nearly five months he has served without pay.

This is estimated at over $4,500.

In a prepared statement, Davis said:

"Inasmuch as the highest court in our state has ruled that I'm unqualified to serve as the director of the Arkansas State Police, I'll begin immediately to move out of my office and

* * *

WR Reacts

Law Change Asked

Gov. Rockefeller said today he was disappointed at the Arkansas Supreme Court's ruling that Lynn Davis is ineligible, in residency requirements, to serve as head of the State Police.

He said that he respects and accepts the ruling and will present legislation to the spe-

Court Rules Davis Ineligible for Job

By GEORGE DOUTHIT
Democrat Staff Writer

State Police Director Lynn A. Davis today was ruled ineligible by the State Supreme Court and was immediately removed from the post. Lt. Col. Carl Miller was made acting director.

The decision was 6-1, with Associate Justice Paul Ward dissenting.

Associate Justice J. Fred Jones, who wrote the majority opinion, said that it was evident that the legislature meant for the State Police director to have actually lived in Arkansas 10 years prior to his appointment.

Davis, who was with the FBI for 5½ years, was outside the state for seven years, having lived 18 months in Texarkana, Tex., prior to going to the FBI.

Davis was in the Supreme Court to hear the decision but would not make any statement immediately.

Gov. Rockefeller was in New York, and Davis planned to talk with him, then meet with the press about his future plans.

Attorney Tom Eisele, one of Rockefeller's top advisors, also was in the courtroom. He confirmed immediately to reporters that Miller was now the acting police director.

Davis' reaction immediately was: "I will not make a statement until I see what the governor says. I am disappointed but not surprised. Carl Miller now becomes the acting director."

Justice Jones pointed out that on June 30, 1967, in response to a request from the governor, the attorney general issued an opinion holding that Davis could not meet the residential qualifications. The governor, nevertheless, appointed Davis as director on Aug. 1.

The director of administration, in view of the attorney general's opinion, refused to approve the payment of Davis salary.

Davis brought the court action for a declaratory judgment finding him to be qualified to hold the office. By intervention, the attorney general sought Davis' ouster.

After a hearing in Pulaski Circuit Court, Judge Warren Wood held that Davis was legally qualified under the statute.

Guilty Plea Entered In Murder

McDonald Given Life Imprisonment In Officer's Death

By BUD LEMKE
Democrat Staff Writer

In a surprise move today, Booker T. McDonald, accused of first degree murder in the shooting of a Little Rock patrolman on Sept. 2, entered a guilty plea in Pulaski Circuit Court.

A jury returned a verdict of life imprisonment after the state waived the death penalty based on requests of the family of the deceased and McDonald's plea.

McDonald was to have gone on trial Dec. 27 for the fatal shooting of Patrolman Lloyd Worthy near 2500 E. Roosevelt.

McDonald, 34, is a Negro, as was the deceased who was 37. The defendant's two lawyers filed a motion declaring that McDonald wanted to plead guilty and when taken before Circuit Judge William J. Kirby, McDonald reiterated the plea.

Pros. Atty. Richard B. Adkisson said the state would waive the death penalty on consideration of the family and what he termed circumstances in the case.

Judge Kirby told the jury that the only question was the matter of punishment since the defendant entered the plea. He told them they could return the death penalty anyway, or else the life term, and in instructing them gave both verdicts. The jury was out seven minutes.

Witnesses Heard Earlier

WRECKAGE REMOVED FROM OHIO RIVER
. . . Crane lifts auto containing 2 bodies

Associated Press

Bodies of 3 More Bridge Collapse Victims Recovered

POINT PLEASANT, W.Va. (AP) — Working in a light rain, a water-borne crane probing the

'Lend Me a Hand!'

Win and my supporters tried but politically failed — bless them for trying.

29 Feb. 1968.

Senator Guy H. "Mutt" Jones of Conway led the movement in the Senate to block Governor Rockefeller's appointment of Lynn Davis as director of the Arkansas State Police. Colonel Davis had grown up in Arkansas, but his employment had taken him out of the state in recent years, and it was decided that he did not fulfill residence requirements.

Hot Springs, the sequel

A little more gambling, but a whole lot different town

BY KANE WEBB
ARKANSAS DEMOCRAT-GAZETTE

HOT SPRINGS — If this city were a movie, it'd be an old-fashioned, big-studio epic with a cast of thousands, produced and directed by Cecil B. DeMille and written by Mickey Spillane. It'd be in colorful VistaVision, with dramatic flashbacks and pauses to the past in grainy black and white.

If this city were a movie, it'd be a series of blockbusters—although, like many serialized dramas, the latest sequel may seem tame compared to the notorious premiere. But it represents a new chapter with an interesting old twist, and it might go something like this:

As opening credits roll, FADE IN to CLOSE-UP shot of a jack hammer grinding into concrete at a construction site.

PULL BACK to reveal the main entrance into Oaklawn Park, the venerable horse racing track. Cars roll by on busy Central Avenue. The hard hats are at work on a track expansion. Another 60,000 square feet is being added to the southwest part of the building. Up and out, it'll [illegible]

[illegible] tion, the new facility will allow Oaklawn to add another 500 machines dubbed Electronic Games of Skill. All perfectly legal and voter-approved, the construction work outside the racetrack represents the biggest expansion of machine-style—some might say casino-style—gambling in Hot Springs since the days of Owney Madden and the Southern Club, Dane Harris and The Vapors, the good ol' bad ol' colorful days when the town was built on illegal gambling and precious little else. It was 40 years ago this spring that the last gasp of illegal gambling in the Spa City was snuffed out by Carl Miller and Ken McKee, the heads of the Arkansas state police who carried on the clean-up work of the legendary Lynn Davis and his boss, Governor Winthrop Rockefeller.

DISSOLVE to a shot of Eric Jackson in his general manager's office at Oaklawn.

VOICE OVER: Jackson is not a stereotypical racetrack breed. His affection for his hometown, and his civic involvement in it, runs deeper than the groundbreaking of his employer's newest expansion. A native of Hot Springs, he holds an economics degree from [illegible]

[illegible] merce and the rotary club. He was a founder and early president of Fifty for the Future, a group key to turning around the city's economic fortunes. He now sits on the board of the Sisters of Mercy Health System. He played a part in getting the so-called Hamburger Tax passed in the 1990s, as well as several other publicly-funded projects, including the city's civic center and Summit Arena.

He was a cub reporter at the *Hot Springs Sentinel-Record* when Rockefeller and Davis finally played the one-armed bandits.

"It was a strange town then," Jackson remembers. "There was one set of laws for some people, and a different set of laws for other people."

VOICE OVER: These days, the law is clear enough. Pari-mutuel betting is allowed at Oaklawn and Southland Greyhound Park in West Memphis as are the new Electronic Games of Skill—a euphemism that's impossible to say without laughing. Even the locals call 'em slot machines.

CUT to Orval Allbritton, town historian, [illegible]

illegal gambling in the Spa City was snuffed out by Carl Miller and Ken McKee, the heads of the Arkansas state ~~police who carried~~ on the clean-up work of the legendary Lynn Davis and his boss, Governor ~~Winthrop Rockefeller~~.

Latter-day comment by the *Arkansas Democrat Gazette* (2009)

Fisher

'From this angle, I'd say it came from above.'

Courtesy Arkansas Democrat Gazette

This outcome of attempts to reappoint me to a second four-year term as US Marshal was a rampant theory advanced by the newspapers and others.

APPOINTMENT AS U.S. MARSHAL FOR THE EASTERN DISTRICT OF ARKANSAS

Could It Be??? It's Who You Know Rather Than What You Know?

The following are excerpts from the book, *The English Godfather, Owney Madden* and other sources, verbal and otherwise.

In August 24, 2007, I found excerpts which were most enlightening and possibly had something to do with my reappointment as United States Marshal or lack thereof. I had been appointed by President Richard Nixon and confirmed by one hundred votes in the United States Senate in 1970.

As everything else I write in this book you can take it or leave it. Having been in the law business, on one end or the other, I know that it is much easier to report "hearsay" than it is to provide written proof or witness testimony, and that without more proof, on the following, you must be my jurors.

The foregoing expressed my attitude all these years because I honestly believed that the reasons given by Senator John McClellan for the lack of his support for a re-appointment to a second four-year term as United States Marshal, even if they were petty, were genuine. That was my belief until I read The English Godfather, Owney Madden.

The scuttlebutt (an old army term) was, from the Director of the Marshals Service to the local people, "in the know", that the Senator was not asking for my reappointment in 1974 for a second four-year term to the U.S. Marshal's position and, as a matter of fact, was opposing my reappointment. When I heard these comments, I was sure they were simply misunderstandings. I had served as the Marshal for a four year term plus one year for a total of five years, becoming, in the meantime, an Inspector for the Service. I discounted these rumors at each turn, telling these people, including the Director of the Marshal's Service and the news reporters, that this couldn't be, as the Senator was one of my main supporters.

I had discounted the reporters' theory that Win Rockefeller was alive when I was first appointed and confirmed by the Senate, by 100 votes, unanimous consent, whereas Win had died in the meantime in 1973. I had been appointed by a Republican President, Richard Nixon in 1970. In 1975 neither Win nor Nixon was around to sponsor my appointment for a second term.

Other reporters advanced the theory that Senator John McClellan had not only received support from the rackets in Garland County, but had, according to their sources, received heavy contributions to the senator's campaigns from Owney Madden and others in the gambling fraternity.

In 1953, J. Edgar Hoover and the Immigration Bureau had begun to re-examine Owney Madden's US citizenship for flaws, with the prime intention of revoking it and deporting him back to England. Jack Kennedy, Bobby Kennedy, and J. Edgar Hoover were convinced that Hot Springs' Owney Madden was either the Number One or Number Two criminal in the United States. To insure that every effort was made, the FBI Director issued orders that Owney Madden's file should be upgraded and given "Top Hoodlum" status in the Bureau's highest criminal category. He liberally used Agents to track Madden and others like him or at least like those of his stature, including members of the Mafia who came to Hot Springs. (Ibid, p. 180)

On July 10, 1954, Owney and Agnes Madden wrote a private note to Senator McClellan:

> "Walter Ebell is attending your rally today so we are taking this opportunity of asking him to carry our contribution to you for your campaign. We decided this more prudent than going to any committee in Hot Springs, as it seems every two-bit politician and newspaper writer tries to make capital of everything connected with our name."

On July 15, 1955, a year and five days after Owney and Agnes' contribution letter, the House Subcommittee on Immigration recommended that deportation proceedings against Martin A. Madden aka (Marty), Owney's brother, should be discontinued. And they were. *(The English Godfather*, p. 181)

This came not from the Bureau of Immigration, the professionals, but the House Subcommittee on Immigration, the politicians.)

On August 12, 1955, Private Law 487, Chapter 875, *an act* for the relief of Martin Aloysius Madden was enacted by the United States Senate and U.S. House of Representatives of the United States of America.

Now, Martin, aka Marty as well as Owney would have no fear of deportation. It seemed apparent that Marty had never done anything other than working in the rackets but that didn't keep him from being citizenized, being sponsored by someone in the United States Senate. (Read the Private Bill above)

Fact or fiction?

(Any history buffs who want to learn more about the United States Marshals Service would do well to visit the U. S. Marshals Service Museum in Fort Smith, Arkansas. There you will find the real heroes of the frontier, those who would take their guns and on horseback go into the Indian Territory to get really bad guys. In the territories they not only enforced federal laws but all laws, what we would consider state laws now. There were Indian policemen, but they still needed the help of the Marshals Service to keep the peace.)

Things haven't changed all that much. The Marshal's Service is still responsible for finding and arresting the bad guy—federal fugitives, terrorists and assorted no-goodniks wanted by not only the federal government but some wanted by states as fugitives from justice.

At the present time there are 92 federal judicial districts which have one Marshal each and hundreds of loyal, hard working, fearless deputy United States Marshals. (And they are still looking for a few good hunters and gatherers!)

LITTLE CHOICE BUT TO LEAVE... GREENER PASTURES OR JUST MARKING TIME?

Leaving the State Police was another chance to make some changes, which I hope we did.

When I became the founding Director of the Arkansas Crime Commission, after I left the ASP but before being appointed U.S. Marshal for the second four-year term, I knew that one day we would have what would become a super sophisticated communications system, but I had no idea that system would become so all encompassing, so far reaching and so available. From myself, one secretary and two desks and a one-room office in 1968, the Crime Commission had a name change along the way, becoming the Arkansas Crime Information Center (ACIC) connected to all States through the National Crime Information Center (NCIC).

The present Director of ACIC recently advised me that there were over 2,000 devices in state and non-state law enforcement vehicles, stations and offices in Arkansas which provide instant contact from these devices to state and national sources of information.

The present Director of the Arkansas State Police, Colonel Winford Phillips, says that each of the State Police cruisers has a computer program which will, when provided with measurements, draw an accident scene to scale.

Leaving that office was not easy but knowing what I knew, I expected something. I prepared for it and waited.

Art for Heart's Sake Sells For Fraction of Valuations

By BILL LEWIS
Of the Gazette Staff

Art patrons would do well next year to ante up the $25-per-couple door tab for the third annual "Art for Heart's Sake" auction, if the bidding at the second annual one Friday night at the Top of the Rock Club was prophetic.

There were some fantastic buys.

About 25 couples, most in evening dress, sipped champagne and nibled hors d'oeuvres for an hour or more before the bidding, ably handled by Tom Davis, got under way.

The first sale seemed to set the trend: United States Marshal Lynn A. Davis, former FBI agent and former State Police director, whose artistic talent apparently has been buried until now, had donated an oil he'd done in the manner of Utrillo, and he'd put a valuation of $150 on it. It went for $40.

Four superb color photographs, framed in ancient cypress and depicting rural Arkansas scenes, had been given by the Dungan-Allen photography firm. They were said to be worth $500 the set, and they went for $210.

A Bruce Anderson watercolor priced at $150 was sold by auctioneer Davis for $80. A large and handsome oil by Maurice Kellogg of the Little Rock skyline, viewed from across an Arkansas River whose width the painter took some artistic license with, sold for $185, which was $315 below the artist's price.

Another prize purchase was an oil by Josephine Graham, an established artist who gets her price. This one, "Munich Fountain," was marked at $150 and it sold for $40 — about the cost of the frame itself.

A delicately executed watercolor still life by Catherine Tharp Altvater of New York, a Little Rock native now well-established as a leading water colorist, sold for $135, a third of its $400 price.

One of the few that exceeded the asking price was an ink drawing of a lone tree, by Ellan McKenzie, which went for $5 above the $50 price.

Two of the major offerings of the evening, a portrait to be painted by Mallie McAninch and a Rembrandt etching, were sold at a fraction of their value. Mrs. McAninch, probably the state's finest portrait painter, usually gets $1,500; the one auctioned Friday night will go at $750, the subject to be the purchaser's choice.

The Rembrandt, given jointly by London Graphica and the Seventh Street Galleries, Graphica's local agent, was valued at $1,000 — a realistic figure. It was bought by Don Couch, president of Union National Bank, for $350.

Most of the paintings, which admittedly included some mediocre works, had been donated by the artists, a few of whom reserved the right to collect 25 per cent of the sale price. Some drew no opening bids on first offering and had to be set aside. All of the purchase prices were contributions to the Arkansas Heart Association, and thus tax-deductible. The paintings, in effect, were gifts.

The auction of the art raised $2,600 for the Heart Fund. In all, including donations and the portion of the $25-a-couple admission price that goes to the funds, some $3,000 was collected for the Fund. Mrs. Harlan Lane was chairman of the event.

Staff Photo

A Lynn Davis Original -- $40

Auctioneer Tom Davis of Union National Bank marks "sold" on a painting, after Utrillo, by United States Marshal Lynn Davis at Friday night's benefit art auction at the Top of The Rock, where evening-dressed couples had their choice of works from Rembrandt down.

Then, from 1976–77 as the Director of the *Pulaski County Child Support Enforcement Unit*, the first county unit of its kind in Arkansas went to a *statewide agency* that now collects some $250,000,000 per year from absent parents.

YOU MAY ASK, "HOW I'M DOING"
(Now the Bragging Starts)

I must tell you I am the luckiest person in the world.

Raised and nurtured in the back of my family's service station with my bedroom window right outside the Dew Drop Inn Honky-Tonk parking lot on East Street in Texarkana, Arkansas, listening to Hank Williams, blaring out from the well-lit juke box, it was exciting. If you were old enough to go in (I wasn't) and didn't have a knife they would issue you one just to keep the fights fair; having rheumatic fever twice and having to learn to walk three times with the untiring help of my sainted Mother and Father who kept quilts on the floor while I was learning; being a Razorback cheerleader at Texarkana, Arkansas, High School; being accepted at the University of Arkansas as a remedial student after not listening to good advice as to the importance of junior high math; getting a degree from Henderson State College; marrying into a family that matched mine for love and devotion; being declared the #1 Hog caller in 1969, shortly before the Big Shootout between the Razorbacks and the Texas Longhorns; working for and with some of the greatest people in the world; and being referred to as the "Legendary" Lynn Davis by the *Arkansas Democrat Gazette*, my favorite newspaper that just happens to be the oldest newspaper West of the Mississippi; and having the Associated Press naming the "Lynn Davis story," the #1 news story in Arkansas in 1967, as well as so many newspapers covering that story fully, honestly and courageously without fear or favor.

As a thespian, I had little experience, but they say, "As long as they spell your name right." Etc., etc.

, Friday, Dec. 5, 1969.

5,000 Hog-callers Rally; Lynn Davis Yell Victorious

By JOHN WOODRUFF
Of the Gazette Staff

About 5,000 hog-calling Razorback fans shouted, sang and shivered their way through an hour-long pep rally at War Memorial Stadium Thursday night.

Eight University of Arkansas cheerleaders arrived at 7 p.m., just as the rally was starting, to lead the crowd in cheers and the U of A Alma Mater, and to judge a hog-calling contest.

At the slightest provocation—a mention of the word "Texas" for example—the crowd went into another hog-calling session.

Even 9-year-old Alan Bellamy's high, piercing hog call over the public address system was quickly drowned out during the hog-calling contest as the fans couldn't help but join in the cheer.

Alan and about a dozen other contestants—the youngest being 3-year-old Becky Brewer of 96 Indian Trail—gave way to former State Police Director Lynn A. Davis of 38 Scenic Drive, North Little Rock, who placed first, and Julius Ketcher of North Little Rock second and Central High School Pep Band upwind from a large bonfire. Fuel for the fire was a five-foot tall, 25-foot long mound of shredded paper, cardboard and scraps of lumber.

The temperature was 37 degrees.

Gusts of wind occasionally blew the flaming paper onto the heads of the onlookers and into the nearby Stadium. Four Little Rock firemen from the station at West Fourteenth and Pulaski Streets stood by at a 1,250-gallon pumper truck but were not needed.

Texas Rally Much Larger

While the spirit of the group fit the nationwide anticipation of the Arkansas Razorbacks football game with the No. 1 ranked Texas Longhorns Saturday, many fans at the rally wished for a much larger group. Texas had a similar rally Wednesday in which 25,000 participated.

Little Rock Police Lt. Harold R. Zook, who estimated the number of fans at 5,000, re- the other cheerleaders drove in from Fayetteville), a few former Razorbacks cheered the Razorbacks to victory with remarks from the platform.

"I'm a man of few words," 1958 Razorback Gerald Nesbitt told the crowd. "The time for talking is over: Give 'em hell!" His former teammate, Dr. Billy Kyzer, president of the Camden Booster Club, also spoke.

Rockefeller Gets Razorback Hat

While state Senator Oscar Alagood of Little Rock led one of the many hog calls, Governor Rockefeller climbed onto the platform. Mr. Rockefeller accepted an under-sized red western Razorback hat but put it on anyway and promised that he would wear one at the game at Fayetteville Saturday "even though I'm a cattle man."

He said the rally was "wonderful" and then read the proclamation. The document was accepted by Brad Scott on behalf of the University of Arkansas. Scott is president of the Letterman's Club, one of the

—Staff Photo by Morris White

Lynn Davis cuts loose with the winning hog call.

But as for cheerleading for the Hogs! Notice that one of the facts that I didn't point out to the judges (UA Cheerleaders) was that I was a cheerleader for the Arkansas High School Razorbacks in Texarkana. (Neither they nor the sponsoring Little Rock Jaycees ever asked me about *that* experience! I won 50,000 Green Stamps for winning the competition. That's the reason my tongue is ¼ inch shorter than before!

Six and ½ years Special Agent, FBI, 120 days as Director of the Arkansas State Police; Five years as the United States Marshal, Eastern District Arkansas; working with some of the best and most courageous people in the world; and practicing law 33 years without being disbarred is quite satisfying.

Being blessed with three children, Tony, Kristi Lynn and Clay, one son-in-law Brian Lilje, three grandchildren, Ross Davis, Nathan Davis and Lydia Sue Lilje and married to Sue Thomas Davis, my conscience, adviser and bellwether wife for 56 years—a chicken in every pot and a car in every garage, is what I always wished for—and I have had it all these years. (Look for them in your own kitchen and garage.) You might have to search for your good memories, but they are there.

Oh yes, my Brother Gene and the rest of my family have always stood with me … I had better quit or you might accuse me of being boisterous and/or braggadocios! I must admit to some of that.

Oh yes, don't forget, possibly my most difficult endeavor in life, writing my first and *last book*—this one. I told you something good was going to happen! I finished it!

On the other hand, this one has been so much fun, I might write another one.

Now you know why they call me LUCKYLYNND.

Author's Note

Many people, young and old, have for years encouraged me to write a historical book, on facts and impressions of the 1967 era. They pointed out many reasons I should write about these events forty two years later. One compelling reason for writing the book was that I was the only one at each of the events described and that if I didn't point out the characters, impressions and the nuances, that period of history would be lost.

The only promise I made to myself and others was that I would write truthfully about the events and the characters involved, verifying my facts and impressions from newspaper articles. I also promised that the book would be a book of history and not a history book.

I promised myself that the newspapers, the *Arkansas Democrat* and the *Arkansas Gazette* would be the arbiters of any dispute in facts. As always they are fair and balanced and sources I could depend upon. (The *Democrat* merged with the *Gazette* a number of years ago becoming the *Arkansas Democrat Gazette*.)

The editors, writers and staff kindly gave me permission to use their sources and contributors, including the cartoons of Jon Kennedy and George Fisher. These two people could put into an ink and pen impression, facts and opinions and tell a story that made a lasting impression, day by day, year after year, in a space no bigger than 2x2 column inches. Thanks too, to Jon, for his present day contributions and bless George who has passed on to the big easel in the sky.

My thanks to the *Democrat Gazette* and all of those who helped me remember and write about those 120 days in 1967, what I hope is an interesting story. I hope I have done it and them justice. (At 75 years of age, I'm afraid I don't have time for a re-write!)

Colonel Lynn A. Davis